PEACE
of SOUL

PEACE
of SOUL

FULTON J. SHEEN

LIGUORI/TRIUMPH
Liguori, Missouri

Published by Liguori/Triumph
An Imprint of Liguori Publications
Liguori, Missouri
http://www.liguori.org

This edition published by special arrangement with the Estate of Fulton
J. Sheen.

Library of Congress Cataloging-in-Publication Data

Sheen, Fulton J. (Fulton John), 1895–1979.
    Peace of soul / Fulton J. Sheen.
        p.   cm.
    Previously published: New York : McGraw-Hill, 1949.
    Includes bibliographical references.
    ISBN 0-89243-915-7
    1. Apologetics. 2. Philosophy, Modern—Controversial literature.
3. Catholic Church—Apologetic works. 4. Conversion. 5. Peace of
mind—Religious aspects—Catholic Church. I. Title.
    BT1200.S5   1996
    230'.2—dc20   95-26419

Printed in the United States of America

Mariæ Gratiæ Divinæ
Matri Dei Incarnati
Hoc qualemcumque est opus
Dedicat auctor indignus
Filiali obœdientia
Alteri si possit nemini
Libertiori animo placiturus

CONTENTS

Chapter 1

FRUSTRATION

U NLESS SOULS ARE SAVED, nothing is saved; there can be no world peace unless there is soul peace. World wars are only projections of the conflicts waged inside the souls of modern men and women, for nothing happens in the external world that has not first happened within a soul.

During World War II, Pius XII said that postwar humanity would be more changed than the map of postwar Europe. It is this postwar frustrated human, or the modern soul, who interests us in this volume.

Such a person is, as the Holy Father predicted, unlike the people of earlier periods. For one thing, the modern soul no longer looks to find God in nature. In other generations, man, gazing out on the vastness of creation, the beauty of the skies, and the order of the planets, deduced the power, the beauty, and the wisdom of the God Who created and sustained that world. But modern man, unfortunately, is cut off from that approach by several obstacles: He is impressed less with the order of nature than he is with the disorder of his own mind, which has become his main preoccupation; atomic [warfare] has destroyed his awe of a nature that can now be manipulated so as to destroy other people or even to commit cosmic suicide; and, finally, the science of nature is too impersonal for this self-centered age. The old approach not only makes man a mere spectator of reality, instead of its creator, but also demands that the personality of the seeker after truth shall not intrude itself in investigation. But it is

1

the human personality, not nature, that really interests and troubles people today.

This change in our times does not mean that the modern soul has given up the search for God, but only that it has abandoned the more rational — and even more normal — way of finding Him. Not the order in the cosmos, but the disorder in themselves; not the visible things of the world, but the invisible frustrations, complexes, and anxieties of their own personality — these are modern humanity's starting point when people turn questioningly toward religion. In happier days, philosophers discussed the problem *of* man; now they discuss man *as* a problem.

> Through his scepticism the modern man is thrown back upon himself; his energies flow toward their source and wash to the surface those psychic contents that are at all times there, but lie hidden in the silt as long as the stream flows smoothly in its course. How totally different did the world appear to medieval man! For him, the earth was eternally fixed and at rest in the center of the universe, encircled by the course of a sun that solicitously bestowed its warmth. Men were all children of God under the loving care of the Most High, who prepared them for eternal blessedness; and all knew exactly what they should do and how they should conduct themselves in order to rise from a corruptible world to an incorruptible and joyous existence. Such a life no longer seems real to us, even in our dreams. Natural science has long ago torn this lovely veil to shreds. That age lies as far behind as childhood, when one's own father was unquestionably the handsomest and strongest man on earth.[1]

Formerly, humanity lived in a three-dimensional universe where, from an earth one inhabited with one's neighbors, one looked forth to heaven above and to hell below. Forgetting God, a person's vision has lately been reduced to a single dimension; one now thinks of one's activity as limited to the surface of the earth — a plane whereon one moves not up to God or down to Satan, but only to the right or to the left. The old theological division, of those who are in the state of grace and those who are not, has given way to the political separation of rightists and leftists. The modern soul has definitely limited its horizons; having negated the eternal destinies, it has even lost its trust in nature, for nature without God is traitorous.

Where can the soul go, now that a roadblock has been thrown up against every external outlet? Like a city that has had all its outer ramparts seized, a person must retreat inside himself. As a body of water that is blocked turns back upon itself, collecting scum, refuse, and silt, so the modern soul (which has none of the goals or channels of the Christian) backs upon itself and in that choked condition collects all the subrational, instinctive, dark, unconscious sediment that would never have accumulated had there been the normal exits of normal times. People now find that they are locked up within themselves, their own prisoner. Jailed by self, they now attempt to compensate for the loss of the three-dimensional universe of faith by finding three new dimensions within their own mind. Above their *ego,* their conscious level, they discover, in place of heaven, an inexorable tyrant whom they call the *superego.* Below their consciousness, in place of hell, they substitute a hidden world of instincts and urges, primitive longings and biological needs, which they call the *id.*

This conception of the human person as consisting of three layers or regions has been emphasized by Sigmund Freud. It forms an essential element in the psychoanalytic doctrine of human nature. The most important feature of this doctrine is the belief that one's conscious mental life, one's experiences, and one's conduct are determined, not by what one knows, feels, or intends, but by forces largely hidden from one's consciousness. The ego, or consciousness, is only the battlefield where an incessant war is fought between a person's biological, primitive urges and the powers embodied in the superego. These powers take the place of conscience; they originate, not in an awareness of a natural law and of a person's obligation in face of the divine law, but from social pressure, environmental influences brought to bear on the plastic mind of the small child. Because the fulfillment of the primitive urges is placed under control by society (as in the training of toilet habits), these urges become "frustrated." Their original aims cannot persist in our consciousness because of their intolerable conflict with environmental standards. Thereby they become "repressed." The child thus takes over all laws, viewpoints, and values of the adult world when he accepts these standards as his own. He does this by identifying himself with the person whom he would view as an antagonist in a primitive society. Thus, the superego arises and acquires its contents — the rules, taboos, and ideals that happen to be those of the child's surrounding world.

According to such a modern conception of the subjective life, the human appears as a captive within his own mind and as a victim of forces that he or she cannot recognize. To free themselves, if that be possible, the persons must know more about their prison. This is one reason for the great popularity psychiatry enjoys today. This science promises to explain humans to themselves, to enable them to cope better with their tragic situation. A certain type of psychiatry tries to explain man by a theory that the conscious is devoid of value, that only through the unconscious may modern man hope to discover a way out of his unhappiness. The conscious, in this belief, is both forced from below by the id and put under pressure from above by the superego. Conscious man is help-less between them. Psychiatry then becomes a sort of iron file, whereby a person hopes to escape out of this mental prison where he has locked himself, acting as his own turnkey. This psychoanalytic theory sees the clue to all human behavior as buried *within* the minds of individual human be-ings. But the parallel between modern theories of the inner and the outer world is striking. Both systems of thought emphasize tension and the possibility of an upheaval. The prophet of the one is Marx, whose philosophy centers in so-cial conflict; the prophet of the other is Freud, whose main concern is with individual conflicts. In both conceptions, the chaotic and unhappy state of human affairs is said to spring from the tension between the surface appearance, on the one hand, and, on the other, from the hidden, dark, irrational forces that, though unknown, are the true determinants of all that happens. As in Marxism the manifest social, polit-ical, cultural status is but a "superstructure" erected upon the underlying economic forces, so in Freud's system con-scious conduct is only a product of forces located in the unconscious. "In both, human situations are seen in terms of *conflicting interests*. Freud's psychology analyzed neuroses as issuing out of a dialectical clash between desire and law. While Freud deals with contradictions within the psychic pro-cesses, his method for explaining these contradictions follows a materialistic strategy."[2]

When the conflict between the unconscious forces and the conscious ego reaches a certain intensity, according to Freud, the effect is upheaval, with a disruption of life and conduct. For Marx, in an analogous fashion, social peace is disrupted when the proletariat arises, and that [occurs] when economic forces from below are strong enough to overthrow the ex-isting social, political, and economic order. Freud and Marx agree, too, that all events, social and personal, are strictly determined. Both deny spiritual freedom. The Marxist holds that history is determined by economic forces; the Freudian, that man's personal fate depends on instinctual forces. Both envision the abolishment of inhibitions as the way toward a better state of affairs. The very existence of this parallel in thinking indicates how modern humanity understands or misunderstands itself within the general cultural, intellectual, and philosophical "climate" of the times. Historical materialism, the philosophy of Marx, and psychological materialism, the philosophy of Freud, are children of the same age and express the same basic attitudes.

The complexes, anxieties, and fears of the modern soul did not exist to such an extent in previous generations because they were shaken off and integrated in the great social-spiritual organism of Christian Civilization. They are, however, so much a part of modern man that one would think they were tattooed on us. Whatever his or her condition, the modern soul must be brought back to God and happiness. But how? Should the Christian, with his eternal verities, insist that modern souls go back to the traditional approach, which started its argument with nature? That the modern soul must approach God through the five arguments of Saint Thomas? It would be a saner world if that were possible. But it is the point of this book that we must make a start with modern man as he is, not as we should like to find him. Because our apologetic literature has missed this point, it is about fifty years behind the times. It leaves the modern soul cold, not because its arguments are unconvincing, but because the modern soul is too confused to grasp them.

But we who are heirs of twenty centuries of sound thinking must not deal with the supernatural as a dog with a bone. If the modern soul wants to begin its quest for peace with its psychology instead of with our own metaphysics, we will begin with psychology. God's truth would have few facets if it could not start with human nature in any degree of perfection, or even of degradation. If the modern man wants to go to God from the Devil, why, then, we will even start with the Devil: that is where the Divine Lord began with Magdalene, and He told His followers that, with prayer and fasting, they too could start their evangelical work there.

The psychological approach offers us no difficulty; for Christian theology is, in a certain sense, a psychology, since its primary interest is the soul, the most precious of things. Our Lord balanced a universe against a soul and found the soul worth more than gaining the world. To study souls is nothing new; in the whole gamut of modern psychology there is nothing written on frustration, fears, and anxieties that can even faintly compare in depth or breadth with Saint Thomas's treatise on the Passions, Saint Augustine's *Confessions,* or Bossuet's treatise on Concupiscence.

But, it may be asked, is not the modern soul so different from that of previous ages that the older writers lacked experience of such a phenomenon — so that not even the Gospel can offer a cure? No. There is nothing really new in the world; there are only the old problems happening to new people. There is no difference except that of terminology between the frustrated soul of today and the frustrated souls found in the Gospel. Modern man is characterized by three alienations: He is divided from himself, from his fellow human beings, and from his God. These are the same three characteristics of the frustrated youth in the land of the Gerasenes.

SELF-ESTRANGEMENT. The modern person is no longer a unity, but a confused bundle of complexes and nerves. He is so dissociated, so alienated from himself, that he sees himself less as a personality than as a battlefield where a civil war rages between a thousand and one conflicting loyalties. There is no single overall purpose in his life. His soul is comparable to a menagerie in which a number of beasts, each seeking its own prey, turn one upon the other. Or he may be likened to a radio that is tuned in to several stations; instead of getting any one clearly, there is received only an annoying static.

If the frustrated soul is educated, it has a smattering of uncorrelated bits of information with no unifying philosophy. Then the frustrated soul may say to itself: "I sometimes think there are two of me — a living soul and a Ph.D." Such a person projects his own mental confusion to the outside world and concludes that, since he knows no truth, nobody can know it. His own skepticism (which he universalizes into a philosophy of life) throws him back more and more upon those powers lurking in the dark, dank caverns of his unconsciousness. He changes his philosophy as he changes his clothes. On Monday, he lays down the tracks of materialism; on Tuesday, he reads a best-seller, pulls up the old tracks, and lays the new tracks of an idealist; on Wednesday, his new roadway is Communistic; on Thursday, the new rails of Liberalism are laid; on Friday, he hears a broadcast and decides to travel on Freudian tracks; on Saturday, he takes a long drink to forget his railroading and, on Sunday, ponders why people are so foolish as to go to Church. Each day he has a new idol, each week a new mood. His authority is public opinion; when that shifts, his frustrated soul shifts with it. There is no fixed ideal, no great passion, but only a cold indifference to the rest of the world. Living in a continual state of self-reference, his conversational "I's" come closer and closer, as he finds all neighbors increasingly boring if they insist on talking about themselves instead of about him.

ISOLATION FROM OTHERS. This characteristic is revealed not only by two world wars in twenty-one years and a constant threat of a third; not only by the growth of class conflict and selfishness wherein everybody seeks their own; but also by one's break with tradition and the accumulated heritage of the centuries. The revolt of the modern child against his parents is a miniature of the revolt of the modern world against the memory of 1900 years of Christian culture and the great Hebrew, Grecian, and Roman cultures that preceded them. Any respect for that tradition is called "reactionary," with the result that the modern soul has developed a commentator mentality that judges yesterday by today, and today by tomorrow. Nothing is more tragic in an individual who once was wise than to lose his memory, and nothing is more tragic to a civilization than the loss of its tradition. The modern soul that cannot live with itself cannot live with others. A person who is not at peace with himself will not be at peace with his fellow human beings. World wars are nothing but macrocosmic signs of the psychic wars waging inside microcosmic muddled souls. If there had not already been battles in millions of hearts, there would be none on the battlefields of the world.

Given a soul alienated from self, lawlessness follows. A soul with a fight inside itself will soon have a fight outside itself with others. Once a person ceases to be of service to neighbors, he or she begins to be a burden to them; it is only a step from refusing to live *with* others to refusing to live *for* others. When Adam sinned, he accused Eve, and when Cain murdered Abel, he asked the antisocial question, "Am I my brother's keeper?" (Gen. 4:9). When Peter sinned, he went out *alone* and wept bitterly. Babel's sin of pride ended in a confusion of tongues that made it impossible to maintain fellowship.

Our personal self-hatred always becomes hatred of neighbor. Perhaps this [was] one of the reasons for the basic appeal of Communism, with its philosophy of class struggle: Communism [had] a special affinity for souls that [were] already undergoing a struggle inside of themselves. Associated with this inner conflict is a tendency to become hypercritical: Unhappy souls almost always blame everyone but themselves for their miseries. Shut up within themselves, they are necessarily shut off from all others except to criticize them. Since the essence of sin is opposition to God's will, it follows that the sin of one individual is bound to oppose any other individual whose will is in harmony with God's will. This resulting estrangement from one's fellow humans is intensified when one begins to live solely for this world; then the possessions of the neighbor are regarded as something unjustly taken from oneself. Once the material becomes the goal of life, a society of conflicts is born. As Shelley said: "The accumulations of the materials of external life exceed the quantity of power of assimilating them to the internal laws of our nature."

Matter divides, as spirit unites. Divide an apple into four parts, and it is always possible to quarrel as to who has the biggest part; but if four persons learn a prayer, no one deprives the others of possessing it — the prayer becomes the basis of their unity. When the goal of civilization consists, not in union with the Heavenly Father, but in the acquisition of material things, there is an increase in the potentialities of envy, greed, and war. Divided people then seek a dictator to bring them together, not in the unity of love, but in the false unity of the three p's — Power, Police, and Politics.

ESTRANGEMENT FROM GOD. Alienation from self and from one's neighbors has its roots in separation from God. Once the hub of the wheel, which is God, is lost, the spokes, which are human beings, fall apart. God seems very far away from modern man: This is due, to a great extent, to humanity's own God-less behavior. Goodness always appears as a reproach to those who are not living right, and this reproach on the part of the sinner expresses itself in hatred and persecution. There is rarely a disrupted, frustrated soul, critical and envious of his neighbor, who is not at the same time an antireligious individual. Organized atheism is thus a projection of self-hatred; no one hates God without first hating himself. Persecution of religion is a sign of the indefensibility of the antireligious or atheistic attitude, for by the violence of hate it hopes to escape the irrationality of Godlessness. The final form of this hatred of religion is a wish to defy God and to maintain one's own evil in the face of His Goodness and Power. Revolting against the whole of existence, such a soul thinks that it has disproved it; it begins to admire its own torment as a protest against life. Such a soul will not hear about religion, lest the comfort become a condemnation of its own arrogance, and so it defies it instead. Never able to make sense of its own life, it universalizes its own inner discord and sees the world as a kind of chaos in the face of which it develops the philosophy of "living dangerously." "He functions as a distracted atom in a growing chaos made poor by his wealth, made empty by his fulness, reduced to monotony by his very opportunities for variety."[3]

Does such a confused soul exist in the Gospel? Is modern psychology studying a different type of person from the one our Divine Lord came to redeem? If we turn to Saint Mark, we find that a young man in the land of the Gerasene is described as having exactly the same three frustrations as the modern soul.

He was self-estranged, for when Our Lord asked, "What is thy name?" (Mark 5:9), the young man answered, "My name is Legion, for we are many" (Mark 5:9). Notice the personality conflict and the confusion between "my" and "we are many." It is obvious that he is a problem to himself, a bewildered backwash of a thousand and one conflicting anxieties. For that reason he called himself "Legion." No divided personality is happy. The Gospel describes this unhappiness by saying that the young man was "crying and cutting himself with stones" (Mark 5:5). The confused person is always sad;

he is his own worst enemy, as he abuses the purpose of nature for his own destruction.

The young man was also separated from his fellow men, for the Gospel describes him thus: "And he was always day and night in the monuments and in the mountains" (Mark 5:5). He was a menace to others. "For having been often bound with fetters and chains, he had burst the chains, broken the fetters in pieces, and no one could tame him" (Mark 5:4). Isolation is a peculiar quality of Godlessness, whose natural habitat is away from other human beings, among the tombs, in the region of death. There is no cement in sin, its nature being centrifugal, divisive, and disruptive.

He was separated from God, for when he saw the Divine Savior, he shouted, "What have I to do with Thee, Jesus the Son of the most high God? I adjure Thee by God that Thou torment me not" (Mark 5:7). That is to say, "What have we in common? Your presence is my destruction." It is an interesting psychological fact that the frustrated soul hates goodness and wants to be separated from it. Every sinner hides from God. The very first murderer said, "And I shall be hidden from thy face, and I shall be a vagabond and a fugitive on the earth" (Gen. 4:14).

It appears that the modern soul is not so modern, after all. Like the Gerasene youth he is estranged from himself, others, and God. But there is a difference, nonetheless, and it is this: The Gerasene youth was pre-Christian, the modern soul is post-Christian. Fundamental as the distinction is, it still leaves the problem: How deal with the person of today?

One thing is certain: The modern soul is not going to find peace so long as he remains locked up inside himself, mulling around in the scum and sediment of his unconscious mind, a prey of the unconscious forces whose nature and existence he glorifies. It is interesting that Freud, who thought such a self-centered solution the right one, took as the motto for one of his earlier works, "If I cannot bend the gods on high, I will set all hell in an uproar." His is not the answer! In dethroning the conscious values of the world, one does, indeed, set hell in an uproar and end in neuroses worse confounded.

The true answer is that humanity must be released from its inner prison. A person will go mad if he must be content to chase the tail of his own mind, being both seeker and sought, rabbit and hound. Peace of soul cannot come from the person, any more than the person can lift himself by his own ears. Help must come from without; and it must be not merely human help, but Divine help. Nothing short of a Divine invasion that restores humans to ethical reality can make them happy when they are alone and in the dark.

The frustrated youth of the Gerasenes was cured only when Our Lord restored him to himself, others, and God. He then recovered the purpose of life. No longer calling himself "Legion," the Gospel describes him as "sitting, clothed and well in his wits" (Mark 5:15). In our language, he was feeling "like his own self." Instead of being isolated from community life, we find him restored to fellowship by Our Lord, Who told him, "Go into thy house to thy friends" (Mark 5:19). Finally, instead of hating God, we find that he begins to "publish in Decapolis how great things Jesus had done for him, and all men wondered" (Mark 5:20). It is similar with people today. If the modern soul is too harassed with fears and anxieties to come to God through the loveliness of a star, then it can come to Him through the loneliness of a heart saying with the Psalmist, "Out of the depths have I cried unto Thee, O Lord" (Ps. 130). If it cannot find God through the argument of motion, it can reach Him by way of its own disgusts — even through the handle of its sins.

The important question is not, What will *become* of us, but What will we *be?* It will always be true today that how one gets *out* of time is not so important as how one *is* in eternity. A bomb in the hands of a Francis of Assisi would be less harmful than a pistol in the hand of a thug; what makes the bomb dangerous is not the energy it contains, but the person who uses it. Therefore, it is modern humanity who has to be remade. Unless one can stop the explosions inside one's own mind, one will probably — armed in some fashion — do harm to the planet itself. Modern man has locked himself in the prison of his own mind; and only God can let him out, as He let Peter out of his dungeon. All that a person must do is contribute the desire to get out. God will not fail; it is only our human desire that is weak. There is no reason for discouragement. It was the bleating lamb in the thickets, more than the flock in the peaceful pastures, that attracted the Savior's heart and helping hand. But the recovery of peace through His grace implies an understanding of anxiety, the grave complaint of imprisoned modern humanity.

Notes

1. C. G. Jung, *Modern Man in Search of a Soul,* p. 235.
2. Harry Slochower, *No Voice Is Wholly Lost,* p. 316, Creative Age Press, Inc., 1945.
3. Lewis Mumford, *The Condition of Man,* p. 418, 1944.

Chapter 2

THE PHILOSOPHY
OF ANXIETY

ONE OF THE FAVORITE psychological descriptions of the modern age is to say that it has an anxiety complex. Psychology is more right than it suspects but for a more profound reason than it knows. There is no doubt that anxiety has been increased and complicated by our metropolitan and industrialized civilization. An increasing number of persons are afflicted with neuroses, complexes, fears, irritabilities, and ulcers; they are, perhaps, not so much "run down" as "wound up"; not so much set on fire by the sparks of daily life as they are burning up from internal combustion. Few of them have the felicity of the good country woman who said, "When I works, I works hard; when I sits, I sits loose; and when I thinks I goes to sleep."

But modern anxiety is different from the anxiety of previous and more normal ages in two ways. In other days people were anxious about their souls, but modern anxiety is principally concerned with the body; the major worries of today are economic security, health, the complexion, wealth, social prestige, and sex. To read modern advertisements, one would think that the greatest calamity that could befall a human being would be to have dishpan hands or a cough in the T-zone. This overemphasis on corporal security is not healthy; it has begotten a generation that is much more concerned about having life belts to wear on a sea journey than

we raise our voice in plea. It is evident that, even though we escaped all the anxieties of modern economic life, even though we avoided all the tensions that psychology finds in the unconsciousness and consciousness, we should still have that great basic fundamental anxiety born of our creatureliness. Anxiety stems fundamentally from irregulated desires, from the creature wanting something that is unnecessary for him or contrary to her nature or positively harmful to one's soul. Anxiety increases in direct ratio and proportion as man departs from God. Everyone in the world has an anxiety complex because each of us has the capacity to be either saint or sinner.

Let it be not believed that a person has an anxiety complex "because he still has traces of his animal origin"; indeed, animals left to themselves never have anxieties. They have natural fears, which are good, but they have no subjective anxieties. Birds do not develop a psychosis about whether they should take a winter trip to California or Florida. An animal never becomes less than it is; but a human being can do just that, because a human is a composite of both spirit and matter.

When we see a monkey acting foolishly, we do not say to the monkey, "Do not act like a nut"; but when we see a person acting foolishly, we do say, "Do not act like a monkey." Because a person is spirit, as well as matter, he can descend to the level of beasts (though not so completely as to destroy the image of God in his soul). It is this possibility that makes the peculiar tragedy of man. Cows have no psychoses, and pigs have no neuroses, and chickens are not frustrated (unless these frustrations are artificially produced by people); neither would man be frustrated or have an anxiety complex if he were an animal made *only for this world*. It takes eternity to make a person despair. "Man is both strong and weak, both free and bound, both blind and farseeing. He stands at the juncture of nature and spirit; and is involved in both freedom and necessity. It is always partly an effort to obscure his blindness by overestimating the degree of his sight and to obscure his insecurity by stretching his power beyond its limits."[2]

Dread arises because a human becomes aware, however dimly, of his contingency and finiteness. He is not the absolute, though he wants it; he is not even all that he is or all that he could be. This tension between possibility and fact, this oscillation between wanting to be with God and wanting to be God is a deeper side of his anxiety. Alfred Adler has always emphasized that behind neuroses is the human's striving to become like God, a striving as impotent as the goal is impossible. The root of every psychological tension is basically metaphysical.

Despair and anxiety are possible because there is a rational soul. They presuppose the capacity of self-reflection. Only a being capable of contemplating itself can dread annihilation in face of the infinite, can despair either of itself or of its destiny. Despair, Kierkegaard tells us, is twofold. It is a desperate desire either to be oneself or to be not oneself; a person wants either to make himself into an absolute, unconditioned being, independent, self-subsistent; or else he wants desperately to get rid of his being, with its limitation, its contingency, and its finiteness. Both these attitudes manifest the eternal revolt of the finite against the infinite: *Non serviam.* By such a revolt, the person exposes himself to the awareness of his nothingness and his solitude. Instead of finding a support in the knowledge that he, though contingent, is held in existence by a loving God, he now seeks reliance within himself and, necessarily failing to find it, becomes the victim of dread. For dread is related to an unknown, overwhelming, all-powerful something — which may strike when or where one knows not. Dread is everywhere and nowhere, all around us, terrible and indefinite, threatening us with an annihilation that we cannot imagine or even conceive. Such fear is humanity's alone. Because an animal has no soul capable of knowing perfect love, because it has to render no account of its stewardship beyond the corridors of the grave, because it is not like a pendulum swinging between eternity and time, it is devoid of those eternal relationships that the human possesses; therefore it can have only a sick body, never a sick soul. Thus a psychology that denies the human soul is constantly contradicting itself. It calls man an animal and then proceeds to describe a human anxiety that is never found in any animal devoid of a rational soul.

Since the basic cause of human anxiety is the possibility of being either a saint or a sinner, it follows that there are only two alternatives: The person can either mount upward to the peak of eternity or else slip backward to the chasms of despair and frustration. Yet there are many who think there is yet another alternative, namely, that of indifference. They think that, just as bears hibernate for a season in a state of suspended animation, so they, too, can sleep through life without choosing to live for God or against God. But hibernation is no escape; winter ends, and one is then forced to make a decision — indeed, the very choice of indifference itself is a decision. White fences do not remain white fences by having nothing done to them; they would soon become black fences. Since there is a tendency in us that pulls us back to the animal, the mere fact that we do not resist it operates to our own destruction. Just as life is the sum of the forces that resist death, so, too, man's will must be the sum of the forces that resist frustration. A person who has taken poison into his system can ignore the antidote, or he can throw it out of the window; it makes no difference which he does, for death is already on the march. Saint Paul warns us, "How shall we escape if we neglect..." (Heb. 2:3). By the mere fact that we do not go forward, we go backward. There are no plains in the spiritual life; we are either going uphill or coming down. Furthermore, the pose of indifference is only intellectual. The will *must* choose. And even though an "indifferent" soul does not positively reject the infinite, the infinite rejects it. The talents that are unused are taken away, and the Scriptures tell us, "But because thou art lukewarm, and neither cold nor hot, I will begin to vomit thee out of my mouth" (Apoc. 3:16).

Returning to the supreme alternatives, humanity can choose between an earthly love to the exclusion of Divine Love, or it can choose a Divine Love that includes a healthy, sacramental, earthly love. One can either make the soul subject to the body, or he can make the body subject to the soul. Consider first those who resolve their anxiety in favor of Godlessness. They invariably end by substituting one of the false gods for the true God of Love.

This god can be the ego, or self. This happens in atheism when there is a denial of dependence on the true God, or when there is an affirmation of one's own wish and pleasure as the absolute law, or when freedom is interpreted as the right to do what one pleases. When such a false god is adored, religion is rejected as a rationalization or an escape, or even as a fear to affirm one's own self as supreme.

Atheists commit the sin of *pride*, by which someone pretends to be that which he is not, namely, a god. Pride is inordinate self-love, an exaltation of the conditional and relative self into an absolute. It tries to gratify the thirst for the infinite by giving to one's own finitude a pretension to divinity. In some, pride blinds the self to its weakness and becomes "hot" pride; in others, it recognizes its own weakness and overcomes it by a self-exaltation that becomes "cold" pride. Pride kills docility and makes a person incapable of ever being helped by God. The limited knowledge of the puny mind pretends to be final and absolute. In the face of other intellects it resorts to two techniques: either the technique of omniscience, by which it seeks to convince others how much it knows, or the technique of nescience, which tries to convince others how little they know. When such pride is unconscious, it becomes almost incurable, for it identifies truth with *its* truth. Pride is an admission of weakness; it secretly fears all competition and dreads all rivals. It is rarely cured when the person himself is vertical — i.e., healthy and prosperous — but it can be cured when the patient is horizontal — sick and disillusioned. That is why catastrophes are necessary in an era of pride to bring people back again to God and the salvation of their souls.

The false god of the atheist can be *another* person, cherished, not as a bearer of human values, but as an object to be devoured and used for one's own pleasure. In such a case, the vocabulary of religion is invoked to solicit the object, such as "adore," "angel," "worship," "god," and "goddess." From it is born the sin of *lust,* or the adoration of another person's vitality as the end and goal of life. Lust is not the inevitable result of the flesh, any more than a cataract is directly caused by eyesight; it is due, rather, to the rebellion of the flesh against the spirit and of the person against God. As Saint Augustine says,

> If any man say that flesh is the cause of the viciousness of the soul, he is ignorant of man's nature. This corruption, which is so burdensome to the soul, is the punishment for the first sin, and not its cause. The corruptible flesh made not the soul to sin, but the sinning soul made the flesh corruptible; from which corruption, although there arise some incitements to sin, and some vicious desires, yet are not all sins of an evil life to be

laid to the flesh, otherwise, we shall make the devil, who has no flesh, sinless.[3]

Flesh in revolt (or lust) is related to pride. The conquest of the one desired may serve the individual's need of excessive self-exaltation; but consummated lust leads to despair (or the opposite of self-exaltation) by the inner tension or sadness resulting from an uneasy conscience. It is this effect that divorces it from a purely biological phenomenon, for in no creature except the human is there any act that involves such an interactivity of matter and spirit, body and soul. It need hardly be noted that lust is not sex in the ordinary sense of the term but, rather, its deorientation — a sign that someone has become ex-centric, isolated from God, and enamored of the physically good to such an excess that he or she is like the serpent that devours its own tail and eventually destroys itself.

The unbeliever's god can be things by which he seeks to remedy his own sense of nothingness. Some people seek this compensation in wealth, which gives them the false sense of power. External luxury is pursued to conceal the nakedness of their own souls. Such worship of wealth leads to tyranny and injustice toward others, and thus is born the sin of *avarice*.

Avarice is the material expression of one's own insufficiency and a challenge to the sublime truth that "our sufficiency is from God." Filling up its own lack at the storehouse of the earthly, the soul hopes to find at least a temporary escape from Divinity itself. All intense interest in luxury is a mark of inner poverty. The less grace there is in the soul, the more ornament must be on the body. It was only after Adam and Eve fell that they perceived themselves to be naked; when their souls were rich with original justice, their bodies were so suffused with its reflection that they felt no need for clothes.

But once the Divine-internal was lost, they sought a compensation in the material, the external. Excessive dedication to temporal security is one of the ways a society's loss of eternal security manifests itself. The quest for wealth and luxury can be infinite, and for the moment it satisfies the godless souls. A person can reach a point of marginal utility in the accumulation of ice-cream cones, but not in the accumulation of credits, for there is an infinity to these ambitions. Thus does a person seek to become God in gratifying limitless desires for riches, when he impoverishes himself from within. "Life wants to secure itself against the void that is raging within. The risk of eternal void is to be met by the premium of temporal insurance . . . social security, old age pensions, etc. It springs no less from metaphysical despair than from material misery."[4]

Pride, lust, avarice; the devil, the flesh, and the world; the pride of life, the concupiscence of the flesh, and the concupiscence of the eyes — these constitute the new unholy trinity by which humanity is wooed away from the Holy Trinity and from the discovery of the goal of life. It was these three things Our Lord described in the parable of those who offered excuses for not coming to the banquet. One refused because he had bought a farm, another because he had purchased a yoke of oxen, and the third because he had taken unto himself a woman. Love of self, love of person, and love of property are not in themselves wrong, but they do become wrong when they are made ends in themselves, are torn up from their true purpose, which is to lead us to God. Because there are some who abuse love of self and love of person and love of property, the Church has encouraged the three vows of obedience, chastity, and poverty to make reparation for those who make gods out of their opinions, their flesh, and their money. Anxiety and frustration invariably follow when the desires of the heart are centered on anything less than God, for all pleasures of earth, pursued as final ends, turn out to be the exact opposite of what was expected. The expectation is joyous, the realization is disgust. Out of this disappointment are born those lesser anxieties that modern psychology knows so well; but the root of them all is the meaninglessness of life due to the abandonment of Perfect Life, Truth, and Love, which is God.

The alternative to such anxieties consists in letting oneself go, not by a surrender of the spirit to the world, the flesh, and the Devil, but by an act of proper abandonment, in which the body is disciplined and made subject to the spirit and the whole personality is directed to God. Here the basic anxiety of life is transcended in three ways, each of which brings a peace of soul that only the God-loving enjoy: (1) by controlling desires; (2) by transferring anxiety from body to soul; (3) by surrender to the Will of God.

1. By CONTROLLING DESIRES. Anxieties and frustrations are due to uncontrolled desires. When a soul does not get what it wants, it falls into sadness and distress. In other generations human desires were less numerous or else were controlled; today even luxuries are considered necessities. Disappointment increases in direct ratio and proportion to our failure to obtain the things we believe essential to our enjoyment. One of the greatest deceptions of today is the belief that leisure and money are the two essentials of happiness. The sad fact of life is that there are no more frustrated people on the face of the earth than those who have nothing to do and those who have too much money for their own good. Work never killed anybody, but worry has. It is assumed by many reformers that the principal and major cause of unhappiness is economic insecurity, but this theory forgets that there are economic problems only because people have not solved the problems of their own souls. Economic disorder is a symptom of spiritual disorder.

To conquer anxiety does not mean eliminating our desires, but rather arranging them in a hierarchy, as Our Lord reminded us when He said that life is more than the raiment. This pyramid of values places things at the bottom — and things include everything material in the universe, from a star that inspires a poet to wheat used for the baker's bread. Above things comes humanity, and at the peak of the pyramid is God. A religious person orders his or her life by the pattern of the pyramid. Such a person overcomes anxiety by making all material things subject to the human, by disciplining the body until it is subject to the spirit, and by submitting the whole personality to God. "For all are yours; and you are Christ's; and Christ is God's" (1 Cor. 3:22, 23). Once the soul recognizes that it is made for God, it abandons the bourgeois idea that every person is to be judged by what he or she has. There follows, not only a renunciation of evil, but even a voluntary surrender of some things that are lawful, in order that the spirit be freer to love God. When the sacrifices of Our Lord become the inspiration of a life, then its burdens are borne with more than resignation — they are accepted as providential calls to greater intimacy with Him.

But quite apart from Christian motivations — even viewed from a purely natural point of view, it is wise for a person to renounce some desires, simply because the soul cannot find satisfaction in fulfilling them. The desire for wealth is one of these. There are two kinds of wealth: *natural* wealth, which takes the form of the necessary food, clothing, and shelter to sustain the life of the individual or family; *artificial* wealth, which is money, credit, stocks, and bonds. It is possible for a person to satisfy his desires for natural wealth, because his stomach soon reaches a point where it can consume no more food. But there is no limit to the desire for artificial wealth. Someone who has a million dollars is never satisfied with that million. There is a certain false infinity about artificial wealth because a person can always want more and more of it. Because natural wealth imposes its own limitations, farming and gardening are among the most satisfying experiences of human life. If we desire possessions, we never have enough of them. We become frustrated. There is a psychological difference between "frustration" and "renunciation." Frustration occurs only when a person feels himself a passive victim of extrinsic forces, against which he is powerless; renunciation springs from a person's own free decision. Parents recognize this difference: A child who has got hold of something he is not allowed to have is told by his parent, "Give it to me, or else I shall have to take it away from you." Often the child will renounce the thing rather than be compelled. The words addressed to the child have left him this way to safeguard his dignity and independence: He does what he must do in any case, but he does it with at least the semblance of freedom. And this freedom makes all the difference. If a person can convince himself that he does not truly need this or that (although he may desire it), to abandon his striving will not frustrate him. It is only if he is forced to renunciation that he feels frustrated.

Uncontrolled desires grow like weeds and stifle the spirit. Material possessions bring a relative pleasure for a time, but sooner or later a malaise is experienced; a sense of emptiness, a feeling that something is wrong comes over the soul. This is God's way of saying that the soul is hungry and that He alone can satisfy it. It is to such modern, frustrated, starved, and anxious souls that the Savior extends the invitation, "Come to me, all you that labor, and are burdened, and I will refresh you" (Matt. 11:28).

2. By transferring concern from the body to the soul — by being wisely anxious. For there are two kinds of anxieties, one about time, the other about eternity. Most

souls are anxious about the very things they should not be anxious about. Our Divine Lord mentioned at least nine things about which we should not worry: about having our body killed; about what we shall say in days of persecution when we are called on the carpet before commissars; about whether we should build another barn (or another skyscraper); about family disputes because we accept the faith; about mother-in-law troubles; about our meals, our drinks, our fashions, our complexion (Luke 12). He did tell us that we should be very anxious about one thing and one thing only: our souls (Matt. 16:24–28).

Our Lord does not mean that worldly activities are unnecessary. He only said that if we were anxious about our souls the lesser anxieties would dissolve: "Seek ye *first* [not *only*] the kingdom of God and His justice, and all these things shall be added unto you" (Luke 12:31). It used to be that the true Christian was set apart from others by the intensity of his healthy anxiety about his soul. (Now he is differentiated by the mere fact that he believes he has a soul to save.) Anxiety is present in all love. And every human being must love or go crazy, because no person is sufficient for himself. Direct love toward God, and peace comes over the soul; turn it from God, and the heart becomes a broken fountain where tears fall, "from the sighful branches of mind." The nobler the heart that breaks, in its refusal to be anxious about God's love, the meaner it becomes in its lovelessness and ungodliness. But there is hope: The greater the frustration, the more complex the anxiety of the godless heart, the more capable it is of being metamorphosed to a saint.

There is hope for everyone. The things a person has done pass away; the doer remains, responsible for his future acts. He can begin to cultivate healthy anxiety now. If the modern souls only knew it, the things they have been most anxious about are only trashy substitutes for Him Who alone can calm their spirits. Charlatans advise us to forget eternity and to satisfy our bodily desires — but who would want to be a contented cow? The Lord's way to be happy is to concentrate on the narrow gate: "Enter ye in at the narrow gate; for wide is the gate, and broad is the way that leads to destruction, and many there are who go in by it. How narrow is the gate, and strait is the way that leads to life, and few there are that find it" (Matt. 7:13–14).

3. By increasing our trust in God. Love is reciprocal; it is received in proportion as it is given. We generally trust only those who trust us; that is why there is a special Providence for those who trust in God. Contrast two children, one child in a happy family, well provided with food, clothing, and education, the other a homeless orphan of the streets. The first child lives in an area of love; the second is outside of that area and enjoys none of its privileges. Many souls deliberately choose to exclude themselves from the area of the Heavenly Father's Love where they might live as His children. They trust only in their own resourcefulness, their own bank account, their own devices. This is particularly true of many families, who consider the rearing of children solely an economic problem, never once invoking the Heavenly Father's Love: They are like a son who in time of need never called on his wealthy father for assistance. The result is they lose many of the blessings reserved for those who throw themselves into the loving arms of God. This law applies to nations as well as individuals: "Because thou hast had confidence in the king of Syria, and not in the Lord thy God, therefore, hath the army of the king of Syria escaped out of thy hand" (II Par. 16:7). Many favors and blessings are hanging from heaven to relieve our temporal anxieties if we would only cut them down with the sword of our trust in God. Relief from all wrong anxiety comes, not from giving ourselves to God by halves, but by an all-encompassing love, wherein we go back, not to the past

in fear or to the future in anxiety, but lie quietly in His Hand, having no will but His. Then the former shadows of life are seen as "The shade of His Hand outstretched caressingly."[5]

Everyone has anxiety. A complex, according to the usage of contemporary psychology, is a group of memories and desires of which we are not conscious but which nevertheless affect our personality. An anxiety complex would be a system of unhappy memories submerged in the unconscious and producing many kinds of symptoms. Everyone has anxiety; fortunately, everyone does not have an anxiety complex. The difference between peace of soul and discontent comes from the *kind* of anxiety we have; the broadest division of all is between anxiety over the things of time and the values of eternity. Of the first, Our Lord said, "Be not anxious, for your Heavenly Father knows you have need of these things" (Matt. 6:8). The second kind of anxiety is normal because it is bound up with human freedom and is a result of our creatureliness. This anxiety is a restlessness with anything short of the perfect happiness that is God.

Ultimately, anxiety, or dread, is related to human finiteness and to a person's vague awareness of an infinite being in comparison with which he or she is almost nothing. A human being, it has been said, may falsely try to overcome his finiteness either by denying his creatureliness (which is pride) or by escaping into an idolatry of sensuality. Then his anxiety still remains in the form of dread — which is not the same as fear. For fear is a response to a human danger and, as Saint Thomas says, is always mixed with a certain degree of hope. But dread knows no hope; it expresses itself in purposeless ways, for it has no obvious cause and comes from a person's half-conscious sense of the precariousness of his being. In this way dread is related to the idea of death, the great unknown, the one inescapable thing of which the person has no experiential knowledge. When this dread is properly resolved by recognizing our dependency on God, it becomes the pathway to peace of soul. But no one in the world, even then, escapes the fact of anxiety or outgrows a feeling of the tension between the finite and the infinite. Such normal anxiety may be covered over, but it will break out somewhere and somehow. Alfred Adler had a glimpse of this truth when he said that neurotics are animated by an unruly ambition to be "like God." The various tensions that psychology studies are very often the reflections of the deeper metaphysical tension, inherent in every human being, between his contingent and limited being and the Infinite and Absolute Being. This tension would not be felt unless man were free and had the responsibility of choosing between self-frustration and self-perfection through the use of creatures as a means to God.

Peace of soul comes to those who have the right kind of anxiety about attaining perfect happiness, which is God. A soul has anxiety because its final and eternal state is not yet decided; it is still and always at the crossroads of life. This fundamental anxiety cannot be cured by a surrender to passions and instincts; the basic cause of our anxiety is a restlessness within time that comes because we are made for eternity. If there were anywhere on earth a resting place other than God, we may be very sure that the human soul in its long history would have found it before this. As Saint Augustine has said, "Our hearts were made for Thee. They are restless until they rest in Thee, O God."

Notes

1. Anxiety is a phenomenon of both consciousness and unconsciousness. An "unconscious" anxiety may mean two things. Either it may mean that the objective seat of the anxiety is unknown to consciousness, in which case the consciously experienced emotional state is related, e.g., by

way of a "secondary rationalization," to some fictitious object in a manner that appears unfounded and nonsensical to the individual but that nevertheless imposes itself with a compulsory force, as in phobias. Or it may mean that the emotional state itself is relegated into and kept in the unconscious, so that it becomes manifest, not as anxiety, but as some other "symptom." Anxiety is also conscious and when experienced is a subject of psychological study, in children and adults, in normal and in abnormal people.

2. Reinhold Niebuhr, *The Nature and Destiny of Man,* p. 181, Charles Scribner's Sons, 1941.

3. *De Civitate Dei,* Book XIV, Chap. 3.

4. Franz Werfel, *Between Heaven and Earth,* p. 71, Hutchinson & Company, Ltd., London, 1947.

5. Francis Thompson, "The Hound of Heaven."

Chapter 3

THE ORIGIN OF CONFLICTS AND THEIR REDEMPTION

THE INTELLECTUAL WORLD has suddenly rediscovered that man is a seat of conflict. Marx found conflict in society, Kierkegaard in the soul, Heidegger in man's being, and psychologists in the mind. To the credit of all of them, it must be said that they come much closer to an understanding of man than did the Liberals of the last few centuries, who taught that man was naturally good and progressive and on the high road to becoming a god without God. Anyone who would say today that modern man (who has fought two world wars in two decades) needs only evolution and education to become a deity would be less observant than the ostrich with its head in the sand. It is apparent to all that the Godless man of the twentieth century has somehow got himself and society into a condition of disorder and chaos. The psychiatrists who have investigated these conflicts and tensions have described them in various ways. To some of them, the conflict is between the conscious and the unconscious mind; to others, it is a tension between ego and environment; to others, a duel between instincts and ideals; to others, a war between the id and the superego.

The cause of the tension is most often traced to personal experience; for example, the blame is placed on the way a child was treated by his parents, or on the fact that the child was denied certain opportunities to satisfy his natural and legitimate desires, or on insufficiency of playgrounds and Grade B milk. Bodily defects are also accused of causing tension and disorders of behavior. Because of the relations established between temperament and the ductless glands, the latter have also been made responsible for our state of tension. Other students lay the blame on certain conflicts that arise inevitably within a family. Freudian psychoanalysis thus speaks of the Oedipus situation. As the hero of the Greek legend killed his father and married his mother, so every male child is supposed to desire his mother and to be jealous of his father, even to the extent of wishing him dead. A daughter is said to play the corresponding role toward her mother; she hates her mother, and she would like, after the fashion of Electra, to kill her in order to marry her father. This situation has been called the Electra situation, or mother complex.[1]

Other schools lay the blame for conflict and tension on something like a racial memory, on the persistent influence of some events that happened in the past of the race; they may go even further back and discuss a "collective unconscious" that human evolution is said to have transmitted to every individual as part of his unconscious psychic equipment. This collective unconscious is traced back even to the "animal ancestors of man."[2]

Common to all these theories is the idea that influences outside of the individual, common to the race itself, condition people presently and cause their conflicts. Though psychiatrists have rediscovered humanity's conflict and described it on the unconscious level, the human race has always known about it. Plato, for example, described personality as a charioteer driving two headstrong steeds. One of the steeds is appetite, or instinct; the other is spirit. The driver is reason, who has the greatest difficulty in keeping both steeds headed in the same direction. Sophocles, the ancient Greek dramatist, spoke of some great primeval disharmony gray with age that infected all men. Ovid, the Latin poet, wrote, "I see and approve the better things of life, the worse things of life I follow." Saint Paul described the human conflict as waged between the law of the mind and the law of the members. Every human being can bear witness to the experience that victories are not all on one side, either of the body or of the spirit. Good people sometimes act like bad people, and very bad people sometimes act better than good people. Goethe regretted that God had made only one man of him when there was enough material in him for both a rogue and a gentleman. Stevenson's *Doctor Jekyll and Mr. Hyde,* a story of the conflict inside of man and of his possible duality, is too well known to need retelling. The Little Catechism, summarizing the best wisdom of the ancients and Christianity, asks the question, "Of which should we take more care, the body or the soul?" — a question that assumes that it is possible for either one to gain the primacy or mastery of life.

The fact of conflict in human personality is not new. It is only its detailed description on the psychological level that is new. Psychiatry pronounces that there is some primordial tendency to evil in the collective unconsciousness that influences all the members of the human race. In throwing new light on this tension it has added new knowledge to what humanity has generally known about itself, namely, that it is not all that it ought to be. It may very well be that the new apologetic to the modern soul will start with the contributions of modern psychology on the subject of conflict, that it will be a kind of preface to the tract, *De peccato originali,* which is relatively the most important treatise on theology for the modern mind.

We are interested here, not in the conflict on the unconscious level, but in the underlying cause of *all* conflict in the body or soul, the will or the heart, society or the individual, of which the psychological is a superficial manifestation. We can eliminate immediately the antiquated idea that poverty is the cause of inner disharmony — for if that were so, all the rich would be normal. Yet there is more abnormality among the rich than the poor. Nor is the cause of conflict to be found in the animal background of man, for man marks a complete break with the animal, as is evidenced by the fact that humans can laugh and animals cannot, that humans can create art, which animals cannot. Laughter and art are impossible without ideas on the one hand and ideals on the other. The cause of conflict is not environment, because the golden bit does not make the better horse. Judas, who had the best environment in history, died in ignominy and shame. Conflict is not due to ignorance; otherwise every D.D. would be a saint. The conflict *is not due to the person alone.* Personal sins do intensify one's complexes; but the inescapable fact is that all human persons in the world have a conflict going on inside themselves. Since it is not you, or I, or he, or she alone that has a tension, it must be that the conflict does not have a personal origin but is due to *human nature* itself. The source of the disorder is to be found both in the individual and in humanity itself. A psychology that assumed that all conflicts are due to aberrations in the person himself would fail to account for the universality of conflict. Since everybody is that way, no individual or personal explanation can be the total cause. The personal cause is an effect of the natural cause, as the individual sins because human nature sinned.

If the true origin of the conflict is to be found, not in the individual exclusively, but in human nature, it is well to examine the human nature that is common to all of us. Two facts stand out.

First, the human is neither an angel nor a devil. Humanity is not intrinsically corrupt (as theologians began claiming four hundred years ago) nor intrinsically divine (as philosophers began saying fifty years ago). Rather, the human being has aspirations to good that he finds it impossible to realize completely by himself; at the same time, he has an inclination toward evil that solicits him away from these ideals. He is like someone who falls down a well through his own stupidity. He knows he ought not to be there, but he cannot get out by himself. Or, to change the picture, he is like a clock whose mainspring is broken. He needs to be fixed on the inside, but the repairs must be supplied from without. He is mistaken if he is an optimist, who believes evolution will give him a mainspring, or a pessimist, who believes that nobody can fix him. He is a creature who can run well again, but only if some watchmaker will have the kindness to repair him.

Second, this conflict has all the appearances of being due to an abuse of human freedom. As the drunkard is what he is, because of an act of choice, so human nature seems to have lost the original goodness with which a Good God endowed it, through an act of choice. As Saint Augustine said, "Whatever we are, we are not what we ought to be." The origin of this conflict has been told by medieval and modern theologians through the analogy of music. Picture an orchestra on a stage with a celebrated conductor directing the beautiful symphony he himself composed. Each member of the orchestra is free to follow the conductor and thus to produce harmony. But each member is also free to disobey the conductor. Suppose one of the musicians deliberately plays a false note and then induces a violinist alongside of him to do the same. Having heard the discord, the conductor could do one of two things. He could either strike his baton and order the measure replayed, or he could ignore the discord. It would make no difference which he did, for that discord has already gone out into space at a certain temperature at the rate of about 1,100 feet a second. On and on it goes, affecting even the infinitesimally small radiations of the universe. As a stone dropped in a pond causes a ripple

which affects the most distant shore, so this discord affects
even the stars. As long as time endures, somewhere in God's
Universe there is a disharmony, introduced by the free will
of humanity.

Could that discord be stopped? Not by the human being
himself, for he could never reach it; time is irreversible, and
man is localized in space. It *could,* however, be stopped by
the Eternal coming out of His agelessness into time, laying
hold of that false note, arresting it in its flight. But would it
still be a discord even in God's Hands? No! Not if God wrote
a *new* symphony and made that false note its first note! Then
all would be harmony again.

A long time ago, long before Oedipus and Electra, God
wrote a beautiful symphony of creation; chemicals, flowers,
and animals were subject to man, man's passions were under
the guidance of reason, and man's personality was in love
with Love, which is God. God gave that symphony to a man
and woman to play, with a complete set of directions, down
to the last detail of what to avoid. The man and woman,
being free, could obey the Divine Director and produce harmony, or they could disobey Him. The Devil suggested that,
because the Divine Director had marked the script and told
them what to play and what not to play, He was destroying their freedom. The woman first succumbed to the idea
that freedom is license, or absence of law; she struck a discord to prove her so-called "independence." It was a very
unladylike thing to do. She then induced the man to do the
same — which was a very ungentlemanly thing to do. On and
on through the whole human race this original discord swept;
whenever there was the conjunction of man and woman, it
affected every human being, save one, who ever was born,
for each inherited the effects of that disharmony. The discord
even had its repercussions in the material universe, as this-
tles grew and beasts became wild. As a stream polluted at

its source passes on the pollution through its length, so the original fault was transmitted to humanity.

That original discord could not be stopped by man himself, because he could not repair an offense against the infinite with his finite self. He had contracted a bigger debt than he could pay. The debt could be paid only by the Divine Master Musician coming out of His Eternity into time. But there is a world of difference between a discordant note and a rebellious human. One has no freedom, the other has; and God refuses to be a totalitarian dictator in order to abolish evil by destroying human freedom. God could seize a note, but He would not seize a man. Instead of conscripting man, God willed to consult humanity again as to whether or not it wanted to be made a member of the Divine orchestra once more.

Out from the great white throne of light, there comes an angel of light, down past the plains of Esdralon to the little village of Nazareth to a village maid called Mary. Since a woman struck the first discordant note, so a woman would be given the chance to right it. This woman herself was free from the stain of the original sin through the anticipated merits of the Son she was later to bear. Fitting it was that He, Who is Innocence itself, should come through portals of flesh not polluted with its common sin. This privilege of Mary has been called the Immaculate Conception. Since a fallen angel tempted the first woman to rebel, God now consults through an unfallen angel, Gabriel, with the new Eve, Mary, and asks, "Will you give me a man? Will you give me freely a new note out of humanity with which I can write a new symphony?" This new man must *be* a man; otherwise God would not be acting in the name of humanity. But he must also be outside the current of infection to which all humans are subject. Being born of a woman, He will be human; being born of a Virgin, He will be sinless. The Virgin was asked if she would consent to be a Mother. Since there can be no birth without love, in the case of the Blessed Virgin Mary, the Power of the Most High, the Spirit of Love, overshadowed her, and He that was born of her is the Son of God, the Son of man, and His name is Jesus, because He saved the world from its sins.

The Immaculate Conception and the Virgin Birth were to the beginning of a new humanity something like what a lock is to a canal, the former in a special way. If a ship is sailing on a polluted canal and wishes to transfer itself to clear waters on a higher level, it must pass through a device that locks out the polluted waters and raises the ship to the higher position. Then the other gate of the lock is lifted, and the ship rides on the new, clear waters, taking none of the polluted waters with it. Mary's Immaculate Conception was like that lock, inasmuch as, through her, humanity passed from the lower level of the sons of Adam to the higher level of the sons of God.

When this plan was presented to Mary in the greatest charter of freedom the world ever heard, she answered, "Be it done unto me according to Thy Word." And God began taking on the form of man within her chaste body. Nine months later the Eternal established its beachhead in Bethlehem, as He Who is Eternal appeared in time; the bird that built the nest is hatched therein; He Who made the world is born in the world which received Him not. Because He is man, Jesus Christ can act in the name of man and be responsible as man; because He is God, everything He does with that human nature has an infinite value. Through this human nature of His that is sinless, He makes Himself responsible for all the sins of the world, and to such an extent that in the strong language of Saint Paul, "He is made sin." As a rich brother takes on himself the debt of his bankrupt brother, so Our Lord takes upon Himself all the discords, disharmonies, all the sins, guilts, and blasphemies of humanity, as if He Himself were guilty. As gold is thrust into the furnace to have its dross burned away, so He takes His human nature and plunges it into the fires of Calvary to have our sins burned away. To change the figure again — since sin is in the blood, He pours out His Blood in redemption; for without the shedding of blood there is no remission of sins.

Then on Easter Sunday, by the power of God, He rises from the dead with His glorified sinless human nature, becoming the first note in the new creation, the beginning of the new symphony that will be played again by the Divine Conductor through all who freely will to produce harmonies in the new harmony of a Christian world. And how are new notes added to this first note? By the Sacrament of Baptism, by which each person dies to the old Adam and rises again with Christ. This unity of notes in measures and movements constitutes the new symphony. To use the language of Saint Paul, each person who freely, as Mary did, gives himself to Christ becomes as a cell in His new Body, which is the Church.

To be a Christian, then, means to be lifted out of the old humanity of Adam to the new humanity of Christ. As one cannot lead a physical life unless one is born to it, so one cannot lead a spiritual life unless one is born to it. No one is forced to accept that Christ Life any more than Mary was. It is free and consultive. Since that Divine Life in our souls is a pure gift of God, since it is not caused by any human effort or merited in the strict sense by anything we do, it, too, may be said to have had a Virgin Birth. As Saint John tells the story, "He was in the world, and the world was made by him, and the world knew him not. He came unto his own, and his own received him not. But as many as received him, he gave them power to be made the sons of God, to them that believe in his name: Who are born, not of blood, nor of the will of the flesh, nor of the will of man, but of God" (John 1:10–13).

Returning to the subject of conflicts, there are two causes, not unrelated. One of them is personal and is born of some personal rebellion against the moral law, with its consequent disturbance of the equilibrium of mind or body or nerves. The other belongs to human nature. We did not cause it personally, but our human nature is involved in it, just as we became involved in a war declared by the head of our government, though the individual citizens did not make an individual declaration of war. What the head of the human government did, we did. It was not you or I who sinned in Adam, but that which we are. Each person is profoundly the way he is, not because of his parents, or grandparents, or great-grandparents, but because of his first parents. Each person is a possible seat of psychoses or neuroses, with darkened intellect and weak will, with passions rebelling against reason, with good instincts such as sex becoming lust, hunger becoming gluttony, thirst becoming intemperance, and with one's body getting all mixed up with one's soul. For human nature, in losing its union with God, did not simply fall to the natural level; rather, it became a fallen king, never satisfied in exile, always desiring intimacy once again with Him Who alone can restore harmony and peace, provided the *will* cooperates with His saving grace.

Humanity's conflict is deep-seated; psychology touches only the shallow part. It springs not only from a revolt against the moral law but, more fundamentally, from the unwillingness of man to accept his position and role in the order of being. Humans are aware, even if they do not reflect on the fact, that they are placed above all other creatures. They are also aware of their quasi-infinite potentialities, of having an intellect powerful enough to solve the puzzles of nature and to enslave its forces, and of a capacity to conceive the most astonishing plans and carry them out. They know themselves capable of creating wonderful things, the beauty of which can never perish. But they also realize that their existence is limited and that there are set boundaries to their power. They may push these boundaries farther out, but however far they go they never see an end. Human beings can never hope to make themselves absolute masters of their existence and their destiny.

Legends of many peoples tell of the fate that overcame those who tried "to be like gods." In the Greek myth, Prometheus fell a victim to the wrath of the supreme Zeus. In the *Arabian Nights,* there is the story of the City of Brass; the expedition that sets out to discover this mysterious city comes to a deserted castle, beautiful but empty. An inscription tells of the might and power of the king who once ruled there, his treasures, and the immensity of his realm. But then came death, and the gold was of no avail.

However great a person becomes, there is something greater than he is. But he is great enough to resent this and to revolt against his fate, which forever condemns him to be less than he wants to be. Yet to revolt against one's own nature and being is an enterprise obviously bound to fail and to end in a catastrophe; and human reason itself sees it to be devoid of sense. But so deeply ingrained is this pride and lust of power and greatness that humanity again and again succumbs.

The human revolt against the moral law may be only a manifestation of this deeper rebellion against one's finitude. The moral law (and secondarily any law) imposes restrictions, and this brings home to the human being the fact that he does not possess boundless power; it renders him aware in a more poignant manner of his finitude and his contingency. Forever there rings in the darkest and most hidden places of a person's soul the seductive promise of the serpent, "You shall be like gods."

There is some truth in the paradoxical saying that pride comes after the fall: Because fallen and deprived of his original state, man has become more proud than ever. But dark-ened though his reason be, it sees with sufficient clarity that revolt against the Infinite is equivalent to revolt against his own nature. This is the most fundamental of all conflicts. The root of all sins is pride, says Saint Augustine. Pride stands at the beginning, dominates man's presence, and creates for him an illusory future. Torn between pride and weakness, striving for the Infinite with the consciousness of finiteness, man is thrown into the turmoil of a conflict that will never end un-less, wholeheartedly and fully, he accepts his true situation. Only when he has secured to himself, by such an acceptance and surrender, a firm basis whereon to stand, can he progress toward his glorious end. As long as he stays in the attitude of revolt, he is the victim of unsolvable conflicts whose manifold forms are only disguises of the one basic revolt.

Plutarch tells the story of a man who attempted to make a dead body stand upright. He tried various schemes of bal-ancing, experimented with different postures. Finally he gave up, saying, "There is something missing on the inside." This is the story of Everyman. A psychiatrist, a doctor, and a teacher may be able to relieve certain superficial complexes and conflicts, but no one is able to remove the basic cause of all complexes except God Himself. He does this by bringing to humanity something that humans cannot produce of and by themselves. And that one thing is God's grace. Saint Paul describes this tension and the ultimate release of it through grace when he writes,

> For that which I work, I understand not. For I do not that good which I will; but the evil which I hate, that I do. If then I do that which I will not, I consent to the law, that is good. Now then it is no more I that do it, but sin that dwells in me. For I know that there dwells not in me, that is to say, in my flesh, that which is good. For

to will, is present with me; but to accomplish that which is good, I find not. For the good which I will, I do not, but the evil which I will not, that I do. Now if I do that which I will not, it is no more I that do it, but sin that dwells in me. I find then a law, that when I have a will to do good, evil is present with me. For I am delighted with the law of God, according to the inward man: But I see another law in my members, fighting against the law of my mind, and captivating me in the law of sin, that is in my members. Unhappy man that I am, who shall deliver me from the body of death? The grace of God, by Jesus Christ Our Lord. Therefore I myself, with the mind serve the law of God; but with the flesh, the law of sin (Rom. 7:15–25).

Physical diseases may be cured by physicians, and mental diseases by psychiatrists, but no good psychiatrist will start with the assumption that all mental disorders and all conflicts are rooted in those instincts that man shares with animals. He will realize that problems must be taken seriously, if they are serious problems. Even a neurotic person runs into problems that demand to be dealt with by means of rational analysis, and not by means of an analysis searching only for instinctual causes.[3] Dr. Karen Horney warns, "Freud's discarding of moral values has contributed toward making the analyst just as blind as the patient."[4] And Dr. Fritz Kunkel writes, "The physical and mental diseases certainly belong to the realm of medicine, and therefore the ethical valuation of these cases must be avoided. But if vices are diseases, they cease to be vices, and theology in sending the drunkard or the gambler to the physician, relinquishes its last connection with reality: the ethical task."[5]

If a person has a moral disease that is sin, then wholeness can come only through the means which God has divinely instituted to restore that person to spiritual peace. It sometimes is true that the body and the mind are affected because the conscience is affected. In that case peace of conscience will bring peace both to mind and to body. The ultimate resolution of all conflicts will not be accomplished until after the Resurrection of the Body, when the bodies of the just who died in the state of grace will reflect and enjoy the beauties of the soul.

When a person is tempted to evil, he must not think there is anything abnormal about him. A person is tempted, not because he is intrinsically evil, but because he is fallen man. No individual has a monopoly on temptation; everybody is tempted. Saints do not find it easy to be saints, and devils are not happy being devils. Not everybody is tempted in the same way: Some are tempted to pervert the good instinct of self-preservation into egotism and selfishness; others, to pervert the good instinct of self-perpetuation through sex into lust; others are tempted to pervert the good instinct of self-extension through private property into avarice. And if one is tempted in any one of these three ways or in the way of intemperance, anger, envy, jealousy, gluttony, it is not because that person is diseased: It is because, since the fall, goodness does not "come naturally," but with difficulty, and is overcome thoroughly only thanks to the supernatural.

People would be in a less unhappy state if they realized that conflict, struggle, effort are inescapable in Adam's progeny. Temptation is not evil, but only the consent to temptation, and since we are the way we are because we rejected God's help, we cannot be happy again except by accepting it. No one can understand human nature, and no one can treat it adequately, who thinks that a conflict is exclusively individual or who thinks that the basic conflict can be healed by human nature itself. Superficial conflicts sometimes yield to natural cures, but even some of these can be remedied only by the Divine Physician. Every theory that discredits the true nature of man or denies the need of a Divine Remedy is only intensifying the disease it attempts to cure. The psychopathic messes into which many tumble are due either to a want of a knowledge of human nature or to a want of genuine religion. Dr. J. A. Hadfield, one of England's greatest psychiatrists, writes, "Speaking as a student of psychotherapy who, as such, has no concern with theology, I am convinced that the Christian religion is one of the most valuable and potent influences for producing that harmony and peace of mind and that confidence of soul which is needed to bring health and power to a large proportion of nervous patients." Dr. William Brown, Wilde reader in mental philosophy at the University of Oxford and psychotherapist at King's College Hospital, says, "I have become more convinced than ever that religion is the most important thing in life, and that it is essential to mental health."

Dr. C. G. Jung, who broke with Freud because of the latter's overemphasis on sex, wrote,

> During the past thirty years, people from all the civilized countries of the earth have consulted me. I have treated many hundreds of patients, the larger number being Protestants, a small number Jews and not more than five or six believing Catholics. Among all my patients in the second half of life — that is to say, over thirty-five — there has not been one whose problem in the last resort was not that of finding a religious outlook on life. It is safe to say that every one of them fell ill because he had lost that which the living religions of every age have given to their followers, and none of them has been really healed who did not regain his religious outlook.[6]

If there is a fear that is born of wrongdoing, even though one denies guilt; if one lacks an inner serenity of soul and despises those who morally reproach him; if there is a harboring of grudges and one has three jeers for everybody and three cheers for nobody; if one "gets mad" every time one hears the name of God; if one calls great Christian truths, which one does not understand, "myths"; if one accuses his neighbor of hypocrisy to cover up his conceit, pride, and "cockiness"; if one thinks he ought to get a divorce because he has found greener pastures and therefore his present spouse is "incompatible"; if one is given to excesses under the disguise of self-expression; if one likes to throw responsibility for his unhappiness on economic conditions — then it is certain that no amount of hours or weeks or years spent on couches and being told one's fear of God's justice is due to a father complex will ever help — any more than the mystical advice of a priest will help a maniac — because the cure, in neither case, is appropriate to the cause of the disorder.

This is not criticism of those who study the psychic manifestations of human conflict, but it is criticism of those who deny that a human conflict or an anxiety can spring from any cause except an instinct common to all animals. The recovering of a person's peace of soul and the mastery of his conflict are not easy. The truly integrated self is won by hard efforts and in cooperation with the resources that pour into us from without. William James once said that most of us live habitually far below the maximum of our energy, and this is particularly true of those powers placed at our disposal through the Incarnation. The more serious diseases of human nature are cured in the presence of God. If man cannot trust in his own *goodness* to discover God, then perhaps his weariness will cast him to His Bosom.

Notes

1. The whole theory of the Oedipus situation, or the Oedipus complex, is open to the most serious objections. The proof that is produced rests exclusively on conclusions drawn from the results of psychoanalysis. If the presuppositions of this doctrine fall, the theory of the Oedipus complex loses its foundation. (It is a fallacious reasoning that claims that the existence of the Oedipus complex proves the truth of the Freudian doctrine, since this proof presupposes that the whole doctrine be accepted first.) Second, the notion that the so-called "Oedipus situation" is a common one in human life and mirrors actual events that have happened in early stages of civilization lacks factual foundation. Were it so, as psychoanalysis pretends, that murder of the father, or patriarch, by his envious sons and marriage of the successful murderer to his mother were a regular event in prehistory, one would expect to encounter the Oedipus myth in many places. In truth, however, it exists only in Greek legend and perhaps, in a somewhat similar form, in one tribe in India. The whole construction of prehistoric society and its habits that Freud and his disciples worked out is without any factual foundation and has been rejected by all competent students of cultural anthropology. For a fuller refutation of this fallacy, consult Rudolf Allers, *The Successful Error;* Emil Ludwig, *Doctor Freud,* Chaps. 8–10.

2. The theory of the collective unconscious has been proposed by C. G. Jung and forms one of the least acceptable parts of his "analytic psychology."

3. The younger psychoanalysts have come to realize that in dealing with a human person, more has to be considered than instincts and their constellations. The slight progress toward a more human interpretation of man's nature is outbalanced by the tendency of many psychiatrists to envision moral conflicts as nothing else but symptoms and to see their cure, not in an acceptance of the moral law, but rather in proclaiming its relativity or denying it altogether. They assume that, if these instincts conflict with the moral precepts, then it is the latter that are wrong and in need of reform. Moral precepts are conceived by these psychiatrists, not as formulations of everlasting obligations, but as results of social and historical situations. Hence the moral law has to change when these conditions become different. The precepts that have been in force are no longer proportionate to man's present state; hence they become the sources of conflicts. The old ideas, they say, have to be given up and replaced by others more congenial to man's present state. Psychology is thus doing what philosophers did a generation ago: finding men who break the law, they change the law to suit the evil way men live. Back of this doctrine

is the notion that conflicts are unhealthy and avoidable and should be prevented at any cost. This notion is but an offspring of the general mentality that esteems comfort and pleasure more highly than anything else and dreams of a life smooth, agreeable, entailing a minimum of effort and a maximum of pleasure. This is what Pitirim Sorokin calls "sensate liberty," which holds that a person may do what he wants. If his desires are satisfied, he is free; if not, he is unfree. "Such a liberty leads to an incessant struggle of men and groups for as large a share of sensate values — wealth, love, pleasure, comfort, sensory safety, security — as one can get. Since one can get them mainly at the cost of somebody else, their quest accentuates and intensifies the struggle of individuals and group" (*The Crises of Our Age,* p. 174).

4. *Our Inner Conflicts,* p. 134.
5. *In Search of Maturity,* p. 7.
6. *Modern Man in Search of a Soul,* p. 164.

Chapter 4

IS GOD HARD TO FIND?

G OD IS NOT HARD TO FIND, for He may be quickly discovered by reason, or by our strivings, or by His own gift.

Saint Thomas tells us that our reason looking out upon the order of the universe _immediately_ concludes there is some governor behind it. As the mind concludes to a watchmaker on seeing the watch, so, too, it concludes to a Divine Mind on seeing the order of the cosmos. This immediate knowledge of God, however, is not clear and distinct; that is why a more refined study is necessary to bring out the nature of God. The distinction between this confused knowledge of God and the reflex-refined knowledge that comes with the formal proofs for His existence is very much like the difference between the knowledge that most people have of water and the knowledge that the chemist has of it as composed of two atoms of hydrogen and one of oxygen. Reason clearly used can prove that there is a Power behind the universe, which made it, a Wisdom directing its laws, and a Will to make all things attain their goal. God is closer to us than we know, "For in him we live, and move, and are" (Acts 17:28). Saint Teresa once said, "Some unlearned men used to say to me that God was present only by His Grace. I could not believe that because as I was saying, He seemed to me to be present Himself. Finally a learned man delivered me of his doubt for he told me that He was present in the world and in us and how He communed with us, and this was a great comfort to me."

Francis Thompson, the poet, elaborating on the idea of Saint Thomas that God is in all things *intimately,* wrote,

> O world invisible, we view thee,
> O world intangible, we touch thee,
> O world unknowable, we know thee,
> Inapprehensible, we clutch thee![1]

God is easy to discover in at least a confused and primitive sort of way through every striving and aspiration of our will and our heart. For the great difference between an animal and a human is that an animal can have its desires satisfied but a human cannot. All that any animal wants is to have its *immediate* needs granted; this is never the case with man. Man is animated by an urge, an unquenchable desire to enlarge his vision and to know the ultimate meaning of things. If he were only an animal, he would never use symbols, for what are these but attempts to transcend the visible? No, he is a "metaphysical animal," a being ever longing for answers to the last question. The natural tendency of the intellect toward truth and of the will toward love would alone signify that there is in man a natural desire for God. There is not a single striving or pursuit or yearning of the human heart, even in the midst of the most sensual pleasures, that is not a dim grasping after the Infinite. As the stomach yearns for food and the eye for light and the ear for harmony, so the soul craves God.

There are many who mistake the nature of this Infinite and seek to satisfy the craving elsewhere than in God, just as there are those who know that food is necessary for the stomach and nevertheless ruin their stomachs by a constant diet of gin. Many a soul is like a magnetic needle that quivers first here, then there, seeking at morning when it flees at night, and then, finding all the other compass points to be a fraud, it comes at last to rest in God alone.

God is not hard to find, because He gives Himself to us

as the Divine Gift. Natural life itself is a gift. The soul has to come into the body from without, directly as a gift from the hands of God. And the supernatural life, too, is given to us from without. The whole meaning of Christianity is contained in the simple phrase of the creed, "He descended from Heaven." To each single soul, Our Lord addresses the words He spoke to the Samaritan woman at the well: "If you knew the gift of God, and who it is that is saying to you, 'Give me a drink,' you would have asked him, and he would have given you living water" (John 4:10). As Saint Paul told the Romans, "The grace of God, life everlasting, in Christ Jesus our Lord" (Rom. 6:23). And later on, to the Ephesians, "By grace you are saved through faith, and that not of yourselves, for it is the gift of God" (Eph. 2:8).

God is presented simultaneously through the Scriptures as both the Gift and the Giver, for such is the nature of Love. No one can buy the Divine Gift (though one may sell it, after it has been received, as Judas did). If God's gift were truth alone, some feeble minds might shrink from seeking it. If the gift were justice alone, our sins might arise and frighten the gift away. But when God's gift is love, then there should be none who would not take His Heart as theirs.

If, then, God is so easy to find and can be discovered either through the beauty of the stars or in every tiny pleasure of earth, which like a seashell speaks of the ocean of Divinity, why is it that so few souls come to Him? The fault is on our side, not God's. Most souls are like people living in a dark room during the daytime and complaining that the light is hard to find — when all that they need do to discover it is to raise the blinds.

God is the most obvious fact of human experience. If we are not aware of Him, it is because we are too complicated and because our noses are lifted high in the air in pride, for lo! He is at our very feet. We need only to "turn a stone and start a wing." The grace of God comes to us in just the degree that we open our souls to it; the only limit to our capacity to receive Him is our willingness to do so. Some thirsty hearts open up only a crevice, while others, with complete abandon, surrender their empty cisterns to be filled with the waters of life. A few souls suffocate, locked in their own unconscious minds with their loathesome frustrations and fears, refusing to open the door and let in the refreshing air of God's grace. "Listen! I am standing at the door, knocking; if you hear my voice and open the door, I will come in to you and eat with you, and you with me." (Apoc. 3:20). The latch is on our side and not on God's, for God breaks down no doors. We bar His entrance. Sometimes we even run away from Him, like chicks in flight from a mother hen. "How often have I desired to gather your children together as a hen gathers her brood under her wings, and you were not willing!" (Matt. 23:37).

Why do we behave so? It is hard to believe, but we have the Divine warrant for it that some people "love darkness rather than light." The added tragedy of sin is that after we do wrong we may not let God help us do what is right and good. We smash the bow so that He cannot play on our violin. We keep Him at arm's length because we refuse to be loved. We are drowning and will not clutch at His helping Hand because in our pride we say that we must "work this thing out for ourselves." The truth of the matter is, not that God is hard to find, but rather that we are afraid of being found. That is why we so very often hear in Sacred Scripture the words "Fear not." At the very beginning of Divine life in Bethlehem, the angels found it necessary to warn the shepherds, "Fear not." In the midst of Our Lord's public life He had to tell his frightened Apostles, "Fear not." And after His Resurrection He had to preface His words on peace with the same injunction, "Fear not."

Our Lord finds it necessary to warn us not to fear because

there are three false fears that keep us away from God: (1) We want to be saved, but not from our sins. (2) We want to be saved, but not at too great a cost. (3) We want to be saved, but in our own way, not God's.

We want to be saved, but not from our sins. The great fear that many souls have of Our Divine Lord is for fear He will do just what his name, "Jesus," implies — be "He Who saves us from our sins." We are willing to be saved from poverty, from war, from ignorance, from disease, from economic insecurity; such types of salvation leave our individual whims and passions and concupiscences untouched. That is one of the reasons why social Christianity is so very popular, why there are many who contend that the business of Christianity is to do nothing but to help in slum clearance or the development of international amity.

This kind of religion is, indeed, very comfortable, for it leaves the individual conscience alone. It is even possible that some persons are prompted to courageous reforms of social injustices by the very inquietude and uneasiness of their individual consciences: Knowing that something is wrong on the inside, they attempt to compensate for it by righting the wrong on the outside. This is also the mechanism of those persons, who, having accumulated great fortunes, try to ease their consciences by subsidizing revolutionary movements. The first temptation of Satan on the Mount was to try to induce Our Lord to give up the salvation of souls and to concentrate upon social salvation by turning stones into bread — on the false assumption that it was hungry stomachs and not corrupted hearts that made an unhappy civilization. Because some people think that the primary purpose of Divinity is to relieve economic adversity, they go to God in the moment of trial and then rebel against God because He does not fill their purses. Sensing a broader need for religion, others are willing to join a Christian sect so long as it concentrates on social "uplift" or the elimination of pain but leaves untouched the individual need of atoning for sin. At the average dinner table people do not object to the subject of religion being introduced into a conversation — provided that religion has nothing to do with the purging of sin and guilt. Thus many frightened souls stand trembling at the gate of bliss and dare not venture in, "fearful lest having Him they have naught else besides."

We want to be saved, but not at too great a cost. The God Who dungs His fields with sacrifice to bring forth the Vine of Life always frightens the timid. The rich man went away sad from the Savior, because he had very great possessions. Felix was only willing to hear Paul "at another time," when Paul spoke of judgment and the giving up of evil. Most souls are afraid of God precisely because of His Goodness, which makes Him dissatisfied with anything that is imperfect. Our greatest fear is not that God may not love us enough but that God may love us too much. As the lover wants to see his beloved perfect in manners and deportment, so, too, God, in loving us, desires that we be perfect as His Heavenly Father is perfect. As the musician loves the violin and tightens the strings with sacrificial strain that they may give forth a better tone, so God submits us to sacrifice to make us saints.

This fear that God's love will make exorbitant demands accounts for the many learned men and women who have come to a knowledge of God, yet have refused to venture in His sheepfold. The world is full of scholars who speak about extending the frontiers of knowledge but who never use the knowledge that has already been acquired; who love to knock at the door of truth but would drop dead if that door ever opened to them. For truth implies responsibility. Every gift of God in the natural as well as in the supernatural order demands a response on the part of the soul. In the natural order, people refuse to accept the gift of friendship because it creates an obligation. God's gift likewise involves a moment of decision. And because accepting Him demands a surrender of what is base, many become bargain hunters in religion and dilettantes in morality, refusing to tear false idols from their own hearts. They want to be saved, but not at the price of a cross; there echoes through their lives the challenge of old, "Come down from the Cross and we will believe."

We want to be saved, but in our own way, not God's. Very often one hears it said that people ought to be free to worship God, each in his own way. This indeed is true, so far as it implies freedom of conscience and each person's duty of living up to the special lights that God has given him. But it can be very wrong if it means that we worship God in *our* way and not in His. Consider an analogy: The traffic situation would be tangled and desperate if we said that the American way of life allowed every person to drive a car in *his* or *her* way and not according to the traffic laws. Catastrophe would result if patients began saying to the doctor, "I want to be cured in my own way, but not in yours," or if citizens said to the government, "I want to pay my taxes, but in my own way and not in yours." Similarly, there is a tremendous egotism and conceit in those popular articles and lectures entitled "My Idea of Religion," or "My Idea of God." An individual religion can be as misleading and uninformed as an individual astronomy or an individual mathematics.

Persons who say, "I will serve God in my way, and you serve God in your way," ought to inquire whether it would not be advisable to serve God in God's Way. But it is precisely this prospect of a stable, universally true religion that frightens the modern soul. For if his conscience is uneasy, he wants, instead, a religion that will leave out hell. If he has already married again against the law of Christ, he wants a religion that does not condemn divorce. Such a reservation means that a person wants to be saved, not in God's way, but in his. In thus refusing to moult his vain desires, he misses the flight to that "Love that leaves all other beauty pain."

If many souls fail to find God because they want a religion that will remake society without remaking themselves, or because they want a Savior without a cypress crown and a cross, or because they want their own blueprints and not God's, it remains to inquire what happens to a soul when it *does* respond to God. Among many other effects several may be mentioned.

First, such a soul passes from a state of speculation to *submission*. It is no longer troubled with the *why* of religion, but with the *ought*. It wishes to please, not merely to parse Divinity. There is a world of difference between knowing about God through study and knowing God through love — as great as the difference between a courtship carried on by mail and one by personal contact. Many skeptical professors know the proofs of the existence of God better than some who say their prayers; but because the professors never acted on the knowledge that they had, because they never loved the God Whom they knew by study, no new knowledge of God was given to them. They liked to *talk* about religion but *did* nothing about it, and their knowledge remained sterile as a result.

With the God-responsive soul on the contrary, a little knowledge about God was received with love. As a result, new portals of wisdom and love were opened. In such souls, the love of God brings a knowledge of God that in its certitude and reality surpasses the theoretical information of the professor. This sublime truth is expressed in Sacred Scripture: "If any man love God, the same is known by him" (1 Cor. 8:3). (The woman at the well was an early skeptic: Wanting to keep religion on a purely speculative level, she raised the question as to whether one should worship in Jerusalem or Samaria. Our Blessed Lord took the discussion out of the realm of theory by talking about her five husbands, reminding her that she had avoided making the moral amendments that true religion demands.)

The God-responsive soul thinks of religion in terms of submission to the will of God. He does not look to the Infinite to help him in his finite interests but, rather, seeks to surrender his finite interests to the Infinite. His prayer is "Not my will, but Thine, be done, O Lord." No longer interested in using God, he wants God to use him. Like Mary, he says, "Be it done unto Me according to Thy Word," or like Paul he asks, "What will you have me to do, O Lord?" or like John the Baptist he says, "I must decrease, he must increase." The destruction of egotism and selfishness so that the whole mind may thus be subject to the Divine Personality does not entail a disinterest in the active life; it brings a greater interest, because the person now understands life from God's point of view. Because of his unity with the Divine Source of energy, he has greater power to do good — as a soldier is stronger under a great general than a poor one. "If you abide in me, and my words abide in you, you shall ask whatever you will and it shall be done unto you. In this is my Father glorified; that you bring forth very much fruit" (John 15:7, 8). It is hard for self-centered creatures to realize that there are some souls that are really and truly passionately in love with God. But this should not be so hard to understand; whoever loves the light and heat of the candle should surely love the sunlight even more.

Life for God-responsive souls now begins to move from a circumference to a center. The externals of life, such as politics, economics and its daily routine, matter less, while God matters more. This does not mean that humanity is unloved, but only that it is loved more in God. The now-moment becomes a servant to the Eternal-moment. The uninteresting, the unreal, is now what is not used or cannot be used for

God's purpose. There is no dart in the quiver of a Godly soul for anything but the Divine Target.

The very reproaches the egotists hurl upon the saintly are devices for covering up their own self-reproach — they suspect they ought to understand. Yet they scoff, as sometimes people say of human lovers, "I cannot understand what he sees in her." Of course not — for love is blind! It is blind not only to defects in the beloved; it is also blind to all but the beloved. Love has its own eyes. All others but the lover see only with the eyes of the body and wonder what there is to love. But the lover sees through the eyes of the heart and finds in the other a sweetness and a love that blind hearts do not perceive. Lift this analogy to the Divine level, and one understands why the unconverted souls think Divine Love is foolishness; they cannot see what a saint can see in God.

The secret of our happiness is centeredness. The God-responsive soul becomes deaf to the promptings of the senses, for to him *God is everything*. Like great cosmic dynamos these souls generate energy by which other souls on the circumference can live. Pius XI, speaking of the contemplative souls, said,

> It is easy to understand how they who assiduously fulfill the duty of prayer and penance contribute much more to the increase of the Church and the welfare of mankind than those who labor in the tilling of the Master's field. For unless the former drew down from heaven a shower of Divine graces to water the field that is being tilled, the evangelical laborers would indeed reap from their toil a more scanty crop.[2]

The truly God-centered soul is not governed merely by its own habits of goodness or even by its virtues; it is moved directly by the Spirit of God. There is a difference between a person rowing a boat and the same person being driven by a sail full of wind; the soul that lives by the Gifts of the Spirit is swept forward directly by God, rather than by its own reason. Such a soul has a wisdom that surpasses all book learning, as was the case of young Catherine of Alexandria, who confounded the philosophers. Such a soul is endowed with a prudence and a counsel that is wiser than anything derived from its own experience.

Philosophy explains this in greater clarity. Every mind has two sides, a speculative side, which studies theory, and a practical side, which directs and guides human affairs. A sinful life does not destroy the first; that is why an evil person can be as good a mathematician as can a saint. But an evil life ruins the practical intellect; hence a learned mathematician who turns to writing on morals and religion is often a bundle of confusion. The God-directed person, because his practical intellect as well as his speculative intellect is illumined by God, is capable of guiding and directing others better than persons who know more, but in a purely theoretical fashion.

Not everyone can give guidance — the divorced cannot guide the married; the teacher or psychologist whose heart is unpurified cannot guide the young. "If the blind lead the blind, both fall into the pit" (Matt. 15:14). Counsel involving right and wrong should never be sought from someone who does not say his prayers, even though he or she might know a thousand times more about a ganglion or a thyroid than the person of prayer. As the eye with the telescope can see the stars better than the naked eye, so the faith-illumined reason understands reality better than the naked reason.

Divinely wise souls often infuriate the worldly-wise because they *always* see things from the Divine point of view. The worldly are willing to let anyone believe in God if he or she pleases, but only on condition that a belief in God will mean no more than belief in anything else. They will allow God, provided that God does not matter. But taking God seriously is precisely what makes the saint. As Saint Teresa put it, "What is not God to me is nothing." This passion is called snobbish, intolerant, stupid, and unwarranted intrusion; yet those who resent it deeply wish in their own hearts that they had the saint's inner peace and happiness.

And so this question of whether God is hard to find puts the answer solely up to us. Most of us are like the man who had lain at the Pool of Probatica for thirty-eight years and was not cured. His excuse was that, when the waters were stirred, there was no one to put him in: He *needed* healing, but he really did not *want* it. There are many like him, who remain just as they are, blaming others for their condition. But when Our Lord appeared, He told this man to do the very thing he had thought was impossible, namely, to take up his bed.

What had been wanting was his will. He was moribund because he did not want to be better. So many failures in life are, like his, avoidable, needless; they persist only because no effort is made to remedy the condition. We today say we do not want war; but we want the things that cause war. In the same way, there are many who say they want to be happy, but they refuse to want that which will bring them happiness. "You shall seek me, and shall find me, when you shall seek me with all your heart" (Jer. 29:13). The basic reason why people are unhappy in this life is because they do not truly desire happiness.

In all literature, there is nothing so expressive of the inescapable presence of God as Psalm 138. The argument seems to be that we can escape from anything that is finite: Space and time are the environment of every escape, but the inescapable is the Infinite. To take one's life offers no escape, for the suicide falls into the hands of the living God. Self-destruction is possible only because one can contemplate another "state" preferable to this, even though he calls it nonexistence. Death through any other cause is still no escape, for He, from Whose hands we came, awaits to take us back, bearing with us the responsibility of all our deeds. Atheism, which rejects this majestic fact, is not the knowledge that God does not exist, but only the wish that He did not, in order that one could sin without reproach or exalt one's ego without challenge. The pillars upon which atheism mounts are sensuality and pride. An atheist may be moral in the popular acceptance of the term, but he is not humble. As Franz Werfel says, "The atheist primarily and always betrays his own psychology when he thinks he is unveiling the mystery; and his denial unwittingly becomes the proof of God by confirming, against his own troubled will, the tremendous and vital importance of the metaphysical content of perception."[3]

As atheism offers no escape from God, neither does darkness, whether it be the dark of a cave or of our own unconsciousness. We may drive God out of our minds, argue against Him, but we know that if He did *not* exist, we should be stupid indeed for spending our energy fighting against the nonexistent. "Whither can I go to hide from Thy Face?" implies that someone is an escapist: He would never seek to fly from a God Who approved his way of thinking, living, and acting. Such a God would be according to man's own image and likeness and therefore something to be embraced.

If we fly from God, it is because His Goodness is our reproach and because union with Him demands disunion and divorce from evil. We cannot long stand a God Who looks into our soul and sees its ugliness without falling to our knees; even the flight from Him witnesses to our need of beauty, our love of the Beautiful. As light reveals all things and yet is not a part of that upon which it shines, so do God's Power, Wisdom, and Love suffuse us, for in Him we live and move and have our being. We know Him, but few want to be known by Him. We love created things because He put some of His love in them; otherwise they could not be lovable. Yet few want to love *Him,* because He loves too much. He wants us to be perfect, and we do not want to be perfect. But even in our escape from the perfect, we are driven back to it in our discontent with the mediocre, our weariness of the ordinary. God is all-wise, therefore our condition is revealed; God is ever-present, therefore our hidden sins are seen. There is no escape from God.

These ideas are but a feeble commentary on the above-mentioned psalm.

Lord, I lie open to thy scrutiny; thou knowest me, knowest when I sit down and when I rise up again, canst read my thoughts from far away. Wake I or sleep I, thou canst tell; no movement of mine but thou art watching it. Before ever the words are framed on my lips, all my thought is known to thee; rearguard and vanguard, thou dost compass me about, thy hand still laid upon me. Such wisdom as thine is far beyond my reach, no thought of mine can attain it.

Where can I go, then, to take refuge from thy spirit, to hide from thy view? If I should climb up to heaven, thou art there; if I sink down to the world beneath, thou art present still. If I could wing my way eastwards, or find a dwelling beyond the western sea, still would I find thee beckoning to me, thy right hand upholding me. Or perhaps I would think to bury myself in darkness: night should surround me, friendlier than day; but no, darkness is no hiding place from thee, with thee the night shines clear as day itself; light and dark are one.

Thine are my inmost thoughts. Didst thou not form me in my mother's womb? I praise thee for my wondrous fashioning, for all the wonders of thy creation. Of my soul thou hast full knowledge, and this mortal frame has no mysteries for thee, who didst contrive it in secret, devise its pattern, there in the dark recesses of the earth. All my acts thy eyes have seen, all are set down already in thy record; my days were numbered before ever they came to be.

A riddle, O my God, thy dealings with me, so vast their scope! As well count the sand, as try to fathom them; and, were that skill mine, thy own being still confronts me. O God, wouldst thou but make an end of the wicked! Murderers, keep your distance from me! Treacherously they rebel against thee, faithlessly set thee at defiance. Lord, do I not hate the men who hate thee; am I not sick at heart over their seditions? Surpassing hatred I bear them, count them my sworn enemies. Scrutinize me, O God, as thou wilt, and read my heart; put me to the test, and examine my restless thoughts. See if on any false paths my heart is set, and thyself lead me in the ways of old.[4]

Yet ever since the days of Adam, humanity has been hiding from God and saying, "God is hard to find." The truth is that, in each heart, there is a secret garden that God made uniquely for Himself. That garden is locked like a safety-deposit vault: It has two keys. God has one key; hence the soul cannot let in anyone else but God. The human heart has the other key; hence not even God can get in without man's consent. When the two keys of God's Love and human liberty, of Divine Vocation and human response, meet, then Paradise returns to a human heart. God is always at that Garden Gate with His key. We pretend to look for our key, to have mislaid it, to have given up the search; but all the while it is in our hand, if we would only see it. The reason we are not as happy as saints is because we do not wish to be saints.

Notes

1. "The Kingdom of God," *Poems of Francis Thompson,* rev. ed., p. 293, Appleton-Century-Crofts, Inc. *A.A.S.,* Oct. 25, 1924.

2. *A.A.S.,* Oct. 25, 1924.

3. *Between Heaven and Earth,* p. 73, Hutchinson & Company, Ltd., London, 1947.

4. Ps. 138, translation by Ronald Knox.

Chapter 5

MORBIDITY AND THE DENIAL OF GUILT

THERE HAS BEEN no single influence that has done more to prevent man from finding God and rebuilding his character, has done more to lower the moral tone of society than the denial of personal guilt. This repudiation of personal responsibility for one's action is falsely justified in two ways: by assuming that man is only an animal and by giving to a sense of guilt the tag "morbid."

The excuses are new — the effort to escape responsibility for our ills is ancient. Through the ages, man has always tried to find something to blame besides himself, e.g., poverty, environment, systems of economics, politics, finances, or society in general. But all these failed wholly to convince — they were obviously too unrelated to the *person,* for all of them are extrinsic. Recently, the materialists hit upon a new scapegoat — not in nature, nor in society, but inside of man himself, namely, his unconscious. The fault was now, not in the stars, but in that part of ourselves that could not be held responsible. Furthermore, it was claimed that the trouble could be controlled solely by lifting the unconscious quirk to the level of consciousness through psychoanalysis.

To prevent a misunderstanding, let it here be stated unequivocally: There is nothing wrong, there is even something commendable, about a psychological method that cures *mental disorders* by making the unconscious conscious. And, even apart from true derangements, people may be disturbed by a complex that has no ethical or moral cause. In treating such cases, medical science has a vast area in which it can legitimately operate. We are concerned and concerned only with methods of treatment that deny all moral responsibility and attack the patient's admission of personal sin and guilt by telling him that the idea of sin induces morbidity or a guilt complex and makes him abnormal.

Such psychiatrists would make all people *nice people,* complacent in their freedom from guilt or sin. By one magic stroke, the world would be rid of *nasty people,* or those who recognize they are sinners. This conception shows a shocking ignorance of human nature. The truth is that there is an increase of mental disorders largely because too many people think they are nice, when really they are nasty. This was the message Our Lord drove home in the parable of the two men who went into the temple to pray. Paraphrasing the story of the Pharisee (who was a very nice man) we can imagine him praying in the front of the temple as follows: "I thank Thee, O Lord, that my Freudian adviser has told me that there is no such thing as guilt, that sin is a myth, and that Thou, O Father, art only a projection of my father complex. There may be something wrong with my repressed instincts, but there is nothing wrong with my soul. I contribute 10 percent of my income to the Society for the Elimination of Religious Superstitions, and I diet for my figure three times a week. Oh, I thank Thee that I am not like the rest of men, those nasty people, such as the Christian there in the back of the temple who thinks that he is a sinner, that his soul stands in need of grace, that his conscience is burdened with extortion, and that his heart is weighted down with a crime of injustice. I may have an Oedipus complex, but I have no sin."

All the while, in the back of the temple, a nasty individual then and now strikes his breast and says, "O God, be merciful to me a sinner" (Luke 18:13). Our Lord tells us that he goes back to his house justified.

The Pharisee who went up to the temple to pray has millions of lineal descendants in this generation who say, "I have no need of a code or a creed." In this they are like the five-year-old child playing the piano who makes up the notes as he goes along; having no standard, he can never be reproached for hitting a "wrong note." By professing no ideal in morality, these *nice* people can never be accused of not living up to their creed. This is the great advantage that they have over the Christians — whose creed is so lofty that they can often and truly be accused of failing to meet its demands.

Very harmful effects can follow accepting the philosophy that denies personal guilt or sin and thereby makes everyone *nice*. By denying sin, the nice people make a cure impossible. Sin is most serious, and the tragedy is deepened by the denial that we are sinners. If the blind deny that they are blind, how shall they ever see? The really unforgivable sin is the denial of sin, because, by its nature, there is now nothing to be forgiven. By refusing to admit to personal guilt, the nice people are made into scandalmongers, gossips, talebearers, and supercritics, for they must project their real if unrecognized guilt to others. This, again, gives them a new illusion of goodness: The increase of faultfinding is in direct ratio and proportion to the denial of sin. (The *nasty* people do not like to gossip about the failings of others, because they are only too conscious of their own failings.)

It is a fact of human experience that the more experience we have with sin — our own sin — the less we are conscious of it. In all other things, we learn by experience; in sin, we unlearn by experience. Sin gets into the blood, the nerve cells, the brain, the habits, the mind; and the more it penetrates a person, the less he knows of its existence. The sinner becomes so accustomed to sin that he fails to recognize its gravity. This was the sinister idea behind Satan's temptation of Eve: Satan told her that if she possessed the knowledge of good and evil, she would be like God. Satan did *not* tell her the real truth — that God knows evil only negatively, intellectually, as a physician who has never had pneumonia knows it as the negation of health. But a human being, knowing evil at all, must know it experimentally — i.e., evil would enter into his system and become a part of him. As a cataract in the eye blinds the vision, so sin always darkens the intellect and weakens the will and leaves a bias toward the committing of another sin. Each sin makes the next more easy, conscience less reproachful, virtue more distasteful, and the attitude toward morality more scornful. In some persons, sin works like a cancer, undermining and destroying the character for a long time without any visible effects. When the disease becomes manifest, it has progressed so far that one almost gives up the hope of a cure.

Kierkegaard, with his usual penetration, has pointed out there is a despair that humans do not easily understand. It prevails in the sinner who sets himself against God, who wants to be his own god and lawgiver and, hence, to be more than his or any one's nature can permit. He wants desperately to be himself (to possess a fullness of being the like of which is only God's) and as desperately *not* to be himself (not to be the finite creature that he cannot help knowing that he is, however much he may try to conceal this fact from his own consciousness).

Seldom will a person revolt openly against the Infinite: If someone knows that he has revolted and sinned and still does not accept the consequences, he tries to minimize the sin by excuses, as Cain did. But modern humanity has lost the understanding of the very name "sin." When a person sins and somehow feels the effects (as everyone must), he or she seeks relief in escapist cults or escapist habits of drink or drugs. That person also puts the blame for his malaise on his spouse, on his work, on his friends, or on the economic, social, and political order. He will often complain of overwork and "tension," develop symptoms of physical distress — all contrived efforts to avoid facing the fact that he has sinned. He may — frequently does — become a neurotic. If his neurosis has advanced far enough, he will be told by some psychoanalyst that he is not fully responsible for his actions because he is "a patient." This gives him a further pretext for not acknowledging his sins.

If we remain in sin through the denial of sin, despair takes possession of our souls. A sinner can sin so much that he does not recognize the totalitarian character of his sinning. He never considers that the present sin is adding to thousands of other sins. Traveling at seventy miles an hour in an automobile is already excessive; but if twenty more miles are added, the danger mounts. Unrepented sins beget new sins, and the dizzying total brings despair. The soul then says, "I am too far gone." The drunkard becomes afraid of a sober day because of the clarity of vision of his own state that it brings. The greater the depression, the more a sinner needs to escape from it through further sins, until he cries out with Macbeth in his despair,

> I had liv'd a blessed time; for, from this instant,
> There's nothing serious in mortality,
> All is but toys; renown and grace is dead. . . .

The condition of despair induced by unrepented sin often reaches a point where there is a positive fanaticism against religion and morality. Anyone who has fallen away from the spiritual order will hate it, because religion is the reminder of his guilt. Husbands who are unfaithful will beat their wives who are faithful. Wives who are unfaithful will accuse their husbands of infidelity. Such souls finally reach a point where, like Nietzsche, they want to increase evil until all distinction between right and wrong is blotted out. Then they can sin with impunity and say with Nietzsche, "Evil, be thou my good." Expediency can now replace morality, cruelty becomes justice, lust becomes love. Sin multiplies itself in such a soul until it becomes a permanent residence of Satan, cursed by Christ as one of the whited sepulchers of this world.

Such is the history of "nice" persons, who believe they never sin.

The nice people do not come to God, because they think they are good through their own merits or bad through inherited instincts. If they do good, they believe they are to receive the credit for it; if they do evil, they deny that it is their own fault. They are good through their own goodheartedness, they say; but they are bad because they are misfortunate, either in their economic life or through an inheritance of evil genes from their grandparents. The nice people rarely come to God; they take their moral tone from the society in which they live. Like the Pharisee in the front of the temple, they believe themselves to be very respectable citizens. Elegance is their test of virtue; to them, the moral is the aesthetic, the evil is the ugly. Every move they make is dictated, not by a love of goodness, but by the influence of their age. Their intellects are cultivated — in knowledge of current events. They read only the best-sellers; but their hearts are undisciplined. They say that they would go to Church if the Church were only better — but they never tell you how much better the Church must be before they will join it. They sometimes condemn the gross sins of society, such as murder; they are not tempted to these because they fear the opprobrium that comes to those who commit them. By avoiding the sins that society condemns, they escape reproach, they consider themselves good par excellence.

Yet what moved Our Blessed Lord to invective was not badness but just such self-righteous goodness as this. We find no words of condemnation spoken against Magdalene, who was overwhelmed by the problem of sexual promiscuity, or against the penitent thief, who found it difficult to respect possessions; but we find Him inveighing against the Scribes and Pharisees, who were nice and self-righteous men. Against them, He pronounced His woes: "Woe to you Scribes and Pharisees, hypocrites..." (Matt. 23:15). "Blind guides, who strain at a gnat, and swallow a camel" (Matt. 23:24). "You serpents, generation of vipers, how will you flee from the judgment of hell?" (Matt. 23:33). "Woe to you Scribes and Pharisees, hypocrites; because you are like to whited sepulchres, which outwardly appear to men beautiful, but within are full of dead men's bone, and of all filthiness" (Matt. 23:27). He said that the harlots and the Quislings would enter the Kingdom of Heaven before the self-righteous and the smug. Concerning all those who endowed hospitals and libraries and public works, in order to have their names graven in stone before their fellow men, He said, "Amen I say to you, they have received their reward" (Matt. 6:2). They wanted no more than human glory, and they got it. Never once is Our Blessed Lord indignant against those who are already, in the eyes of society, below the level of law and respectability. He attacked only the sham indignation of those who dwelt more on the sin than the sinner and who felt pleasantly virtuous, because they had found someone more vicious than they. He would not condemn those whom society condemned; his severe words were saved for those who had sinned and had not been found out. That was why He said to the woman taken in sin, "He that is without sin among you, let him first cast a stone at her" (John 8:7). Only innocence has a right to condemn. He would not add His burden of accusation to those that had already been hurled against the winebibbers and the thieves, the cheap revolutionists, the streetwalkers, and the traitors. They were everybody's target, and everybody knew that they were wrong.

And the people who chose to make war against Our Lord were never those whom society had labeled sinners. Of those who sentenced Him to death, none had ever had a record in the police court, had ever been arrested, was ever commonly known to be fallen or weak. But among His friends, who sorrowed at His death, were converts drawn from thieves and prostitutes. Those who were aligned against Him were the *nice* people who stood high in the community — the worldly, prosperous people, the men of big business, the judges of law courts who governed by expediency, the "civic-minded" individuals whose true selfishness was veneered over with public generosity. Such men as these opposed Him and sent Him to His death.

Why did they hate Him? Because, all during His life, He had been tearing the masks of false goodness from nice people, exposing the evil of men and women who lived in accordance with the conventional standards of His time. Finally a time came when the accused could no longer tolerate His reproaches of what they were. Our Lord was crucified by the nice people who held that religion was all right in its place, so long as its place was not *here,* where it might demand of them a change of heart. The Cross of Calvary stands at the crossroads of three prosperous civilizations as eloquent testimony to the uncomfortable truth that the successful people, the social leaders, the people who are labeled *nice,* are the ones most capable of crucifying the Divine Truth and the Eternal Love.

The gravest error of the *nice* people in all ages is the denial of sin. Yet this is always a hopelessly illogical stand for any person to take. Even in the natural order, laws cannot be broken without disastrous consequences. Gravitation will help a person if he builds the side of his house straight and plumb; but gravitation will oppose him and make his house fall down if he builds it out of plumb. Disobedience to natural law brings punishment. Astronomy reveals that now and then certain stars get out of their orbits; as a penalty for that deordination, they burn themselves out in space.

It is a law of nature that the higher shall control the lower object in God's whole hierarchy. In the biological order, *death is the domination of a lower order over a higher order.* For death ensues when the vital forces no longer can integrate, in the interests of the whole being, those physical and chemical processes that go on continuously in the cells of the organism. Life has been defined as the sum of the forces that resist death, that prevent this revolution of the amoeba. Gradually, as we grow old, the process of life wears away the substance of the cells and diminishes the power of our various vital functions. Our chemical processes become more and more independent of the controlling vital forces; and their rebellion makes it increasingly difficult for the organism to harmonize their activities in the interests of the whole person. At that precise point where there is a balance of forces in favor of the purely chemical processes as against the vital controlling powers, death ensues; the chemical processes, having achieved full independence, have been able to disrupt the integrity of the organism. Such is the history of all terrestrial beings.

In human life the hierarchy extends higher — there is a superstructure above the physical, and the same great law applies here, too. For man is so made that, when all is in order, the moral order holds supremacy over the instinctive and the physical. At that moment when the carnal gains mastery over the spiritual in a person — when the ego overcomes the social impulses, when the material dominates the ethical — a domination of a lower order over a higher order has occurred.

Again, this results in death — the death called sin. "For the wages of sin is death" (Rom. 6:23).

Humanity cannot with impunity break the laws of its own nature; the punishment that invariably follows such attempts at rebellion may be most apparent in the psychological order. For example, it is clear that every self-centered person is a frustrated person. Why must this be? It is because frustration results when a natural longing encounters an insurmountable obstacle. Every natural longing, to find satisfaction, needs to be turned toward an object; until that occurs, it remains a longing — an inclination for a certain sort of performance. But actualization of the longing can come only through something that is itself actual; the longing, as such, being a mere potency, cannot procure its own satisfaction. What does procure it is the object toward which the potency is ordained. As long as the person remains concerned exclusively with himself, instead of giving himself to the objective world of tasks and duties, such actualization cannot take place. Frustration and discontent ensue.

Every man and woman alive experiences a sense of guilt when they break a natural law. As Seneca said, "Every guilty person is his own hangman." Every guilty person is also fearful, for "Conscience doth make cowards of us all." Instead of calling it a fiction, it would be truer to call it a friction, a "rubbing the wrong way." Guilt over unadmitted sins accounts for many of modern man's psychological ills. Yet it would be unsound to say that the moral factor is *always* behind mental disorders; for it is not. Mental diseases, using the phrase in the strict sense of the term, may have physical causes, such as organic alterations of the brain, disturbances in the endocrine glands, malformations of the central nervous system, and the like. Here we abstract entirely from all theories concerning the origin of schizophrenia, such as that which holds it is due to abnormalities on the "molecular level," and the theory of psychogenetic causes of "manic-depressive insanity." We are here treating the philosophy of frustration; we criticize only those psychiatrists who, acting as philosophers, go beyond their proper medical or scientific sphere to deny the possibility of guilt and sin. To use a razor to hew down a mountain, to direct our lives toward any other road than that which ends in our ultimate perfection, is not only to damage our minds, but it is also to miss the happiness that comes from living right.

Yet it is sometimes asserted by psychiatrists and sociologists that sin is nothing more than a deviation from the accepted ideals of society at any given moment. Now, there is no doubt that a person's ethical code is to some extent determined by the society in which he lives; but this is not to say that sin and guilt are products of a "herd instinct" or of the environment-made decisions of society. If this were true, how could the individual conscience often call itself wrong and know itself to be wrong, even when society says that it is right? Conscience knows that right consists sometimes in repudiation of the social standards of a given time (such a time as 1938 in Nazi Germany). If someone can be right when he acts against the herd and wrong when he acts with the herd, or with society, then it follows that there is something more to sin than social disapproval.

The denial of the existence of objective guilt by materialist psychologists is due to a false understanding of human nature. About four hundred years ago, some errant theologians said man was intrinsically corrupt and therefore was incapable of justification by works. From this flowed the idea that man is justified by faith in Christ, Whose merits are imputed to the corrupt man. Later, other errant theologians said that, since man is intrinsically corrupt, he is incapable of being justified *either* by faith or by works: His restoration was made dependent on predestination, or the Sovereign Will of

God Who elects or damns. The false conception spread and did much to destroy man's belief in human freedom. Finally, totalitarianism came on the scene to say that, since man is intrinsically corrupt, he cannot be justified by faith, or by works, or by the Sovereign Will of God, but only by the collectivity that absorbs man; this, we are told, will do away with human depravity by substituting state conscience for individual conscience and a dictator for God.

The materialist psychologists, in rebelling against the notion of total depravity common to this tradition, were right: Man is not wholly depraved. But the psychologists often erred in not investigating the traditional concept of man, which stands midway between the false optimism that promises to make him a saint by evolution and education and the false pessimism that goes far toward making him a devil.

The sense of sin is a reality everyone knows. It is more than just a violation of law; its poignancy would not be present except for man's intuition that sin also involves a breaking of a relationship between persons. Some people who steal from a great corporation do not feel that they have done anything very wrong (although they actually have), because they cannot think of the corporation as anything but impersonal. They have a flickering intuition of a truth — that the essence of sin is not a negation of a code but a rejection of a person toward whom one feels bound through his goodness and his love. Sin is an affront by one spirit against another, an outrage against love. That is why there is no sense of sin without the consciousness of a personal God. Isaias had a deep sense of guilt when he saw God and said, "Woe is me, because I have held my peace; because I am a man of unclean lips, and I dwell in the midst of a people that hath unclean lips, and I have seen with my eyes the King the Lord of hosts" (Isa. 6:5). "I had heard of you by the hearing of the ear, but now my eye sees you; therefore I despise myself, and repent in dust and ashes" (Job 42:5, 6). "Depart from me, for I am a sinful man, O Lord" (Luke 5:8).

Because sin is the breaking of a relationship with Love, it follows that it cannot be treated exclusively by psychiatry. (We are not here saying that all mental disorders are due to a sense of sin. They are not. But there are some that are; and when materialist psychiatrists assume that distresses due to sin can be treated in exactly the same way as other nervous and psychic diseases, with no reference to spiritual resources, they are adding to the complexities, derangement, and frustration of the patient's life.) It is not enough to *analyze* the sin in order to break down the consciousness of sin or to cure it. If the dentist learns that the decay in the tooth is due to eating candy, it does not follow that the tooth immediately becomes healthy. Digging about an oak tree to discover the rottenness of the acorn from which it originally came is not strengthening the tree itself. To uncover the motives of sin, by studying the patient's past, is no cure. Sin is not in the understanding alone, nor in the instincts; sin is in the will. Hence it cannot be broken up as another complex may be broken up by dragging it into the consciousness. Psychic diseases may arise from repressed complexes; but sin must be regarded as an act of the will that implicates the whole personality. Mere intellectual comprehension will not destroy its effects or restore the patient's health.

It is not true that acknowledging our sins as sins induces a guilt complex or morbidity. Because a child goes to school, does he or she develop an ignorance complex? Because the sick go to the doctor, do they have a sickness complex? The student concentrates, not upon his own ignorance, but upon the wisdom of the teacher; the sick concentrate, not upon their illness, but upon the curative powers of the doctor; and the sinner, seeing his sins for what they are, concentrates, not on his own guilt, but upon the redemptive powers of the Divine Physician. There is *no evidence whatever* to sustain the position of some psychiatrists that consciousness of sin tends to make a person morbid. To call someone an escapist because he asks God for forgiveness is like calling a householder whose home is on fire an escapist, because he sends for the fire department. If there is anything morbid in the sinner's responsible admission of a violated relationship with Divine Love, this is a jovial sanity compared with the real and terrible morbidity that comes to those who are sick and who refuse to admit their illness. The greatest refinement of pride, the most contemptible form of escapism, is to refrain from examining oneself, lest sin be discovered within.

As a drunkard will sometimes become conscious of the gravity of his intemperance only through the startling vision of how much he has wrecked his own home and the wife who loved him, so, too, sinners may come to an understanding of their wickedness when they understand what they have done to Our Divine Lord. That is why the Cross has always played a central part in the Christian picture. It brings out what is worst in us by revealing what sin can do to goodness and love. It brings out the best in us by revealing what goodness can do for sin — forgive and atone at the moment of sin's greatest cruelty. The Cross of Christ does something for us that we cannot do for ourselves. Everywhere else in the world we are spectators; but, facing the vision of the Cross, we pass from spectatorship to participation. If anyone thinks that the confession of his guilt is escapism, let him try once kneeling at the foot of the Crucifix. He cannot escape feeling involved. One look at Christ on the Cross, and the scab is torn from the ulcerous depths of sin as it stands revealed in all of its ugliness. Just one flash of that Light of the World shatters all the blindness that sins have begotten and burns into the soul the truth of our relationship to God. Those who have refused to go up to Calvary are those who do not weep for their sins.

Once a soul has gone there, it can no longer say that sin does not matter.

If the sense of guilt is an estrangement from God and sorrow at having wounded someone we love, if the ache of self-reproach is a symptom of our rejection of love's invitation, then our emphasis must be not so much on the guilt as on the way to remove it and find peace. It takes love to see that love has been hurt. Divine Love always rewards that recognition by forgiveness; and once the forgiveness is given, a relationship is restored in a much more intimate way than ever before. There is more joy, Our Lord said, among the Angels of Heaven for one sinner doing penance than for the ninety-nine just who needed not penance.

When love is understood aright, we do not feel sorry for sin in order that God may forgive; rather, we feel sorry at accepting that forgiveness. God offers to forgive us before we repent. It is the sorrow on our part that makes that forgiveness available. The father did not begin to forgive the prodigal son when he saw him coming down the roadway. The father had already forgiven the son from the beginning. The forgiveness could not become operative until the son became sorry for having broken the relationship with his father and sought restoration. Just as there has always been music in the air that we do not hear unless the radio is attuned to it, so there is always forgiveness available, but we do not receive it so long as our soul lacks sorrow and a purpose of amendment. We find only what we seek: Nature has many secrets to give us, but she will not surrender them until we sit down patiently before her and obey her laws. Only by such submission do we receive. So long as there is no prayerful wish for a different relationship with God than that distant, fearful one that sin has caused, the sin cannot be forgiven. To be a sinner is our distress, but to know it is our hope.

Nice people must see themselves as nasty people before

they can find peace. When they exchange their proud and diabolical belief that they never did anything wrong to a hope for a Divine remedy for their mistakes, they will have attained to the condition of normality, peace, and happiness. In contrast to the pride of those who deny their guilt to escape self-criticism is the humility of God, Who made a world that added not to His glory and then made man to criticize Him. The *nasty* people are the convertible people; aware of their own imperfections, they sense within themselves an emptiness. This may seem to them a meaningless vacuum like the Grand Canyon, but in reality its emptiness is more like that of a nest, which can be filled. They have a hunger and thirst for something not of themselves. Their sense of sin does not beget a forlorn despair but a creative despair, once they know that they can look beyond themselves for loving relief.

Our Blessed Lord was very fond of nasty people. He told so many stories about them. One of the charges the enemies made against Him was that He ate with nasty people and with sinners. One of the greatest of all the Apostles came to Our Blessed Lord through hate. It is the prodigal who was placed before his virtuous brother; the son who rebelled and repented was preferred to the one who pleaded loyalty and then disobeyed. The lost sheep was put upon the shoulders of the Good Shepherd, and the ninety-nine were left in the field. The lost coin was found and made an occasion for rejoicing, but there was never any party or celebration for the other nine. The Savior turns out the buyers and sellers from the Temple and then takes a child upon His knees and says that he will enter the Kingdom of Heaven before the wise university professors. He washes the feet of disciples who seek first place at table, talks freely to women whom the whole nation hates, and intervenes to protect an adulteress from stoning at the hands of those whose adultery has not yet been found out. The announcement of His Incarnation was made to a

Virgin; but the announcement of His Resurrection from the dead was made to a converted sinner.

Because Our Blessed Lord preferred the nasty people to the nice people, it is very likely that if we could look up into Heaven we should see some sights that would scandalize us. We should say, "*Well,* how did that woman get there?" or "How did *he* get in? I knew him when..." There will be many in Heaven whom we never expected to see there. The surprises will be numerous. But the greatest surprise of all will be to find that we are there ourselves.

Nasty people may come to happiness this side of Heaven, too; their humility makes it possible. Many who come to the fullness of Christ, when asked why they embraced the Church, answer, "I joined the Church in order to get rid of my sins." Those who refuse to admit their sins, who deny that they are sinners, will find this very difficult to understand. Indeed, it is difficult for the nice people to understand, for they fail to realize there are two very devastating things that happen to those who come into contact with Our Lord: an overwhelming sense of shame, and a glorious feeling of liberation.

No one who denies personal guilt is happy, but there is not a person who has admitted it, and been forgiven, and lives in the love of God, who is unhappy. A sense of moral unworthiness has never saddened a soul, but many souls are made sad and frustrated by their own self-love. The greater the consciousness of our own misery, the greater our confidence in the goodness and mercy of God. God could not show the attribute of mercy unless there was misery. God would have been Infinite Goodness if He had never made the world; but unless nasty persons had existed, He never could have shown His sweet Mercy for our sins.

Chapter 6

EXAMINATION OF CONSCIENCE

F OR CENTURIES most souls believed, as some still do, in the examination of conscience. This great spiritual exercise was kicked out the front door by modern materialists on the ground that it is vain to examine conscience; they offered three arguments: that there is no sin; that conscience is only our recognition of social conventions and taboos; and that each person is the sole determinant of what is right and wrong. What these materialists threw out the front door some psychiatrists now sneak in through the back door under a new name — examination of the unconscious — but with one difference: With them there is no God, there is no moral law, there is no final judgment.

This examination of the unconscious is commonly called psychoanalysis.[1] Because of a general confusion on the subject, it is important here parenthetically to suggest the difference between psychiatry and psychoanalysis. Psychiatry is a science that treats mental ills; it may be practiced only by doctors of medicine. Psychoanalysis is a particular method of treating such ills, by relieving a hampering evil and by bringing the unconscious to the conscious. One can be opposed to a certain school of psychoanalysis, such as the Freudian, without being opposed to psychoanalysis in general, just as one can be opposed to "swing" without being an enemy of music. Psychiatry as a term covers an even wider territory;

apart from all forms of psychoanalysis, it includes a dozen different methods. Psychiatry as a branch of medicine is not only a perfectly valid science — it is a real necessity today. In the last hundred years, while the population of the United States increased only 671 percent, the percentage of institutionalized mental patients increased 23,328 percent. Doctors qualified to care for, cure, and prevent such maladies are in need. Most of the psychiatrists doing such necessary work today are *not* psychoanalysts.

But even psychoanalysis, understood as mental exploration and treatment, can be a perfectly valid method. To some extent, it could even be viewed as an application of the Christian doctrine of examination of conscience to the examination of the unconscious. Christian faith and morals cannot possibly have any objections to a mental treatment whose aim is the restoration of the sick mind to its human end. But "psychoanalysis" becomes very wrong indeed when it ceases to be a method of treatment and pretends to be a philosophy. It steps outside its legitimate area as a branch of medicine and becomes dangerous when it is made the basis of a philosophical conception of human nature, with such assertions as the statement that man is an animal and has no free will or that "religious doctrines are illusions."[2]

Psychoanalysis (still using this name in a wide sense) cannot be wholly independent of a philosophical outlook on human nature. But a sound philosophy is not derived from the findings of psychoanalysis; rather, the philosophical interpretation precedes the psychological theory and determines its particular aim. If a psychoanalytic school assumes that man is only an animal, this tenet is not something its founder concluded from the facts uncovered by psychological study. It is an assumption that the founder accepted prior to all investigation and built into the foundations underlying the theory. If a psychoanalytic school claims that those mental disorders that are not caused by an organic disease of the brain originate in instincts, sexual or otherwise, such a statement again goes beyond what is justified by and deducible from the observed facts; it pertains to the presuppositions the psychoanalysts accepted as true before they proceeded to develop their theory. When Freud wrote the following, he imposed an irrational prejudice on a theory: "The mask is fallen: it [psychoanalysis] leads to a denial of God and of an ethical ideal."[3]

Freud's school of psychoanalysis often does just that. But there are other schools. And, I repeat, there is no objection to psychoanalysis as such, so long as it remains a mere method and does not bring in influences or ideas that are contrary to truth (although psychoanalysis, at its best, is not a panacea applicable as widely as its more enthusiastic believers claim). But once psychoanalysis asserts that "man is not a being different from the animals, or superior to them"[4] or that sin is a myth, religion an illusion, and God a "father-image," then it ceases to be a science or a method and begins to be a prejudice.

All through the ages there has been some sort of psychoanalysis — an analysis of the psyche, or soul, along with the search for the mental causes of all kinds of human troubles. The ancient Greeks thought that the basis of normal life, of wisdom, and of sanity was "Know thyself." Socrates spoke of the need to "take care of one's soul"; and the Greek words for his saying are precisely "therapy of the soul." Mental cures were applied, as means of healing certain physical disorders, in the sanctuaries of the god Aesculapius. The Stoics of pre-Christian time, and in particular Seneca, recommended a nightly examination of the soul on the assumption that, the more the moral man enters into himself, the greater is his peace. Marcus Aurelius wrote a series of meditations in which he communes with his soul, discusses the problems of

right and wrong, and, generally speaking, examines his conscience, giving an account to himself of how far he has lived
up to his principles. Later, Saint Augustine said, "Do not go
out of thyself; rather return into thyself and thou shalt transcend thyself." And he also said that truth dwells in the inner
man. Saint Augustine is rightly considered the father of self-
analysis in psychology, although scientific psychology, or the
science of mental phenomena, originated with Aristotle.

There are other passages in the writings of many medieval
and later authors that strongly anticipate modern psychological or psychoanalytic conceptions. Dream analysis plays a
great role in several of the modern psychoanalytic schools;
but this is not a new idea, as Freud admitted, although he
claimed to have gone far beyond what had been done before, giving this method a totally new significance. Even Saint
Thomas remarks, "There are some doctors who are wont to
examine dreams in order to determine the dispositions of the
people."[5]

The problem of the mental factors in all sorts of disorders
was one that particularly interested the German Romanticists
in the first part of the nineteenth century. Among the writers whom Freud himself lists as his predecessors there is one
Schubert who wrote extensively on dreams and on what he
called the "night-side" of the soul. Hypnosis and its influence
was another topic that attracted these Romanticists, under
the name of "magnetic influence." W. Grimm (who was at
least close to Romanticism, even if he does not belong strictly
to the narrower group, and whose name is famous as one of
the fathers of modern linguistics) wrote an essay on the unconscious. There is also a story, "The Sanctus," among the
fantastic tales of E. T. Hoffmann; it tells of a girl who lost her
voice because of a sentiment of guilt and regained it when she
overheard a friend explain to her father the mental origin and
mechanism of the whole process.

In the Gospel we find that Our Blessed Lord analyzes the motivations of the people, using not mere psychoanalysis but Divine Analysis — such as seeing the Pharisees as whited sepulchers, clean outside but inside full of dead men's bones. He pierced beneath the pretensions and hypocrisies of their prayers and their almsgiving, saying that they did these things to be seen by others. He analyzed the soul of the hypocrite who went to the front of the temple to pray, revealing how proud he was in his own heart. When a woman came uninvited into the house of Simon and cast herself at the feet of Our Blessed Lord, Simon thought within himself, "If He only knew what manner of woman she is!" which makes us ask, "How did *he* know?" But Our Lord then analyzed the soul of Simon and told him the story of the two debtors, the one who owed five hundred pence and the other fifty, and from that He drew the lesson that many sins were forgiven the woman because she loved much. Saint Paul told the Corinthians, "Let a man prove himself" (1 Cor. 11:28), and again, "Try your own selves if you be in the faith" (2 Cor. 13:5). These words hark back to Jeremias speaking to his own people: "Let us search our ways, and seek, and return to the Lord" (Lam. 3:40).

Our Blessed Lord has reminded us that the world will end with a great "psychoanalysis" in which the secret and hidden sins of every person will be revealed and no one will go out until he has paid the last farthing. Because of this basic relationship between human soul and God, throughout the whole of human history one of the most universal spiritual practices of every saintly soul has been what is known as the nightly examination of conscience. The thoughts, the words, and the deeds of the day are brought to the surface and examined to consider whether or not they are in conformity with the moral law of God. After this examination, there follows a resolution to amend our life, to do penance for failures, and to enter into a greater union with the love that is God. Such self-psychoanalysis is sound.

There is, however, a profound difference between Freudian psychoanalysis and the Christian examination of conscience. For psychoanalysis is supposed to reveal or unveil something not even the most searching examination of conscience could discover. Freud claims that what is hidden in the unconscious is inaccessible to consciousness; it is forbidden to emerge to our conscious view; it is held back in the unconscious by a powerful force called the "censor." Since there is no way for the mind to delve into its own unconscious and uncover what is hidden and shut up there, a peculiar technique has to be employed to bring the contents to light. This technique, known as "free association" and "interpretation," is used by Freudian psychoanalysis.

Psychoanalysts all agree that examination of conscience (or the sincere account a person renders to himself of his actions and intentions) will do much toward freeing the mind of inhibitions and worries. But they consider self-examination a rather superficial process; they contend that the real causes of mental difficulties, inner conflicts, and inhibitions can be discovered only if the unconscious is forced to render back to consciousness what once had been exiled and repressed.

Even if the presuppositions of Freudian psychoanalysis were accepted — which they cannot well be — it is questionable whether this notion of the total inaccessibility of the "unconscious" to our normal examination can be maintained. It is conceivable that the mind, when using the right approach, can achieve almost as much analysis alone as under the guidance of a third person. To this statement Freudian psychoanalysis — at least that of the "orthodox" brand — has, of course, an answer ready. The presence of the third person (or the analyst) is viewed as an indispensable condition for release; it is he who, for a time, becomes the object of the repressed instinctual longings by the so-called process of "transference"; this is thought by Freudians to be a necessary link in the process of rearranging or redistributing the "instinctual energies." But this argument appears less conclusive than the analysts believe it to be. There is no cogent reason to assume the indispensability of the transference mechanism itself. If the latter is viewed as indispensable, it is only in virtue of the peculiar theory of Freud — an unsubstantiated theory at that — of the nature of the unconscious. Indeed, there has been in recent time a tendency among even some followers of Freud to abandon one or the other of the tenets of the original theory. One of these suspected tenets is that of the necessity of transference or the intervention of the analyst. Karen Horney, for instance, speaks of "self-analysis." Such a name makes sense only if it is conceded that the human mind can gain access to its own unconscious.

To the extent that psychoanalysis, in the twentieth century, takes an interest in the inside of a person's soul, it represents a great progress over the sociologies of the nineteenth century, which thought that everything that was wrong in the world was due to poverty, bad economic conditions, free trade, high tariffs, or politics. Furthermore, to the extent that psychoanalysis has revealed the effects of our minds — even of the unconscious mind — on our physical health and behavior, it has confirmed the great Christian truth that an uncontrolled mind (or even an uncontrolled unconsciousness) leads to abnormality.

Saint Thomas has many passages deploring just such repression as the psychoanalysts deplore. Mankind has always recognized the relationship between conscious and unconscious as something like that of a pilot of a ship to an engine room and a rudder. (We do not use unconscious here in the technical sense of Freud.) The pilot on the bridge can see ahead; he sets the direction and the course to be followed.

These directions are transmitted to the engine room below and, finally, to the rudder and on to the water. In like manner, it is consciousness and, more properly, conscience and the will that tell a person the course to follow. But sometimes, when the directions are communicated to the unconscious and to the instincts and to the senses and to the passions, there is a kind of rebellion, a defiance. The result is that, down in the unconscious of the engine room or the unconscious of the rudder, there is a miscarrying of the orders, a rebellion, which is bound to leave its scars upon the mind. Because the traces of such past revolts may still be there, unrecognized, there is no denying that there is sometimes an advantage in analyzing even the unconscious — just as there is value in cleaning out the many articles in the cellar of a home. An emergency may make such cleaning an immediate need: If a cat crawls into a furnace pipe, it smells up a house, making it necessary to examine the so-to-speak unconscious parts of the house in order to have a better smell upstairs. (If, however, the psychoanalyst went on to say that those who live upstairs can disclaim all responsibility either for the mustiness of the cellar or for the presence of the cat in the furnace pipe, they must be reminded that the cellar and the cat that found its way into the pipes were both their own.)

Psychoanalysis, then, has a respectable but limited work to do. We oppose here only those particular psychoanalysts who would deny any validity to the examination of conscience, on the ground that the examination of the unconscious takes its place. The Christian has no quarrel with the psychoanalyst who says that the human mind is very much like a flower, which has roots in the mud and slime and dirt of the earth; but he or she will quarrel with the psychoanalyst who, concentrating upon the roots, denies the existence of the stem, the organic relationship of the leaves to the stem, or the flower's beauty. As the root is not the whole flower, so man is not wholly to be understood in terms of his unconscious. If we are ever so ill that we need a psychoanalyst's help for the examination of unconsciousness, let there be no dispensing with the examination of conscience. The former is sometimes necessary; but it is never a *substitute* for the latter.

A doctor may sometimes give us medicine to cure the blood of its anemia; this does not remove the greater, enduring necessity for us to clear the blood by breathing. Similarly, there may be times when it is necessary to analyze unconsciousness to find out whether an idea has been repressed or suppressed; but it is always necessary for us to examine conscience to find out whether the motive that prompted an action was right or wrong. (And, discovering this, one may also find the reason for the repression.) Sometimes it is useful to analyze attitudes or states of mind; but it is always needful to analyze the will and recognize its guilt, if any. This is a more painful process than psychoanalysis is apt to be: A person can be proud of his mental attitudes, he may boast of his skepticism, his atheism, his agnosticism, and his perversion, but his conscience will never boast of its guilt, its shame, or its misery; even in isolation, a guilty conscience is troubled. It longs to escape the pain of self-knowledge by laying the responsibility elsewhere. Sometimes the blame for an abnormal mental condition is to be laid upon grandmothers and grandfathers, on cruel parents or clumsy kindergarten teachers; but let it never be forgotten that much more often the blame is more justly to be placed on oneself, as one strikes one's breast, confessing, "Through my fault, through my fault, through my most grievous fault." Sometimes it may be helpful to have one's unconsciousness examined as one is stretched out on a couch, but unless one wants to abdicate one's entire personality to another, it is always necessary to reserve the right of the excavation of one's own mental property, to dig in one's own soul. No person is ever made better by having someone else tell him how rotten he is; but many are made better by avowing the guilt themselves.

It is very often the case that, when the unconscious is made conscious, mental difficulties disappear. (But this is not a substitute for righting a wrong committed against some objective standard.) There are times when it is morally helpful to bring into the light of consciousness the contents hidden in the unconscious; if the subject knows about these contents, he becomes able to deal with them and to turn the newly acquired self-understanding to a better use, directing his energies toward more reasonable goals.[6]

No one will deny that the effectiveness of the analysis depends on the technique, but the technique is no substitute for repentance. Nor does a psychology penetrate very deeply into human problems if it interprets man entirely in terms of instincts and the conflict of instincts or if it traces back all conflicts to instinctual sources, claiming that there are *no other elements in the human person.* In animals, there are only instincts, but not in man. The instincts of an animal are so well adjusted to its possible situations that they come into play automatically. As Saint Thomas points out, there cannot be any deliberation in a subrational being (even though we may get the impression that there is); there is only an interplay of forces, the more attractive image proving stronger and becoming a determinant of behavior. Instincts in animals seem to operate according to the pattern of physical forces, where the stronger always prevails; for animals are utterly devoid of the freedom that characterizes man.[7]

Because man is free, he can sin, as animals cannot. Sinners may need self-analysis; but they *surely* need help from beyond themselves to make them well. A profound difference between examination of the unconscious and examination of conscience is that the first remains subjective and may lock the patient inside his own tight ego, like a squirrel in a cage.

As one psychologist has said, "You cannot see what you are looking for because you are standing in your own light" — you are looking for yourself, searching for the very thing that also seeks. Such a process is very much like trying to watch oneself go to sleep. But in the examination of conscience one gets outside self as quickly as possible by letting the light of God shine in. It is Christ Who looks into the soul and Who peers into the conscience. That is why Sacred Scripture is full of the idea, "Search my soul, O God." And when the Divine Light looks into the mind, it takes the mind off itself, avoiding the many miseries that spring from too much introspection.[8] That is why Our Blessed Lord urged us to forget our mental states, when such a thing is possible. "No man putting his hand to the plough, and looking back, is fit for the kingdom of God" (Luke 9:62). "Follow me, and let the dead bury their dead" (Matt. 8:22).

Some mental disorders, however, refuse to be ignored, even after guilt as a cause and examination of conscience as a cure have been applied. There remain many mental ills that have a purely psychological and neurological, even a physiological, basis; these only a good psychiatrist can cure. But it is important, to effect a cure, to be treated by a *good* psychiatrist. A system of psychoanalysis that starts with the denial of the will, of human responsibility, and of guilt renders its followers incapable of understanding the human nature upon which they operate and increases, in many instances, the very disease it attempts to cure. Sick souls who, up to this time, have denied the possibility of sin and guilt ought to reexamine their consciences rather than their unconscious and consider the possibility that maybe some of their mental troubles are due to an unrecognized sense of human guilt. There are many souls stretched out on psychoanalytic couches today who would be far better off if they brought their consciences to a confessional box. There are thousands of patients on their backs who would be made better today if they were on their knees instead. The very passivity symbolized by being stretched out on a couch is symbolic of the patient's irresponsibility, which the whole theory of Freud assumes. It is in striking contrast to the humility of a man who, kneeling, says not "Oh, what a fool I have been," but "God, be merciful to me, a sinner."

Those souls who deny the possibility of their own guilt do so, usually, because they are either too self-complacent or too snobbish to face the facts. They are "escapists" seeking to sweep their moral dirt under Freudian rugs. Instead of admitting their sins as their own, they project them onto others. Many of the troubles of today come about because all of us looking for someone else to blame for our own wrongdoing.

All scapegoats are the result of efforts to eliminate all concern about the higher self, and thus they atrophy the moral sense. They also put to sleep the critical judgment, which should see the illogic of this theory. For if the unconscious is the cause of abnormal *mental* states and ensuing disorders, we must ask: What makes the unconscious produce these psychoses and these disorders? And if repression is the cause, then why does consciousness *want* to repress that which is wrong?[9] The amoralist psychoanalyst, refusing to admit "right" or "wrong," has difficulty in answering. The explanation, of course, is to be found in the natural moral order, in the existence of an *ethos* to which every person is subject and against which we sometimes rebel. Such a moral order is universal and has been universally recognized. It is hard to find in any literature the assumption that the only difference between a sane person and an insane person lies in the contents of their unconsciousness, but it is very easy to find, throughout the ages, a distinction drawn between what a person appears to be to his neighbor and what he really is in himself or between what he is and what he ought to be.

Man has, indeed, two aspects, often perceived by poets and philosophers. As Browning put it:

> God be thanked, the meanest of His creatures
> Boast two soul-sides, one to face the world with,
> One to show a woman, when he loves her.

These two sides of human nature relate to the yearnings for a greater good than we can realize in our everyday living. There is always an ideal involved.

The Freudian attempt to brush away our moral consciousness as a disguised version of something else has been generally repudiated in Europe; more recently, even in America it is losing its hold as comedians are make it the butt of their jokes and cartoon books deride it. When one thinks about the subject calmly, it becomes clear that few more ridiculous theories have been invented than this, which derived a person's feeling of guilt from the inhibition of a potential desire to kill his father and marry his mother (Oedipus complex) or to kill her mother and marry her father (Electra complex). Such a theory assumes no objective wrongness about either wish but makes only the bald and unproved statement that I am made to feel guilty because of my repressed desire for father slaying or mother slaying.[10]

C. E. M. Joad, commenting on this theory, writes:

> Again the explanation burkes the issue by begging the question to be explained. Why do I feel guilt now? Because, we are told, I or possibly my remote ancestors desired to commit parricide or incest. And therefore? Therefore, presumably, I or my remote ancestors felt guilt because they so desired. Now either parricide and incest were things they thought they ought not to have done, or they were not. If they were, then the feeling of guilt which the theory seeks to explain away is still

found to be attaching itself to that which is invoked as the explanation of it. If they were not, it is impossible to see how the process leading to the feeling of moral guilt can be derived from a remote past in which men did not feel morally, no more than the feelings of awe and reverence can be derived from a universe in which nothing is sacred or awesome, or the feeling of aesthetic appreciation from a universe in which nothing is beautiful."[11]

Dr. Edmund Bergler in his psychiatric study, *The Battle of the Conscience*,[12] breaks with those who consider conscience an illusion. "Everyone has an inner conscience; it is constantly under the influence of that inner department of the personality. The cynic who ridicules conscience forgets that his own cynicism has its reason not unrelated to his conscience. The rabid behavior of the cynic is the expression of defensive warfare against his 'internal enemy.' He strikes others, but he is aiming at himself." The old adage that an easy conscience is the best pillow to sleep on is today confirmed by those who sleep — or spend sleepless nights — on the hard pillow of materialism. Since this philosophy denies the very possibility of guilt, it doses them off from the possibility of cure.

The voice of conscience can be stilled in four ways: by killing it, by denying it, by drowning it, and by fleeing from it. Nietzsche is the inspiration of those who kill conscience. This philosopher frankly advocated sin, to the point where conscience is completely lost and where there is no longer a distinction drawn between good and evil. As an earlier poet put it:

> Why should not conscience have vacation,
> As well as other courts o' th' nation?

> Have equal power to adjourn
> Appoint appearance and return?[13]

Nietzsche urges what he calls a "transvaluation of values," which makes the good evil and the evil good. If such an abuse is continued long enough, conscience can be killed. When one goes to work in a boiler factory, the noise is deafening for the first few months; after that one does not hear it. In like manner, conscience can be drowned out so that we do not notice it until the last waking hours of life, when it revives.

Another way to escape from conscience is by denying it.

> Let not our babbling dreams affright our souls;
> Conscience is but a word that cowards use,
> Devis'd at first, to keep the strong in awe.[14]

This escape generally takes the form of a rationalization by which there is an adjustment of our conscience to the way we live. By denying any ultimate standard outside of self, one can escape all self-blame and go through life on a perpetual mission of face saving. Marxism is one form of the denial of conscience — because it blames our sense of inner tension on economic conditions. Other ideologies trace the existence of the conscience to the influence of the herd. Such philosophies all assume that a person is other-determined, rather than self-determined. They deny that man is free and yet usually claim for every person a right freely to choose his own opinions.

The third escape is by drowning conscience.

> O conscience, into what abyss of fears
> And horrors hast thou driven me; out of which
> I find no way, from deep to deeper plunged.[15]

When one realizes that there are 6 million doses of sleeping tablets sold per day in the United States and that the per capita consumption of alcohol was recently estimated at

more than $50 per man, woman, and child; when one counts
the 700,000 confirmed alcoholics and the 3 million border-
line cases, there is indeed a strong indication that there are
many in our population who are engaged in trying to drown
all sense of their own responsibility and freedom and the
burden of choice.

Not to be ignored is the fourth method of escape —
the flight from conscience. This motivation is also apparent
among the drug addicts and the alcoholics: They have lost
the capacity to put up with any unpleasantness whatsoever.

> Vice is a monster of so frightful mien
> As to be hated, needs but to be seen;
> Yet seen too oft, familiar with her face,
> We first endure, then pity, then embrace.[16]

Fugitives from the demands of conscience have quailed before the effort to make any decision or to overcome their
condition; facing difficulties involves too much unpleasantness. Their trouble has been called the "idolatry of comfort."
It is a common complaint. People today feel that life ought to
run smoothly, that nothing should inconvenience them, that
everything should function as perfectly as the gadgets with
which they love to surround themselves and on which they
depend. Only for special rewards will they accept hardship
willingly. Many people are still able to put up with a certain
amount of unpleasantness for things they believe worthwhile:
They will make great efforts to ensure a higher income or social prestige. But there are others who cannot support even
the small, inevitable sufferings of daily existence. From these
things they seek refuge in intoxication or one of the other
flights from responsibility. In their attempted escape from all
effort they bear out the conception of the Book of Genesis of
work as a punishment man does not enjoy.

It should be pointed out that all four forms of repression

of human guilt have their effects upon the unconscious and upon the human body. Any denial of conscience as the voice of God may be momentarily effective, but a day will come when the abused conscience will turn with fury and will harass its victim, tormenting his waking life and making his dreams a poison, his darkness a nightmare. When night gives our inner vision scope, the guilty conscience lies awake, fearful of being known in all its ugliness. There is nothing that so arouses unhealthy fear as a hidden guilt.

This fear is evidenced in many ways: When a person is not right on the inside, there can be nothing right in his outside activities. He will project his own discontent to others; what should have been an unrevealed self-criticism will express itself in cantankerous, critical faultfinding. If such a person is rich, he may try to make compensation — perhaps for ill-gotten goods — by espousing an ideological cause or founding newspapers. If he is of the intelligentsia (which means he has been educated beyond his intelligence), he will try to solace his conscience by a pretended interest in social justice or by sneering at religion. The guilty person seeks to adjust himself to his environment, although he knows that the cause of his trouble is that he is not self-adjusted. (It may be very wrong for people to adjust themselves to their environment until they are sure that it is the right environment.) Such a soul wearies itself to death as it runs from one psychoanalyst to another, struggling with the problem of the sickened self; in spite of these apparent efforts to find a cure, it is fleeing the truth about itself, as a person may be afraid to open his letters lest they be reminders of his unpaid bills.

Sound psychologists point out that certain emotions have repercussions on the physical nature of man, as psychosomatic medicine bears witness. So too they might point out that immoral repressions of conscience can have still more serious effects. Not only do they destroy character, but they also create disorders in the unconscious mind. As the cock crowed when Peter denied Our Lord, so all nature rises in revolt against us when we have done wrong. One physician in treating one hundred cases of arthritis and colitis found that 68 percent of the patients suffered from a hidden sense of guilt. There is a case on record in England of a nursing mother whose milk poisoned her baby because of the intense hatred that she bore her husband: The wicked spiritual state of her soul had harmed not only her own mind but the body of her child.

In one of the Gospel stories, when a paralyzed man was let down through the roof, Our Blessed Lord said to him, "Thy sins are forgiven." It happened that there were present a number of escapists who laughed at guilt and the moral order, scoffed at giving this public importance to sins. Our Blessed Lord became angry with them; He said, "Which is it easier to say, 'Thy sins are forgiven thee'; or to say, 'Arise and walk' " (Matt. 9:5). And the man immediately walked. But notice the order: *First* the man's sins were forgiven, and *then* he was able to recover. Considerable medical testimony now exists to prove that memories tinged with guilt can increase the probability of fractures, which patients then blame on their "bad luck." The "accident-prone" are always breaking dishes and arms, losing things, falling off ladders, but these accidents are less "accidental" than they seem — they may be secret efforts to escape from the demands of duty, they may be a disguised self-punishment. In the light of this, it is conceivable that a person may even commit suicide as a form of "self-punishment" for a wrong he has done. Self-destruction becomes an extreme case of the attitude that prompts a person to say, "I could kick myself for doing that." Some suicides are clearly expressions of such subconscious drives.

A neglected conscience can revenge itself in many devious

ways. There are many people suffering from physical disorders, finding it difficult to maintain normal relations with one another, nervous and unstrung at home and in the office, simply because they have a repressed guilt. Either this has not been brought to the surface at all, or they have had it explained away by those unscientific charlatans who see in human nature no difference or transcendence over that of a cockroach. But there is no escaping the law of human nature. As it is recorded in Scripture, "Your sins will find you out." Just as a refusal to study in childhood begets an ignorance that finds us out in mature life, when we find ourselves unable to cope with the economic existence, so, too, those sins we thought did not matter or that we rationalized away or denied or thrust down into our unconsciousness will somehow make themselves felt in their effects on our health, our attitude of mind, and our general outlook on life. Sin resides primarily in the soul; but secondarily it resides in every nerve and cell and fiber of our being and in every corner of our brain. A number of individuals living in invalid marriages are not enjoying the physical aspect of their marriage simply because they have to live with consciences that will not give even their bodies rest. This is particularly true of those who once had the faith and gave it up. After the first flush of courtship excitement has died down, conscience begins to reassert itself. They discover that they cannot give themselves completely to one another, because they are not in possession of themselves since committing an obvious and conscious violation of their relationship with God.

There are many people who go about their duties in the daytime with an apparent peace of mind but who at night, because of an unrequited sense of guilt, feel those pangs that make them, like atheists, afraid of the dark. As a person may have a clear head and an active mind but also may have a disease of the brain that will later reveal itself, so many a person may be apparently upright and noble-minded, generous and tolerant, yet be gradually eaten away from the inside by a hidden guilt. That is why the spiritual men of old cried out, "Cleanse thou me from my secret faults, O Lord."

How can we avoid these modern sufferings that stem from secret guilt? Many of them would yield to nightly examination of conscience.

There is no denying the fact that the analysis of unconsciousness is much more popular than an examination of conscience. As a substitute, it seems far more attractive at first. No one minds examining his unconsciousness or even having it examined, but who is there who does not dislike both examining his own conscience and having it examined? An escapist has not the heart or the nerve or the stomach to face his own conscience. For alongside each and every one there stand three pools that give three different reflections. We look into one pool, and we are pleased with ourselves, because in that pool we see ourselves as we are in our own eyes. In the second pool, we see ourselves as our neighbors see us. But in the third pool we see ourselves as God sees us, that is, as we really are. It is to this third pool that the examination of conscience takes us at the close of every day. Just as a businessman at the end of a day takes out of his cash register the record of debits and credits, so, too, at the end of every day, every soul should examine his conscience, not using himself as his standard, but seeing it as it appears in the light of God, his Creator and his Judge.

The examination of conscience brings to the surface the hidden faults of the day; it seeks to discover the weeds that are choking the growth of God's grace and destroying peace of soul. It is concerned with thoughts, words, and deeds, with sins of omission and sins of commission. By omission we mean the good that is left undone — a failure to aid a needy neighbor, a refusal to offer a word of consolation to those who are burdened with sorrow. Sins of commission involve malicious remarks, lies, acts of dishonesty, and those seven sins that are the seven pallbearers of the soul: self-love, inordinate love of money, illicit sex, hate, overindulgence, jealousy, and laziness. In addition to all this, there is the examination for what spiritual writers call our "predominant fault." Every person in the world has one sin that he or she commits more than others. Spiritual directors say that if we blotted out one great sin a year, in a short time we should be perfect.

The examination of conscience, because it is concerned with guilt as an offense against love of God or neighbor, is quite distinct from attempts to cure the pathological forms of guilt that haunt some disturbed minds. The former can never be blotted out by any form of analysis or psychiatry; the latter may fall within that field and may belong to the spiritual domain as well. Hence we must distinguish between guilt in the strict sense of the term and guilt in the broad sense of the term. The sentiment of guilt implies always the awareness of having failed to comply with some demand. The differences in the two forms of guilt arise from the demands recognized by the individual. Guilt, in the broad sense of the term, need not be related to a failure to obey the moral laws; laws broken or tasks left undone may be of another kind and still cause us remorse. If someone sets for himself a high standard for all his achievements and, by his own fault or because of adverse circumstances, fails to live up to them, he may feel guilty. Indeed, a person may feel guilty because he has not given the right answer in a quiz program; a gentleman may feel guilty because he hurt the family reputation; a medieval knight felt guilty because he had failed to observe the code of *noblesse oblige*. Yet in none of these cases was sin necessarily involved.

There is a sentiment of guilt that is related to pride. Some people, because they do not live up to their own expectations, feel guilty. It is difficult to know whether this factor plays a determining role in the development of melancholy, with its excessive sentiment of guilt. Pierre Janet thought that each attack of pathological melancholy was preceded by an experience of defeat. He added, however, that such moods may have a long period of incubation and that the releasing experience may have occurred several months before the melancholic depression developed. In cases where the sentiments of guilt appear to be unfounded, a more searching inquiry into the past of the afflicted person often reveals that there is, in truth, a good reason for his having a bad conscience. One need not go back to early childhood or posit an Oedipus situation to find this. We all have done things we would rather not have done. Nietzsche, long before Freud, remarked, " 'You have done this,' says memory. 'I cannot have done it,' says pride. And memory gives in."

Some psychoanalysts claim that the mere tracing back of a guilt feeling to the unconscious instinctual roots will free the patient from this sentiment. When this effect does not follow, the patient is told that whatever he has so far brought forth is not the right memory — the "trauma" — and that he may not find it unless he goes back to his very earliest experiences. His guilt feeling is explained as the effect of unconscious forces, erasing every action that he may prefer not to remember having done. But this is equivalent to saying that the patient's sense of guilt arose at a period of his life in which we are not responsible — at infancy. This would be a comforting belief if it did not violate the universal human experience that guilt and freedom are inseparable: Only free beings can sin. Only a human can choose between obeying or defying his nature's laws: Ice never sins by melting, nor are fires at fault for going out.

This relegating of our mistakes to our irresponsible babyhood is one more instance of the curious, prejudicial way of thinking that is common to modern psychology with a Freudian basis. It cannot face the fact that man may have a guilt feeling because he knows himself to be guilty of doing something wrong. The Freudian will not even consider the possibility that the sentiment of guilt might disappear once its real (not its "unconscious") roots were revealed, provided the guilty person atoned and made good what evil he or she had done. Such a psychoanalyst will not consider this possibility because he is convinced that only the search of the unconscious can bring improvement — which means, to him, making the "symptom" disappear. Such a psychoanalyst is, naturally, in no position to pass judgment on the efficacy or nonefficacy of confession and atonement.

The Freudian sometimes argues that confession does no good in healing complexes, whether they arise from an offense against the moral law or not. Usually he defines confession wrongly, as a mere "speaking out"; he forgets that confession involves reparation. Money stolen must be paid back. The balance of justice must be restored. When guilt derives from real sin, there is a healing power in this retracing of false steps. In practice, one often does see a morbid sentiment of guilt disappear when its real cause — wrongdoing — is recognized first by oneself, is then admitted to another, and is finally compensated for by an adequate atonement. Even apart from the sacramental character of confession, there is the psychological comfort in "doing penance" so that the evil done in the past can be compensated by some good done now.

Guilt feelings very often have a sound, reasonable cause in a person's memories of unadmitted wrongdoing. Here a helpful distinction made by the Scholastics should be recalled. There are two kinds of evils: *malum culpae*, an act performed with freedom, responsibility, and retreat from God;

and *malum poenae,* which is something that happens to us apart from our deliberate choice — something like a pain in the neck. One is a moral evil; the other is a physical or mental evil. The Sacrament of Penance is concerned only with the first; psychiatry properly deals with the mental evils resulting primarily from nonmoral causes.

Sometimes there are mental or physical repercussions because of sin; *in these cases,* there must be peace of *soul* before there can be peace of *mind.* The two are not the same: Peace of soul implies tranquillity of order, with material things ordered to the body, the body to the soul, the personality to neighbor and to God. Peace of mind is subjective tranquillity — a narrower thing. It requires great moral effort to attain peace of soul, but even those who are indifferent to right and wrong sometimes achieve peace of mind (which the Scriptures call "false peace"). On the other hand, it may be that mental disorders prevent moral and spiritual development. In that case a sound psychiatric examination is a required preliminary to the priest's helpfulness. The sound psychiatrist and the spiritual director can make a mutual contribution one to the other; this is so obvious that to develop it would be as vain as to create a mutual-admiration society. But our primary concern here is to show the difference between guilt and disease, to protest against the reduction of one to the other, and to indicate some advantages of self-examination in cases where it is required.

All of us have a little corner in our heart we never want anyone to venture into, even with a candle. That is why we can deceive ourselves and why our neighbors know us better than we know ourselves. The examination of unconsciousness, if it is used as a substitute for examination of conscience, only intensifies this deceit. We often justify ourselves by saying that we *are* following our consciences, when we are following only our desires. We fit a creed to the way we live, rather than fit the way we live to a creed; we suit religion to our actions, rather than actions to religion. We try to keep religion on a speculative basis in order to avoid moral reproaches on our conduct. We sit at the piano of life and insist that every note we strike is right — because we struck it. We justify want of faith by saying, "I don't go to Church, but I am better than those who do," as one might say, or "I don't pay taxes or serve the nation, but I am better than those who do." If each person is his own judge and standard, then who shall say he is wrong?

Not only will the examination of conscience cure us of such self-deception, it will also cure us of depression. Depression comes, not from having faults, but from the refusal to face them. There are tens of thousands of persons today suffering from fears that in reality are nothing but the effects of hidden sins. The evil conscience is always the fearful conscience. The greatest worries come from our failure to face reality. (That is why a pain that is present is more bearable than an equal worry to come in the future.) Morbidity increases with the denial of guilt, the explaining it away, or the covering up of the ulcerous part.[17] Whence comes the depression of self-pity, if it be not a total unconcern with the interests of others, which is a sin? A soldier on a battlefield does not heed the wound if he loves his cause, and the soul that can cast its anxiety and worry upon an all-loving God is thus saved from self-pity. Many souls are like persons with boils, who could be cured by lancing, which would allow the pus to run out. Their suppressed sins give rise to this form of sadness.[18] There has never been in the history of the Church a saint who was not joyful: There have been many saints who were great sinners, like Augustine, but there have never been sad saints. This is understandable: Perhaps there could not be anything in life more depressing than the knowledge that one has been guilty of a grave sin, without the chance of starting all over again. Saint Paul wisely distinguishes between the sadness of the guilty who know redemption and the depression of those who deny both their guilt and the possibility of forgiveness. "For godly grief produces a repentance that leads to salvation and brings no regret, but worldly grief produces death" (2 Cor. 7:10). "You know that later, when he wanted to inherit the blessing, he was rejected, for he found no chance to repent, even though he sought the blessing with tears" (Heb. 12:17). The examination of conscience not only relieves our sadness, not only gives us a second chance when forgiven. It also restores us to Love.

In the examination of conscience a person concentrates less on his own sin than on the mercy of God — as the wounded concentrate less on their wounds than on the power of the physician who binds and heals the wounds. The examination of conscience develops no complex because it is done in the light of God's justice. The self is not the standard, nor is it the source of hope. All human frailty and all human weakness are seen in the radiation of God's infinite goodness, and never once is a fault separated from knowledge of the Divine Mercy. Examination of conscience pictures sin, not as the violation of law, but as the breaking of a relationship. It develops sorrow, not because a code has been violated, but because love has been wounded. As the empty pantry drives the homemaker to the bakery, so the empty soul is driven to the Bread of Life.

Nor is examination of conscience a concentration on one's own disordered consciousness in the way an Oriental mystic contemplates his navel. Excessive introspection leads to immobility and morbidity. No minds or souls are more helpless than those who say they will "work the thing out alone." The Christian soul knows it needs Divine Help and therefore turns to Him Who loved us even while we were yet sinners. Examination of conscience, instead of inducing morbidity, thereby becomes an occasion of joy. There are two ways of knowing how good and loving God is. One is by never losing Him, through the preservation of innocence, and the other is by finding Him after one has lost Him.

Repentance is not self-regarding, but God-regarding. It is not self-loathing, but God-loving. Christianity bids us to accept ourselves as we really are, with all our faults and our failings and our sins. In other religions, one has to be good to come to God — in Christianity, one does not. Christianity might be described as a "come as you are" party. It bids us stop worrying about ourselves, stop concentrating on our faults and our failings, and thrust them upon the Savior with a firm resolve of amendment. The examination of conscience never induces despair, always hope. Some psychologists, by the proper use of their method, have brought mental peace to individuals, but only because they have found a safety valve from mental pressure. They have let off steam, but they have not repaired the boiler. That is the business of the Church.

Because examination of conscience is done in the light of God's love, it begins with a prayer to the Holy Spirit to illumine our minds. A soul then acts toward the Spirit of God as toward a watchmaker who will fix our watch. We put a watch in his hands because we know he will not force it, and we put our souls in God's hands because we know that if God inspects them regularly, they will work as they should.

It is true that, the closer we get to God, the more we see our defects. A painting reveals few defects under candlelight, but the sunlight may reveal it as a daub. The very good never believe themselves very good, because they are judging themselves by the Ideal. In perfect innocence each soul, like the Apostles at the Last Supper, cries out, "Is it I, Lord" (Matt. 26:22).

The examination of conscience is primarily a concentration upon the goodness and the love of God. Every soul that examines itself looks at a Crucifix and sees a personal relationship between itself and Our Divine Lord. We admit that the Crown of Thorns would have been a little less piercing if we had been less proud and vain and that if we had been less swift in running down the pathways of sin the Divine Feet would have been less pierced with nails; if we had been less avaricious, the hands would not have been so deeply dug with steel, and if we had been less carnal, the Savior would not have been stripped of His garments.

This figure upon the Cross is not a MVD agent or a Gestapo inquisitor, but a Divine Physician, Who only asks that we bring our wounds to Him in order that He may heal them. If our sins be as scarlet, they shall be washed white as snow, and if they be as red as crimson, they shall be made white as wool. Was it not He Who told us, "Just so, I tell you, there will be more joy in heaven over one sinner who repents than over ninety-nine righteous persons who need no repentance" (Luke 15:7)? In the story of the prodigal, did He not describe the Father as saying, "Let us eat and make merry: Because this my son was dead and is come to life again; was lost, and is found" (Luke 15:23, 24)?

Why is there more joy in Heaven for the repentant sinner than for the righteous? Because God's attitude is not judgment but *love*. In judgment, one is not as joyful after doing wrong as before; but in love, there is joy because the danger and worry of losing that soul is past. He who is sick is loved more than he who is well, because he *needs* it more. Some will feign sickness to solicit love and pretend wounds in order that the beloved may bind them.

Those who deny guilt and sin are like the Pharisees of old who thought our Savior had a "guilt complex" because He accused them of being whited sepulchers — outside clean, inside full of dead men's bones. Those who admit that they are guilty are like the public sinners and the publicans of whom

Our Lord said, "Amen, I say to you, that the publicans and the harlots shall go into the Kingdom of God before you" (Matt. 21:31). Those who think they are healthy but have a hidden moral cancer are incurable; the sick who want to be healed have a chance. All denial of guilt keeps people out of the area of love and, by inducing self-righteousness, prevents a cure.

The two facts of healing in the physical order are these: A physician cannot heal us unless we put ourselves into his hands, and we will not put ourselves into his hands unless we know that we are sick. In like manner, a sinner's awareness of sin is one requisite for his recovery; the other is his longing for God. When we long for God, we do so not as sinners, but as lovers.

It is true that, after our examination of conscience, we do often find ourselves unlovable, but it is precisely that which makes us want God — because He is the only One Who loves the unlovable. "Whom wilt thou find to love ignoble thee, Save Me, save only Me?"[19]

Notes

1. The name "psychoanalysis" was coined by Freud, who insisted that it be used for his doctrine and his method *exclusively*. German, French, and also Italian authors have more or less heeded this admonition. Some Americans, too, tried to identify Freudianism and psychoanalysis, but in general, in Anglo-Saxon countries, the name of psychoanalysis is applied indiscriminately to other kinds of medical and mental treatments. C. G. Jung, to indicate the difference between his theory and that of Freud and, at the same time, his indebtedness to it, speaks of his own doctrine as "analytic psychology." Adler named his conception "individual psychology," a theory that is more or less dependent on psychoanalysis but nevertheless rejects one of its fundamental tenets. Because of the growing criticism of Freudianism and psychoanalysis, some psychoanalysts are using the term psychiatry to avoid the criticism. To think clearly on this subject, then, these three distinctions must be kept in

mind: (1) Freudianism is not psychoanalysis, just as Raphael is not painting. (2) There are other systems of psychoanalysis than the Freudian, and
some of them are much more sound. (3) Psychoanalysis is only one small
branch of psychiatry.

2. Sigmund Freud, *The Future of an Illusion*, p. 59, Horace Liveright,
1928.

3. Ibid., p. 64.

4. Sigmund Freud, *Introductory Lectures on Psychoanalysis,* trans.

5. *Summa Theologica*, II–2, Q. 95, Art. 6.

6. Perhaps it should be mentioned that the notion of the unconscious
in the form that is popularly given to it is open to objections. It is difficult to arrive at a final opinion whether or not a certain content is truly
unconscious. The mere fact that the person claims to know nothing about
it is not sufficient, nor is the other fact, that this content came to the surface only in the course of a long and searching analysis. The human mind
has many tricks to get rid of contents that are felt to be troublesome or
that might lead to unpleasant consequences if fully acknowledged. The
mind can sever all connections between some data and the rest of consciousness, isolate certain data or prevent them from turning up because
they are totally unrelated or have been made so to the rest of conscious
contents. This problem is not one of merely theoretical interest but is also
eminently practical. What a person has ejected from his consciousness because he did not want to face it has a more important hearing, in regard
to morality and responsibility, than contents that were relegated to the
unconscious at an early age, when neither understanding nor responsibility were developed. It happens during analysis that allegedly unconscious
material comes to the fore, and the subject acknowledges it; he may even
say that he somehow knew these things always but took care to keep
them out of his way. In such a case, there is obviously a different degree
of responsibility from what there is when the unconscious facts pertain to
the experiences of early childhood.

7. Despite the common jargon about human instincts, it must be
remembered that there is no agreement, among neurophysiologists, concerning the existence and efficacy of instincts in a person in his mature
and normal state. According to K. Goldstein (*The Organism,* American
Book Company, New York, 1939; *Human Nature in the Light of Psychopathology,* Harvard University Press, Cambridge, Mass., 1940), purely
instinctual manifestations are seen in humans only in consequence of a
breakdown of the complex whole. Normally, they have been integrated
into higher functions. In fact, one hardly finds any reaction in a normal adult that might be labeled "instinctive." An instinct in animals is
characterized, according, *e.g.,* to Bierens van Haan (*Die Instinkte*), as
(a) characteristic of the species, not of the individual; (b) immutable or, at

least, mutable only within the narrowest limits; (c) impossible of transformation, into other behavior patterns; (d) purposive, without the animal's knowing purpose. To this, one may add that complex instinctual behavior is an indivisible performance, although it appears to the observer as consisting of partial actions, one following the other. Consider the behavior of the sand wasp: It digs a tiny hole in the sand, flies away to capture a caterpillar, deposits the prey beside the hole, paralyzes it by a well-applied sting, puts it into the hole, deposits the eggs there, and closes the hole with some grains of sand. In whatever phase this performance is interrupted, the animal abandons it to begin anew from the first phase. In other words, for the wasp there is no succession of steps, but only one indivisible performance. Compare this with so-called "instinctual" behavior in man: Any such action can be interrupted at any moment and resumed at that stage, as soon as the circumstances permit. For man, there is a true succession of partial acts. It would seem as if in man instincts were only one kind of motivation, their satisfaction only one kind of goal to be envisioned, not as if they were absolute determinants of behavior. That is why when one studies human behavior one must rise above the purely animal pattern and concentrate upon those two faculties, intellect and will, which separate man from the animal. The analysis of conscience is, therefore, the profoundest analysis one can make of man.

8. The diseased mind becomes unable to communicate with others, and to the degree that this occurs it becomes involved in an excess of subjectivism. One has to distinguish between the psychotic's excessive subjectivism (as it exists in schizophrenia) and one that merely excludes man from communication and encloses him within himself. This milder form exists in many forms of neurotic disturbances. But even in these cases it cannot be stated with absolute certainty that subjectivism is a true cause of the mental abnormality. It is conceivable that a person can be driven into such a subjectivistic attitude by the fear of some threat. He will then be at pains to protect himself, be concerned with himself, and so become more and more subjective in his attitude. One observes such responses in bodily diseases; the vital uncertainty into which a human being is thrown when he realizes the weakening of his body makes him excessively concerned with himself.

Of course, it cannot be denied that such a reaction need not occur. If a person were fully conscious of the relative insignificance of his earthly existence as set against his eternal fate, he would not worry so much and, therefore, would not feel that he had to be concerned with himself alone. But bodily disease may so weaken a person that his best insights and intentions prove ineffective. If someone grew up under the impression that nobody really cared for him, that he was badly equipped to meet the problems of reality, he, too, would become unusually concerned with himself; his subjectivism, accordingly, would be more of an effect than of a cause of his mental abnormality. The question of subjectivism as an attitude for which the person may be held responsible turns up only after he has become aware of the lack of a foundation for his general approach to reality. It is one aim of mental treatment or reeducation that the neurotic be made to realize the fictitiousness of many things he dreads and, therefore, to see that his excessive preoccupation with himself is as unnecessary as it is misguided.

9. Freudian psychoanalysts answer that (1) consciousness does not repress but that it is rather the passive battleground where the superego becomes victorious and manages to expel what it does not tolerate; (2) it refuses to tolerate certain things, not because they are objectively wrong in any moral sense, but because they are contrary to the existing social conventions. These conventions are inculcated in the mind of the small child; they form the superego, which, in virtue of "identification," acquires a fateful domination over the ego and therefore over consciousness. Rebellion is the attempt of the id to reassert itself against the tyranny of the superego. It is in the ego, and consciousness, that the battle for supremacy is fought.

Psychoanalysis may admit that there is an *ethos;* but this ethos, it says, will be dependent on and a product of the existing societal situation. When society takes on another shape, the moral code will change correspondingly. In this Freudianism runs parallel to certain modern sociological theories, as e.g., that of E. Durkheim and his school. Durkheim recognized the role and existence of moral and religious values and precepts; but he believed that they were derived from the societal structures, each of which demands another code according to its nature.

Recently, attempts have been made, on the part of some Freudians, to integrate their standards with those of recognized morals. Edmund Bergler declares in his work *Divorce Won't Help* that monogamy is a natural state, or one that corresponds to human nature. Humans cannot help being basically monogamous and will feel better if they cling to monogamy, because of the Oedipus complex. The Oedipus longings, incestuous by nature, are repressed; the superego keeps them in the vaults of the unconscious and, instead of the primordial indiscriminate instinctual longings, the superego sets up those approved by morality, placing any deviation under sanction. The wife is the substitute for the mother and therefore is irreplaceable. All extramarital vagaries are attempts on the part of the repressed instinct to reassert itself.

In this reasoning, two details deserve consideration. First, it is to be noted that the idea of uninhibited indulgence as conducive to greater happiness and a fuller development of personality is here abandoned. Licentiousness, which, by some psychoanalysts (though not by Freud), has been viewed as a way out of conflicts, is no longer encouraged. Either the psychoanalysts are beginning to realize that there is such a thing as an objectively valid morality and to try to render account of this in their own way, or they have found out that disregarding the moral precepts does not, for one reason or another, result in a happy life. Second, the psychoanalysts, in doing the one or the other, are unaware that they contradict their own principles. A perfectly subjectivistic conception has no place for any sort of objective morality. Subjectivism must be relativistic, by necessity. But the Oedipus complex is not dependent on any particular social structure or form of civilization. It has to occur in any society, primitive or advanced, totalitarian or democratic, atheistic or religious. According to the psychoanalytic theory this complex is an inevitable effect of human nature, therefore prior to all societal forms. If this position is assumed, it follows of necessity that there is some immutable, unchangeable principle of human relations. As soon as this is conceded, the whole notion of the relativity of values, including those of ethics, becomes untenable.

10. Religion is explained by Freud in a similarly fantastic way: "Religion is a general compulsion neurosis like that of a child and derives from the Oedipus complex, the relation of the father. And if the original sin was one against God, the Father, the oldest crime must have been parricide, the slaying of the first father of the primitive human horde, whose memory picture was subsequently transferred into Divinity."

11. *God and Evil,* p. 210, Harper & Brothers.

12. Washington Institute of Medicine.

13. Samuel Butler, *Hudibras.*

14. William Shakespeare, *Richard III.*

15. John Milton, *Paradise Lost.*

16. Alexander Pope, *Essay on Man.*

17. Freudian psychoanalysis believes that certain ideas or emotions are driven into unconsciousness and are "forbidden" by the superego to show themselves. Every painful experience owes its character to the frustration of some instinctual urge, which is relegated to the unconscious because it has been placed under sanction by society and the superego. Thus Freudian psychoanalysis can easily explain that certain experiences (chiefly those causing pain or a sentiment of guilt) are repressed and kept out of consciousness by the "censor." If, however, the Freudian system is not accepted (and it is not helpful on this point), then it becomes questionable whether the "forgotten" evil deeds are truly unconscious. Many a person will admit that he knew about things he ostensibly had forgotten. Perhaps one ought to consider another mechanism in the mind besides repression. There is a tendency in man to disconnect certain events, memories and phases of life from the rest, which is easily reproduced in consciousness. Man turns away from something he knows, tries "to for-

get about it," and after a certain time apparently it is forgotten. But, in truth, he has only acquired the habit of avoiding certain paths of thought, just as the bereaved may put away all things that remind them of their loss. They feel that, the less opportunity there is for being reminded, the better they are. So, also, the mind puts away certain details that might, if aroused, lead to memories of which one does not want to think. But this is not what Freud conceives the unconscious.

18. There are other forms of melancholia, *e.g.,* "symptomatic" melancholia, or depression, occurring not infrequently in organic mental diseases (senile processes, progressive paresis, epilepsy); there are also melancholic states depending on other bodily factors (involuntary melancholia in women). It may be true that mental factors such as the consciousness of guilt are not determinants of melancholia in the strict psychological sense of the term.

19. Francis Thompson, "The Hound of Heaven."

Chapter 7

PSYCHOANALYSIS AND CONFESSION

A FEW DECADES AGO, nobody believed in the confession of sins except the Church. Today everyone believes in confession, with this difference: Some believe in confessing their own sins; others believe in confessing other people's sins. The popularity of psychoanalysis has nearly convinced everyone of the necessity of some kind of confession for peace of mind. This is another instance of how the world, which threw Christian truths into the wastebasket in the nineteenth century, is pulling them out in isolated, secularized form in the twentieth century, meanwhile deluding itself into believing that it has made a great discovery. The world found it could not get along without some release for its inner unhappiness. Once it had rejected confession and denied both God and guilt, it had to find a substitute.

Our particular concern here, as usual, _is not with either psychiatry or the psychoanalytic method, both of which are valid in their spheres._ We limit the discussion solely to that single psychoanalytic group who assert these things: Man is an animal; there is no personal responsibility and therefore no guilt; the psychoanalytic method is a substitute for confession.

To begin positively: The Sacrament of Penance, or Confession, was instituted by Our Divine Lord, and it satisfies the deepest aspirations of the human soul. Experience reveals these three aspirations: When a person does wrong, he wants to avow it. Because he knows it to be a wrong, he will not tell it to anyone who happens by, but only to some representative of the moral order, for what he seeks is pardon. And, to get back on the right track, that person wants some ideal higher than himself or even his neighbor, some unfailing absolute standard, with a spokesman willing to help him to that ideal.

1. AVOWAL. No human being feels satisfied with uneasiness in his heart, where it rankles and festers. All nature speaks for release, and conscience shouts its claim. A foreign substance gets into the stomach that the stomach cannot assimilate; the stomach revolts and casts forth the cause of the trouble. A speck gets into the eye, and through pain and tears the eye demands that the dust be removed. Conscience is no different: Every sin seeks release.

The consciousness of something wrong — of a sin clamoring to be expelled — may be repressed, and many men and women use such a concealment to escape self-reproach. Both from a psychological and from a spiritual point of view this repression is very dangerous, affecting the health of both body and mind. Some try to escape their uneasy consciences by the denial of their particular guilt, while others believe that, if they abandon themselves to evil and forget all moral "totems and taboos," they will have joy. But they are grossly deceived: Nothing in the whole realm of psychology is more destructive of personality than the notion that moral restraints *cause* unhealthy repressions through preventing the release of animal instincts and primitive urges. Destructive impulses *should* be repressed; knowledge of our faults should not. Individuals who have reversed this healthy rule have invariably wound up many times more neurotic than before; indeed, the suppression of the ethical self to permit untrammeled indulgence of the animal self is one of the principal causes of mental disorders in modern humans. The widespread repression of guilt (instead of the proper repression of rage and hate and lust) has had such serious consequences that the modern world has finally come to see the necessity of avowing, or confessing, some of the hidden causes of disturbed mental states.

The Church opposes repression on all levels. She has always said, "Confess your sins; tell them; get rid of them; avow them." Modern psychology has at last seen the wisdom of Christian teaching, and it now says, "Do not repress your complexes. Repression of the mind's contents is bad." Repression of even a physical disorder is dangerous to the body, as repression of a moral disorder is dangerous to the soul. If a piece of glass gets into the hand, the hand will first try to expel it by bleeding; when it cannot get rid of the glass, it then proceeds to surround the glass with fibrous tissue to prevent it from harming the rest of the body.[1] When the doctor later operates and digs out the piece of glass to prevent infection, he is doing what nature first intended, namely, preventing repression and its consequent irritation. In the moral order, Our Divine Lord said that repression of sins was dangerous; if we covered them up, they would cause an irritation with eternal consequences. So He asked His Apostles to go around the world preventing repression by hearing confessions and forgiving sins. Now psychiatry has seen the wisdom of doing for the diseased mind what doctors have always done for the body and what religion has done for the soul from time immemorial — get a release, get a confession.

But to keep sin to oneself is worse than keeping a disease to oneself. A patient confides his physical or mental sickness to the doctor, as a student offers his ignorance to the teacher; why should not sin also have its *confidante?* The memory of wrongdoing, if kept to oneself, will do one of two things: either it will become a temptation to repeated sin, or its remorse will paralyze our moral efforts toward betterment with such despairing words as "Oh, what's the use?" What the hand is to the eye in providing relief from the speck, that the tongue ought to be to the heart in providing release from sin.

> My tongue will tell the anger of my heart;
> Or else my heart, concealing it, will break,
> And rather than it shall, I will be free
> Even to the uttermost, as I please, in words.[2]

It is on this point of avowal that there appears the first difference between psychoanalysis and confession. Psychoanalysis is an avowal of attitudes of mind in unconsciousness; confession is an avowal of guilt in conscience. Psychoanalysis is the probing of mind by mind; confession is the communion of conscience and God. The revealing of mental attitudes asks nothing of our pride and never craves pardon: As a matter of fact, one can be proud of an unhealthy state of mind. Some men delight in boasting of their atheism, their agnosticism, their perversities, but no conscience ever boasted of its guilt. Even in isolation, the sinner is ashamed.[3]

If the moral order is denied, the avowal becomes only the acknowledgment of a mistake or a misfortune, not the acknowledgment of sin. Guilt is moral, not physiological or animal; therefore it cannot be known objectively and scientifically, any more than a poem can be known by a study of its meter alone. As against the escapism of some analysis that makes the self blameless, confession to a priest assumes that the ego can be at fault, that the seething lava of unrest below the surface is due to the repression of a *willful* disorder, and that only by acknowledging it as one's own can one be restored to a fellowship with self, with nature, with others, and with God. It takes no courage to admit that one is guiltless, but it takes a heroism of which few are capable to take the burden of one's guilt to Calvary and to say to the

Christ on the Cross, "That Crown of Thorns my pride placed there; those nails were driven by the hammer of my avarice; the scourges that fell on Thy flesh were swung by my lusts and my cupidities." Guilt is guilt only when it is subjectively felt as one's own. If a person does not know within himself that he is harsh or spiteful or proud, he does not know himself. The Agony in the Garden was the supreme subjective knowledge of the world's guilt, for there it was that Our Lord permitted Himself to feel the guilt due to the sins of man; and the Agony resulted in the Bloody Sweat.

A further difference is this: No person likes to have his mind excavated according to a fantastic, unscientific theory that sex must be at the bottom of all his problems. This was one of the most general complaints of soldiers during World War II against mental examinations; some Army doctors assumed that continence was abnormality. Even in the occasional case where sexual conflicts are really to blame, no one is made better by having someone else tell him how abnormal he is or how rotten he is. Everyone wants to do his own telling, for he knows he can be made better only by avowing the guilt himself. "Let me tell it" expresses a primary right of the human heart. The individual alone has the right to repudiate a part of himself as the condition of betterment. He resents probing and analysis by alien minds. He wants to swing open the portals of his own conscience; he wants no one breaking them down from the outside. The very uniqueness of personality gives him the right to state his own case in his own words. No soul likes to be studied like a bug. No trial is complete unless the defendant has a chance to take the witness stand to testify in his own case. The worst in the self, through self-avowal, ministers to one's betterment and peace. But each person wants to be his own witness for the prosecution — to conduct his case against himself, not that he may be condemned, but that he may not.

In the confessional, one is his own prosecuting attorney and his own counsel for defense. The self-accused is forgiven; people have always recognized that a spontaneous confession is a form of expiation, meriting pardon. We see this on many levels: The mother, who wishes her child to admit openly a fault, says, "Tell me, and I will not punish you"; under the honor systems in our colleges, students are told to "stand up" and acknowledge their guilt; even the judge who interrogates the criminal from his bench shares the sentiment that says that punishment shall be tempered when a person pleads guilty. The penitent analyzes his own faults in admitting them; he does not depend on a psychoanalyst to drive their meaning home.

And there are other differences. In confession the narration of sins is brief and abstract; in psychoanalysis it is generally long, involved, and very definite. The time difference is largely due to the fact that the normal person, going to confession, already has a fixed standard of conduct and judges himself in relation to that standard; the abnormal patient, having no well-defined purpose in life, requires more time to gather up the pieces. And because there is no humiliation in confessing mental oddities — as there is in moral lapses — the patient may enjoy prolonging the story of his "symptoms" and say preeningly, at the end of a lengthy presentation, "Doctor, did you ever hear anything like *that?*" There are also patients who like to talk about themselves above all else; this allows unscrupulous analysts — particularly those who stress sex — to cause their patients to return again and again and have the whole life analyzed (*if they have the money*). It is not a wholly disagreeable process to be analyzed. A person who has been told that everything is a symptom never need accuse or judge himself or ask to be judged. He may come to look upon himself as a curious phenomenon that needs to be investigated — not for the sake of bettering himself or to profit by the knowledge the analyst gives him, but only to satisfy his curiosity.

The spirit of confession is not one of fact-finding, but of mercy. If a human being accords pardon to others who humbly avow their faults, why should not God do the same? That is precisely what Our Blessed Lord has done. He has taken the natural avowal of faults — which already has an expiatory force — and has elevated it to the dignity of a Sacrament. Avowal is only human, but He has divinized it. What is natural, He has made supernatural. The indispensable condition of receiving human pardon — the open avowal of guilt — is the condition upon which Almighty God grants His pardon in the Sacrament of Mercy. With infinite tenderness, He told the story of the prodigal son who came back to his father, acknowledged his guilt, and was rewarded with the embrace and kiss of his father. Such is the joy of God at a sinner's return, for "even so there shall be joy in heaven upon one sinner that does penance, more than upon ninety-nine just who need not penance" (Luke 15:7).

Let no one say that *man* instituted the Sacrament of Penance; no man would ever have given to it such a form. A man is not naturally so reverential or so amiable in regard to another that he would willingly lay open his whole soul even to a stranger, as millions of Christians do each week. Let no one say that officials of the Church invented this Sacrament of Mercy, for if they had, human as they are, they would have surely excluded themselves from its humiliations. Yet no priest, no bishop, no cardinal, not even the Holy Father himself is immune from the necessity of confession. Let those who say that the confessional was instituted by a priest try sitting in the stuffy confessional boxes of our churches for five or six hours on Saturdays and on the eves of the feast days and of the First Fridays, listening to the routine misgivings and failings of human nature, and he will know it is the most trying of all the priest's labors — yet sweet because he knows and feels that he is carrying on the blessed ministrations of Our Lord and Savior Jesus Christ.

2. THE RIGHT LISTENER. Another difference between psychoanalysis and confession concerns the person to whom the avowals are made. Throughout the centuries, the confession of sin has always been made to a representative of the moral order, so that the sick soul might be restored to moral health and union with God. In analysis, there is a telling of symptoms to the analyst; in the Sacrament, there is confession of sins to a priest. It is a notable difference.

Furthermore the analyst represents not the moral but the emotional order. He is the recipient of the client's love and hate in turn. Some analysts have called this process the "transference"; through it, the emotions (libido) of the client are released from their old objects and transferred to new ones. (Obviously this mechanism is poles apart from confession, where through penance, faith, grace, and amendment there is a transference of the soul's center of gravity from creature to Creator, from self to Christ.) In order to understand the role of the analyst, psychoanalysis must be understood on its own terms. Thus viewed, it is a process by which mental energy — stemming from instinctual, libidinous sources and barred from true efficacy because it is directed toward unfulfilled and unfulfillable ends — is freed to aim at realizable goals. When this result has been attained, man, says the analyst, is healed and self-pity yields to altruism, apathy to accomplishment. The person of the analyst plays the role of an intermediary agent in bringing about this change. Early in an analysis the client's repressed urges, which the superego forbids him to acknowledge (his incestuous longings), are freed and become attached to the person of the analyst — who replaces temporarily the parent who was the primordial goal of these desires.

Transference to the analyst is not dependent on faith; it is considered, rather, to be the necessary first step toward a mature reorganization of mental energy. Before this energy is yet capable of being directed toward acceptable goals, it finds in the analyst an appropriate, temporary object. Faith in the analyst results from the transference; because the analyst has become an "object" of deep libidinous longings, he is often credited with all the qualities that the client admires and loves. Freud knew that it was dangerous to make the analyst even the temporary object of the emotional release. "Transference," he said, "especially in the hands of an unscrupulous medical man, is a dangerous instrument." There is a tendency for the "disenchanted" client of the early sessions to become "enchanted"; and if the analyst is of the opposite sex and not too unattractive, there may be a danger of making the transference permanent instead of temporary, physical instead of mental. No one who is familiar with sex analysts is unfamiliar with the danger. But even when there is no true transference to the analyst, there can be a dependence on the analyst that amounts almost to slavery, with the patient refusing to do anything without consulting this adviser.

We need not predicate a universal suppressed desire for incest to explain why many clients develop a deep dependence on their analysts. Almost every neurotic wants attention: He feels alone, isolated from reality and from other people by his inner restlessness. He is preoccupied with himself and fearful of failure. Externally he has often become a perfect nuisance — his complaints are boring to others, his behavior irritates them. He thus loses contact with the people around. It is no wonder, when he finds an analyst or psychotherapist who is willing to listen — whose task it is to listen — that this person begins to play a great role in the patient's life. The therapist becomes the first person with whom the neurotic resumes a human relationship; he is of inestimable value to the neurotic, a value that is utterly out of proportion to his real worth. In this connection, it must not be forgotten that the neurotic mentality retains many traits of adolescence. The client's infatuation resembles, in more than one respect, the schoolgirl "crush."

In confession, however, the relations between the confessor and the penitent are utterly impersonal. The very structure of the confessional protects the penitent from revealing his identity; there are a screen and a veil through which the priest cannot see. So impersonal is the relationship that the penitent may go indifferently, as far as the validity of confession is concerned, to *any* priest; there is nothing personal in the Sacrament. Psychiatry can learn much from the Sacrament of Penance; it, too, will discover that the more impersonal the relations between patient and psychotherapist, the greater the chances of a cure.

It may appear paradoxical that an impersonal relation is more favorable than a personal one in effecting a transference. This is not difficult to understand. By remaining impersonal and, so to speak, outside of all truly human relation, the psychiatrist would become a mysterious figure and therefore a suitable object for imaginary transformation. A person who is well known is less easily idealized than one who is known a little or not at all. The transference is just such an idealization, remote from all reality. For liking a person because of his human qualities, and transference, are two different experiences. Of the first, a person may give a rational account; of the latter, he cannot. If transference is desirable at all, it is more effectively acquired by the unknown priest than by the familiar psychoanalyst.

3. The Objective Standard. More important than the other differences is the fact that, in confession, the avowal and deliverance of sin are made on the *moral* plane; in analysis, by its very nature, this cannot be. If a sin were merely

a mistake someone had made, he might, indeed, confide it to his analyst or to anyone else who cared to hear. Our mental difficulties we are willing to unload on any listening ear; but who cares to talk indiscriminately about his guilt? And since it is conscience that is most often troubled, the healing must be done *on that level*. Since it is God's goodness that is rejected in sinning, a soul refuses to make its avowal of sin to any nonmoral listener. He wants his confession to be heard by a representative of the moral order that he has violated: That representative must stand in the place of God, to whom alone the conscience yields authority. The avowal of guilt must be subject, not to the individual whims and theories, idiosyncrasies, and kinks of the one who hears it, but only to universal Law, Order, and Goodness.

We are not here speaking of the advantages of confession over psychiatry; we are, rather, taking issue with those who offer psychotherapy as a substitute for the Sacrament of Penance. And in this the difference between the priest and the analyst is fundamental. As Dr. William Ernest Hocking has put it,

> Analysis requires that the psychiatrist be the recipient of unreserved self-avowal. The psychiatrist assumes that his scientific attainments justify this demand on his part: he does not raise the question of his personal fitness to receive this confidence. But if he fails to recognize the pertinence of this question, he thereby displays his unfitness for his function. For here the moral issue cannot be merged in the scientific problem. It is neither desirable nor possible to confess all things to all people; it is least of all desirable to display one's sentiments before a gaze that is nothing-but-scientific, from which exposure they can only emerge denatured, because pure science is indifferent to sentiment.

Confession is an act of opening one's life to the eyes of a true judgment. If science is the true judge of life, then confession to one who represents science is possible. If science is a partial judge of life, if science in omitting the moral ingredient, omits an essential part of true judgment, then confession to the scientist must be by its own logic incomplete. Confession exists because at bottom people wish to know themselves as they are before a judgment of complete understanding and complete justice: they confess to those who most nearly reach that ideal, or who can most nearly represent it. The valid confessor must stand *in loca Dei,* where *Deus* means all morality as well as all science. The rankling center of mental disease is that one strives to cloak from himself what he cannot conceal from the universe: it is that pocket which must be lanced before integration can take place, and it requires an eye and hand more unsparing than that of condoning causality to do it.

...May we not say that God is the law of normal mental life? We would mean by this that a life lived on the plan of getting along without God, without a sense of the cosmic demand, is already, whether it knows it or not, sick, off from normal, its values infected with the dry rot of mortality, intrinsically unhappy because unreal, driven subconsciously by a need which some day it is bound to recognize and define. This drive, which can be called psychologically the self-assertion of normal human nature, is in its true nature, the working of a law which is God. If this is the case, we may say of God that he is an unceasing activity, one which interferes in no way with scientific observation, but which is nevertheless indispensable to any complete psychological statement of what the life of man is.[4]

When, on the other hand, the one to whom avowal is made is a sex analyst, the chances are that the last state of the client will be worse than the first. (When I attack sex analysis, I do not mean the theory of Freud,[5] but rather that of the bandwagon climbers who take Freud too seriously and who explain *all* neuroses as repressed sexuality.)

If the one to whom the confidence is made has as his equipment a mere theory about the source of unhappy mental states (e.g., that they are due to repressed libidinous instincts), there is no certainty that the interpretation he makes will be right. The guilty conscience wants to avow its guilt, not to a theorist of a particular system, but to a mediator of Divinity. That is why the Church asks that a priest who absolves a penitent be in the state of grace, a participant, himself, of the Divine Life. (This does not mean, however, that a priest in the state of mortal sin would not possess the power to forgive sins or that when exercised it would not be effective for the penitent; the priest would be morally accountable for such a breach.) Every priest who sits in the confessional must receive authority from his Bishop or Superior; unless he is wise and prudent, the permission is not given. Behind him at the time of his first hearing of confessions is a six-year preparation in moral, ascetical, and dogmatic theology. He is annually reexamined for six to ten years after ordination; in addition he must attend conferences on moral theology to keep his knowledge fresh. The priest himself is counseled to go to confession once a week.

Psychoanalysis never raises the question of the moral fitness of the analyst, but the Church raises that question every time one of her ministers enters a confessional box. The penitent, in avowing sins to him, knows that the priest is another human being, but one who has been endowed with Divine Power to forgive. That a man may administer this Sacrament is logical — the Son of God forgave sins through His *human* nature. He also transmitted the power to forgive to His Church: "Whose sins you shall forgive, they are forgiven; whose sins you shall retain, they are retained." (These words imply the *hearing* of confession, for how would one know which sins to forgive and which sins not to forgive unless they were heard?)

There is another reason why a human confessor is a reasonable necessity: Every sin is an offense, not against God alone, but also against our neighbor. This is most obvious in sins of injustice; it also exists in the most secret and hidden of our sins, because each of these diminishes the content of charity and love that ought to exist between the various members of Christ's Mystical Body. Just as a headache diminishes the general well-being of the whole body, so an individual's sin affects the fellowship of all believers in Christ. And since every sin is an offense against the love of God and brotherhood of Christ, it follows that a representative of that spiritual fellowship should, in God's name, and through God's power, receive the individual back into the fellowship.

Finally, since every sin is a form of pride and rebellion, Our Lord ordained that there be a corresponding humiliation in asking absolution. It would be very nice to bury our heads in a handkerchief and tell God we are sorry — but we know very well that if we committed a crime against the state, it would not accept that kind of reparation. Not even in the Divine Courts may the criminal be both judge and jury; that would be too comfortable. And we know in our hearts that the sins we own should be disowned to someone else who, in God's name, can free us from the tyranny of our ego. As Dr. John Rathbone Oliver observed:

> ...the pastor comes into early contact with the development of faulty mental habits; he, much more than the psychiatrist, holds the key to a patient's confidence; he,

in a much deeper sense than can ever be applied to the physician, is a physician of the soul. He stands, as it were, like a watcher at the gate, the gate that leads to the mental hospital. He can, if he will, turn back hundreds, who, but for him, will have to pass through that same gate, many unfortunate men and women who will not be able to get out of it again until they have indeed "paid the uttermost farthing" in mental torment and despair. He can show to the man or the woman who comes to him in mental illness or difficulty, sources of help that the cleverest psychiatrist cannot give. The priest may not be able to offer his parishioner a course of psychoanalytic treatment, but he may offer him the Sacrament of Penance and the Sacrament of the Altar. He may establish the renowned "transference" of the psychoanalyst, not to himself, but to Our Lord and Savior Jesus Christ. He can show his parishioner, through the Sacrament of Penance, a "catharsis" that is infinitely more powerful than any emotional cleansing of the most enlightened mental sanitarium. He may not be able to teach his mental patient to make baskets or to bind books, but he can teach him to pray. What do we know about the real value of prayer — of mental relaxation in the presence of God — when applied to mental cases? Very little. But here again it is a type of occupational therapy that is worth trying.

For, above all else, the mental patient needs first a human, outstretched hand; secondly, a patient understanding and appreciation of his difficulties; and thirdly, a source of strength and help to which that human hand and that sympathetic understanding can lead him. Teach him to find God — after, and because, he has found you. For he is very lonely. That is the torment of most mental illness. It seems to cut the patient off from contact with the friendly, familiar, normal world. He is often horribly alone.[6]

The great advantage of the confessional is that the confession is kept absolutely secret. Every priest is bound by the *sigillum,* or seal, which forbids him, under penalty of death, to reveal a person's confession in even the most general way. Knowing this is a great consolation for a penitent, who recognizes that his personality has a right to secrecy and who does not want to see his confidences revealed in a book of "case histories." Nothing so much wrecks one's confidence as the discovery that he has divulged his secrets to the wrong persons. Out of that betrayal and prostitution a new shame is born that makes future confidences impossible for him. And since the offenses we commit are against God, it does not belong to any human being to write them in a gossip column or in a book. Human guilt may come to the knowledge of man, but it is not for man's use. It belongs to God; therefore our sins must never be revealed to the judgment of humans. Somehow, somewhere, in these days of gossip, headlines, columnists, there have to be listening ears to act as God's ears, as there are hands that act as God's hands in the pouring of the Baptismal waters. Because the confessor's ears are God's ears, his tongue may never speak what God heard through him. The priest is at the mercy of the penitent in the confessional; he may refuse to accept no confidence, even though it places him in danger or grave embarrassment. He is not even permitted to say that a particular person has been to him in confession, if by so doing he might suggest that the penitent was in need of confession as the result of grievous sin.

But in the confession box the penitent seeks more than release in secrecy. A soul that has confessed its guilt wants an ideal to strive toward — and an ideal more inspiring than "what everyone approves" in our society. This the confessional offers in the Supreme Example of the Person of Our Lord, Who gives us His grace to amend our lives through sorrow and repentance. One authority, recognizing the necessity of an ideal higher than any the analyst alone can give, has written:

> The psychiatrist mutters something about the need for "integration."
>
> The soul replies, "I realize the need; but I cannot integrate myself. I am trying to be modern, and modernity seems to me inwardly contradictory and adrift. How can a broken pot mend its own break?"
>
> The psychiatrist responds, "Take refuge in Society. You are introverted, self-concerned and secretive. Hence you are a divided person. Confess what you are hiding; confess to me, for I represent Society. This act will restore your objectivity toward yourself. Then socialize your impulses."
>
> The soul: "I am not sure that Society is so worthy of respect. It seems the source of the difficulty, not the cure for it. It does not know where it is going."
>
> The psychiatrist: "If you feel this doubt, you must take refuge not in yourself, nor in Society, but in your ideal aims. Everyone has some such aims. Use your imagination to fuse these into a unity. Give yourself to the service of this unity, and you will be integrated: You will again be a soul."
>
> The soul: "I have been taught that ideal aims are but myths."
>
> The psychiatrist: "I cannot assure you that they are not. But even fictions have a healing power. Everyone is helped by having some sort of myth. Give yourself to the healing fiction."

The soul: "I see your difficulty. You believe nothing, and cannot heal me without a belief. The fiction might heal me if I did not know it to be a fiction. Knowing this, I cannot give myself to it. But I see that you have done your best. Farewell."

The sick soul and the psychiatrist are twin features, peculiar features of this end of the modern era. The psychiatrist is the embodiment of applied science, attempting to deal with the ravages of the mistakes of science. What he finds is, that more science is not enough.[7]

In contrast to such a sterile effort to help, we have Christianity, whose Ideal Personality is not merely an Example to be copied but also a life to be lived. When the Divine Life Our Lord purchased for us on Calvary pours into the soul, it not only deletes sin — it also remits some or all of the temporal penalties due to sin. Thanks to its moral counsels, this grace has a tremendous educational value; it gives us an increase of self-knowledge, perfects us in humility, gives a more sympathetic understanding of the shortcomings and failings of others, and makes God a real consolation and Savior rather than a distant ideal; knocks conceit, egotism, "kookiness" out of the soul; strengthens the will and thereby increases self-control. People often sing in their bath because of the joy of purification; a repentant sinner feels like singing after the joy of a good confession. Grace from above has made that person glad and well.

But if we deny that there *is* a Divine Power outside of man, there is left only a human sinner or a human specialist such as the psychoanalyst — as a source of cure. (Atheism, naturally enough, is often the belief of those analysts who would treat sins as mental diseases.)[8] But either position is illogical; to expect the patient to lift his consciousness by the bootstraps of his own unconscious is expecting the impossible.

Such atheist analysts tell the client, at one moment, that he was determined to be the way he is by infantile urgings or by the herd instinct, so that he is not responsible for his wrong; the next moment, they tell him that he is now responsible for his future condition. This is to frustrate a person by telling him both that he is free and that he is not free. To ask the client to adjust himself to his environment is not to cure him, even if he can obey, for the world's environment today is itself in a state of considerable maladjustment. It is conceivable that some patients are too well adjusted to their environment; they need, as Our Lord suggested, "to go into the desert and rest awhile."

How can the psychoanalyst himself be the source of the new and needed power to heal — particularly if he himself has had to be psychoanalyzed? As Our Lord said, if the blind lead the blind, then both will fall into the pit. And who has established the analyst as a prototype for what is normal? Psychoanalysis based on a materialist philosophy can offer no norm, no ideal, no motivation, no dynamism, no purpose in life; it has none of these to give. Yet an ideal there must be — each personality cannot be his own model; otherwise who of us is crazy, who is sane? And if a person lowers his ideals to the demands of his unconscious instincts — if, in psychoanalytic language, he claims that the id must assert itself against the superego — he ends in stagnation and degeneracy. Neither the personal nor the collective nor the analyst can offer the client the pattern he clamors for, the ideal toward which to strive. There can be an ideal for a number of different selves only if there is a Perfect Personality of whom this person and that person both partake and reflect. In personal development, as in art, we cannot progress unless we have the ideal of perfect beauty.

When Humpty Dumpty fell off the wall, all the king's horses and all the king's men could not put Humpty Dumpty together again. But if there had been a model egg, not only would Humpty Dumpty know how much he had disorganized himself, but he would also have a model, a pattern to which he could conform, and thus could become normal. Christianity offers such a release by presenting the Ideal Personality of Christ, Who offers power and resources to all the broken eggs to become normal again: "I have given you an Example" means "I am the Model, the Prototype of a Personality." The falling away from that mind which is in Christ Jesus is the source of abnormalities; the integration to that image is the source of all peace and joy. The precondition of a perfect human life and of a psychology that makes sense is a Divine Image reflected in Christ, Our Lord. It is not the ego ideal but the Christ Ideal that can make the self more than it is. When psychologists talk about an integrated personality, this is the Exemplar they seek. Where there is less than perfection of aim, there is some disintegration.

There are numerous other differences between analysis and confession. Some of these have been pointed out by the Reverend Victor White:

> But the "confession" required of the penitent and the "confession" required of the analysand are two very different things; and the difference lies in the difference of "remote matter" which we have already noted. What a penitent is expected to confess is very clearly defined and restricted to the sins committed since his baptism or his previous confession. No such limitation can bind the analysand. Though no analyst who knows his business will want to exclude such material, he will still seek less to limit his patient's "confessions" to his real or alleged misdeeds. And he will be concerned with them, not precisely as moral offenses, but as causes or symptoms of neurosis, and as providing — together with the

patient's conscious or unconscious attitudes to them —
important elements in the total picture of the personality
with which he has to deal. The patient's "good deeds"
will interest him no less than his "bad" ones (confessors
are notoriously, and rightly, impatient with rehearsals
of the "penitent's virtues") while dreams, free associa-
tions, spontaneous reactions and other manifestations of
the unconscious will interest him still more. His business is less with what the patient does than why he
does it. Only from this totally different standpoint may
there be some overlapping, but never complete identity,
between sacramental and analytical "confession." The
psychological processes demanded by each differ correspondingly: The former requires a certain concentration
of conscious memory and the orderly recital of a selec-
tion of its contents; the second, contrariwise, a mental
and physical relaxation that permits the free flow of
uncontrolled fantasy and the suspension of regular "directed" mental activity. The uncomfortable confessional
box with its hard kneeler, and the couch or armchair of
the analyst's office, admirably express and promote the
two very different kinds of "confession" for which each
is appointed.

Psychological analysis knows nothing of contrition
or satisfaction as predetermined acts to be required of
the patient; it would fail entirely of its purpose were it
to lay down in advance the conscious attitude that the
analysand was to adopt to his material. This can no
more be predetermined than can the material itself.

Still less is there any equivalent in psychological analysis to the form of the sacrament of penance. This
"form" is the words of forgiveness pronounced by the
priest; it is the specifying and determining element that
makes the sacrament of penance to be what it is; it is the

efficacious sign of reconciliation with God, and so the very remedy for the evil that is the sacrament's "remote matter." Nothing of the sort is to be found in psychological analysis. Some very superficial resemblance might be suspected in certain cases in which reconciliation is effected with some imago projected upon the analyst; but there will be no "remedy" except in so far as the transference is resolved, the projection withdrawn and assimilated to the patient's own conscious ego. There is still considerable disagreement among analysts as to what their own precise role in analysis should be. But few, even of those who most strongly advocate his "active" intervention in the process, would maintain that the ultimate remedy comes from the analyst rather than the analysand and his own response to his own material. None certainly would claim divine power and authority to forgive sin.

So the differences between sacramental confession as understood and practiced in the Catholic Church and psychological analysis as known and practiced today are considerable and profound. . . . [9]

The modern world is full of mentally normal but harassed people who seek peace wherever they have heard that it is offered — even from people who have been trained to deal with the insane. But they are sane enough. For them, the world needs a revival of the Rights of Sanctuary: During the ages of Faith, a fugitive from justice was considered immune from prosecution by civil law if he succeeded in grabbing the big iron ring that was attached to the front door of a church. By this token, he threw himself upon the mercies of church laws. Such sure and solitary harbor is needed today for the poor souls who long to pour out their guilt for the sake of pardon and reparation and peace. And the Church does have such a haven in the confessional box, where the Divine Mercy Our Lord extended through His human nature to a penitent thief, Magdalene, and the woman taken in sin is made available to our equally broken hearts. It is not easy to go into that box, but it is a wonderful feeling to come out!

More than any form of psychoanalysis, the world needs psychosynthesis; some psychiatrists have recognized this — Jung, in his idea of "rebirth," and some followers of Freud, who have called their theory "active psychoanalysis." For human beings need to be put together more than they need to be taken apart. Sin divides us against ourselves; absolution restores our unity. Most people today have a load on their minds because they have a load on their consciences; the Divine Psychologist knew how miserable we should be if we could not unload that burden. Hospitals are built because people have sick bodies, and the Church builds confessional boxes because they also have sick souls. Regular confession prevents our sins, our worries, our fears, our anxieties, from seeping into the unconscious and degenerating into melancholy, psychoses, and neuroses. The boil is lanced before the pus can spread into unconsciousness. The Divine Master knew what is in humanity; so He instituted this Sacrament, not for His needs, but for ours. It was His way of giving us a happy heart. The left side of the physical heart and the right side of the heart have no direct communication with each other; they are joined through the medium of the blood circulating through the body. Our hearts become happy, too, by communicating with Christ's Mystical Body and His Blood. We are not made worse by admitting the need for absolution. We are not made worse even by admitting we are all broken-hearted; for unless our hearts were broken, how else could God get in?

Notes

1. In the first period of psychoanalysis, when the theoretical conceptions were mainly those of J. Breuer, he developed the idea that an emotion to which adequate expression, or discharge, had been denied and that had been repressed would act "like a strange body" embedded in the tissues of the organism, irritating these locally and, eventually, causing disturbances also in more distant parts of the body (*Studien über Hysterie*, by J. Breuer and S. Freud, Vienna, 1895, trans. by Brill, *Studies in Hysteria*).

2. William Shakespeare, *The Taming of the Shrew*, Act IV, Sc. III.

3. The psychiatrist, whether he be a follower of Freud or of any other school, has no right to pass moral judgment on the actions, motivations, attitudes that his clients report or that he discovers in their minds. He has no right to do so because he is not ex officio a judge, having never received such a mandate either from society or from God. He would even handicap his work and render his services inefficient were he to condemn what deserves to be condemned from the moral angle. This does not, of course, mean that the psychiatrist ought not to harbor very definite opinions on what is right or wrong. But it means that he has to "bracket" these opinions while dealing with his client, at least during the phase of exploration and explanation. It may be questionable how far the psychiatrist may go in pointing out what is morally right in what might be called the phase of reeducation. Alfred Adler never hesitated to assume such a responsibility. His standard of morality was not very high, being mainly whatever was socially useful, but in applying it he recognized the right of the neighbor, the common good, the need of natural kindness as objective principles of human existence.

The person who seeks help with the psychiatrist considers himself "ill." He wants a cure and not a sermon. His doing of what he ought not to have done he regards as a symptom. Hence there is no sense in telling him that he sins; either he knows this and "cannot help it," or he does not admit it and is scared away because he came to seek out the physician and not the moralist.

Sometimes the exploration of the mind (under the guidance of the psychiatrist, but actually achieved by the person himself) is a necessary condition for the patient's attaining a true understanding of himself and his motivations. This clarification can be brought about, in many cases, by what is called today "nondirective" counseling or psychotherapy (C. Roger, *Counseling and Psychotherapy*, Boston, 1941). It is quite true that many counselors try to force on their clients certain views and principles without caring to find out whether and how far these things can be accepted and may become effective. But, in many cases, mere talking on the part of the counselor or on the part of the client will lead to a gradually progressing clarification. In a person acquainted with the principles of morality, such unburdening will lead also to a return to and a greatest appreciation of the moral precepts, the values of religion, and therewith, in a Catholic, to confession.

4. *Science and the Idea of God,* University of North Carolina Press, 1944.

5. Freud recognized, besides the libido, other instincts. These are (a) the ego instincts, as he called them originally (*Ich-Triebe*), and (b) the death instinct. It is true that the first group play a subordinate role in psychoanalytic thought. And it is also true that the death instinct is a somewhat obscure idea, the proposal of which was not acceptable even to many of Freud's "orthodox" followers. But still there are, within the framework of Freudian psychology, other factors admitted besides those of sex.

If the latter have been given particular emphasis, it is partly because of the wide signification Freud gave to libido or sex. The libidinous instincts are indeed sexual by nature; everything which may possibly become an object of appetition is to some extent a possible object of sexual desire. Perhaps Freud has been influenced by the notion that there are in living beings two basic instincts — that, in man, nature pursues two ends, the preservation of the individual and that of the species. The ego instincts, in Freud's original conception, would correspond to the instinct of self-preservation: libido, to that of the preservation of the species. But the primordial instincts should not be confused with sexual urges or with any experiences observed in the mature individual.

The sexual factors that determine mental troubles must be sought, according to Freud, in infancy and childhood. At this age, they are supposed to manifest themselves in an undisguised manner as sexual urges. Urges that at first sight have nothing in common with sex, as it is usually understood, are still labeled sexual, because of Freud's general presumption that all object-directed urges are fundamentally of the same kind and that the nature of all of them is that of sexuality. Here one observes a certain inconsistency in the doctrine. One of the main passages in Freud's *Three Essays,* in which he pretends to give proof of the existence of sexuality in early infancy, seems not to be in accordance with the general conception of libido as object directed. In this famous passage, Freud asserts that nobody can doubt having before himself the complete expression of sexual satisfaction when he observes a suckling infant, smiling, with rosy cheeks, falling back satisfied from his mother's breast and into sleep. The argument is, of course, highly fallacious. It implies unproved assumptions, such as an identity of causes to explain what may be only a vague similarity of expression. Instead of concluding that all satisfaction, whether of hunger or of sex or of power, etc., produces *similar* expressions, Freud concludes that the satisfaction itself must be the same (not only as experience but also in its causation) because the expression is the same. His argument resembles the following: When a person has taken phenobarbital, he sleeps; here is a person asleep; *ergo,* he has taken a sleeping drug.

Many psychiatrists understand libido as synonymous with sex in the ordinary sense and hence see lifting certain inhibitions as the essence of the cure. This was not Freud's original meaning. Nor does such an idea necessarily follow from his basic assumptions.

6. *Psychiatry and Mental Health,* Charles Scribner's Sons, New York, 1936.

7. William Ernest Hocking, *What Man Can Make of Man,* Harper & Brothers, New York, 1942.

8. There are some psychiatrists who believe that all criminality is the effect of mental disease or of an inborn abnormal condition. This theory, some think, originated with Cesare Lombroso. But the roots go further back. Jean-Jacques Rousseau spoke of humans as being born naturally good; if a person turned bad, it was because of society, for in the state of primitive nature he would have been good always. In Rousseau's day, some philosophers were full of enthusiasm for the "noble savage." Others, like Condorcet, believed less in original goodness than in the infinite perfectibility of man. The idea that there is something intrinsically evil in man, which was the Lutheran notion, and a wrong one, had up until then had a vast popularity. Rousseau revolted against this doctrine; so did the "liberals" of the eighteenth century and of later years. Kant still maintained that man is "radically evil," but he held at the same time that man is capable of good will, which he calls the only goodness on which everyone is agreed. However, the influence of Kant's moral philosophy was less great than one generally assumes. It surely had little effect on French thought, which, through the Revolution and other factors, determined for a long time the Western mentality. Man, having now been elevated into the highest being in an absolute sense, could not well be conceived as "radically evil." But evil there was; hence the need to "explain it away." This could be done by declaring that all evil-doing is contrary to man's sound nature and is thus the product of abnormalities. Lombroso's ideas were admired for a time; they are revived today in other terminologies. Criminality and immorality are now considered as "maladjustment." The well-adjusted person will, by his "enlightened self-interest," behave so that he does not arouse the antagonism of the powers that are. If he is unable to behave so as to hold conflict and unpleasantness down to a minimum, he is maladjusted and has to be reeducated

or "treated." The psychiatrists holding this view consider maladjustment as the effect either of some inborn defectiveness (psychopathic personalities) or of unfortunate influences that worked on the child's mind so as to warp it and rendered the individual unfit for adjustment.

9. The Analyst and the Confessor, *Commonweal*, July 23, 1948.

Chapter 8

SEX AND LOVE OF GOD

S EX HAS BECOME one of the most discussed subjects of
modern times. The Victorians pretended it did not exist; the moderns pretend that nothing else exists. Some critics
place all the blame on Freud. Emil Ludwig in his book,
Dr. Freud, claims that the popularity of Freud is due to the
fact that he made it possible for people to talk about sex
under the guise of science.

> ... Freud's scientific label permits the nicest girl to dis-
> cuss intimate sexual details with any man, the two
> stimulating each other erotically during the talk while
> wearing poker faces, and at the same time proving them-
> selves learned and liberated. What a convenience in
> puritan America![1]

This is, of course, not the total explanation; Freudianism
would never have become popular in a more normal civilization. Marx and Freud would not have written in the
thirteenth century and would have had a trivial audience in
the Elizabethan era; their appeal now is due to the fact that
the climate of the world is more favorable for such a philosophy. There had to be a materialist preparation for Sexism.
Lewis Mumford rightly contends, "Despite the scope Freud
gave theoretically to man's deepest subjective impulses, he
looked to science alone to effect man's improvement. Unconsciously, he accepted as a final revelation of truth the ideology
that was formulated in the eighteenth century; that of Locke,

Hume, Diderot, Voltaire."[2] Dr. Reinhold Niebuhr relates Freud to a reaction against false optimism: "The romantic pessimism which culminates in Freud may be regarded as symbolic of the despair which modern man faces when his optimistic illusions are dispelled; for under the perpetual smile of modernity, there is a grimace of disillusion and cynicism."[3] Thomas Mann makes Schopenhauer the source: "Schopenhauer, as psychologist of the will, is the father of all modern psychology. From him the line runs, by way of the psychological radicalism of Nietzsche, straight to Freud and the men who built up the psychology of the unconscious and applied it to mental science."[4]

It is unhistorical and philosophically unsound to blame Freud for the current overemphasis: Instead of being the creator of the popularity of sex, he was rather its expression and its effect. Far from being the founder of an age, he was its postscript. There are some faithful disciples still writing who consider Freud's method and his philosophy as absolute truth; they bitterly and instantly resent any criticism, calling it "reactionary" or "obscurantist." But many others have already changed or abandoned fundamental Freudian ideas; among these are Karen Horney and Theodor Reik.[5]

The reasons for the exaggerated interest in sex lie deep in our civilization:

> To communicate with Mars, converse with spirits,
> To report the behaviour of the sea monster,
> Describe the horoscope, haruspicate or scry,
> Observe disease in signatures, evoke
> Biography from the wrinkles of the palm
> And tragedy from fingers; release omens
> By sortilege, or tea leaves, riddle the inevitable
> With playing cards, fiddle with pentagrams
> Or barbituric acids, or dissect

The recurrent image into pre-conscious terrors —
To explore the womb, or tomb, or dreams; all these are
　usual
Pastimes and drugs, and features of the press:
And always will be, some especially
When there is distress of nations and perplexity.[6]

The principal reason for sex deification is loss of belief in God. Once people lose God, they lose the purpose of life; and when the purpose of living is forgotten, the universe becomes meaningless. Man then tries to forget his emptiness in the intensity of a momentary experience. This effort sometimes goes so far that he makes someone else's flesh a god; there are idolatry and adoration, which eventually end in disillusionment when the so-called "angel" is discovered to be only a fallen angel and one of no great attraction. Sometimes one's *own* flesh is made the god: Then one tends toward tyranny over the other person and, finally, toward cruelty.

There is no surer formula for discontent than to try to satisfy our cravings for the ocean of Infinite Love from the teacup of finite satisfactions. Nothing material, physical, or carnal can ever satisfy man completely; he has an immortal soul that needs an Eternal Love. "Not by bread alone does man live." Man's need for Divine Love, once perverted, impels him to go on seeking Infinite Love in finite beings — never finding it, yet not able to end the search despite his disappointments. Then follow cynicism, boredom, ennui, and finally despair. Having lost spiritual oxygen, such a person suffocates. Life ceases to mean anything precious to him, and he thinks of doing away with himself as his last and final act of rebellion against the Lord of Life. As E. I. Watkin observes of such moderns,

> ...Rationalism has robbed them of faith in God and the spiritual love-life of union with Him. Being men,

not calculating-machines or vegetables, they must have life, concrete, intense, passionate. They therefore turn to sex, the biological image of spiritual life, its passion and union — not for what it really can give and has given in all ages, but for the content of that other and supreme love-life which it reflects. They are, of course, disappointed, and they will continue to be disappointed. But their search is a judgment, a testimony and a summons. It is in the first place a judgment.... Human ratiocination cannot attain the clear and complete system of truths on which alone a stable world-order of a purely rational description could be constructed. He [man] is devoured by the submarine monster of biological life lurking in his irrational instincts, the whale of sex. For, like the whale, sex should feed man's wants, not swallow him. But the sea-monster may after all prove an instrument of his deliverance. In its belly, dark and confined, he learns, like the prophet, the impotence of his natural powers to satisfy the demands of his spirit, his need of divine illumination and grace. Thus the judgment of sex in its modern idolatry becomes a testimony to man's need of the life and love which God alone can bestow, a witness to the reality it prefigures and reflects.[7]

A second reason for the cult of sex is a desire to escape from the responsibility of living and from the unbearable voice of an uneasy conscience. By concentration upon the unconscious, animal, primitive areas, guilt-ridden individuals feel that they no longer need to fret about the meaning of life. Once God has been denied, then everything becomes permissible to them. By denying the ethical in life, they have substituted license for liberty.

Those who are aware of the evidence brought forward by modern psychology for the large part played in man's opinions and conduct by the conscious or unconscious force of sexuality may well incline to the view that the will to overturn the social order is not due entirely to undiluted love of justice or even to the need of food and property among the hungry and dispossessed; a more or less open wish to get rid of social restrictions on sexual activity is a frequent and important factor.[8]

That is why an age of carnal license is always an age of political anarchy. The foundations of social life are shaken at the very moment when the foundations of family life are destroyed. The rebellion of the masses against social order, which Marx advocated, is matched by the rebellion of the libido and the animal instincts, which the sexists advocate within the individual. Both systems deny responsibility — either because history is believed to be economically determined or because man is called biologically determined. Yet the very individuals who deny all human responsibility and freedom in theory freely blame their cooks for burned bacon in the morning and say "Thank you" at night to the friend who praises their latest book, *There Is No Freedom.*

A third reason for the overemphasis on sex is the modern denial of immortality. Once the Eternal is denied, the Now becomes all-important. When people believe in immortality, they not only seek the continuance of their spirit in eternity, but also the continuance of their flesh, through the creation of families that will survive them and meet the challenge death otherwise presents. The denial of immortality thus gives death a double mastery, first over the person who denies survival, though he needs must die, and second by leading him to repudiate family life, which is now regarded as a mere hindrance to the pleasures of the brief hour of life. It is a historical fact that in times of disaster, epidemic, bombings, etc., some individuals who have no eternal values to sustain them, seeing the lease on life about to run out, plunge into orgies of debauchery; concentration on the perishable things of earth tends to dry up moral enthusiasm and to stimulate cravings for bestial satisfaction when such humans see their ends approaching. But such catastrophes are not needed: Whenever time on earth is seen as all-important, the elders talk about "the future which is in the hands of the young"; everyone is afraid to speak of his age, and the subject of growing old is treated in a manner midway between an insult and a sneer. Like beasts trapped, not in cages but in time, such humans become angry with time for passing: The hastening years diminish pleasure and cast a shadow one must try not to see. But since one cannot hope to escape it forever, the fear of death grows apace. It is no accident that the present civilization, which has emphasized sex as no other age in the history of Christianity has emphasized it, lives in constant fear of death. Baudelaire rightly pictured modern love as sitting on a skull. When the flesh is given a moral value, it produces life; when sex frustrates morality, it ends in death.

A child who is given a ball and told that it is the only ball he will ever have in his life cannot enjoy it much because he is overfearful of losing it. Another child, told that if he is good he will be given another ball, one that will never wear out and will give him unending pleasure, need not be fearful of losing the first. So it is with the person who has only one world, in contrast to the one who believes otherwise. Even in the enjoyment of life the first person walks in fear of its end. His very pleasures are shadowed by death. But the one who believes in a future life, conditioned by morality, has the great advantage of being able to be happy in this world, as well as in the next.

The predilection for sex is characteristic of a profoundly naturalistic age. Even before psychoanalysis was conceived, one can observe notable signs of such a development. The naturalistic literary school of France — which became tremendously influential, starting with Flaubert, Guy de Maupassant, and Zola — emphasized sex. None of these writers was an "immoralist"; but they shared the idea that "nature" must be discussed openly and without restrictions. There is little licentiousness in their writing; but it happened that these works, intended to describe things human as they are, were welcomed by readers who sought quite another effect from them. The naturalistic school thus became, involuntarily, a preparation for a growing licentiousness. The success of psychoanalysis in America — not with the psychiatrists, but with the public — has the same source as the success of certain novelists of sex, like D. H. Lawrence.

A fourth reason for the overemphasis on sex is the *denial of the rational soul* and the equating of humans with animals. This connotes the complete abandonment of the ethical in human relations. Not the will but instinct now reigns supreme, as the standards of morality give way to the practices of the barnyard. The modern tragedy is not that human beings give way more often to their passions now than in previous ages, but that, in leaving the right road, they deny that there is a right road. People rebelled against God in other ages, but they recognized it as rebellion. They sinned, but they knew that they sinned. They saw clearly they were on the wrong road; today people throw away the map.

The equation of man with the animal is a great fallacy; sex in man is not the same as sex in animals.[9] An animal feels, but no animal loves. In the animal, there is no body-mind conflict; in man, there is. In the animal, sex is mechanical, a matter of stimulus and response. In man, it is linked with mystery and freedom. In the animal, it is only a release of tension; in man, its occurrence is determined by no natural rhythm, but by the will. Sex can cause a loneliness and sadness in humans that it cannot cause in animals. The animal can satisfy all its desires below; man cannot do this, and his tension comes from trying to substitute the chaff of sex for the bread of life. As Prinzhorn says, in speaking of Freudianism of a certain type, "It gives to people who are over-intellectualized, out of touch with the living earth, in the grip of a debased sexuality, a false religion, which is admirably suited to their condition."

A totally neglected feature of the sex problem in man is the role that original sin has played in causing it, although it must be said to the credit of modern psychology that it has implicitly reaffirmed the fact under the name of "tension." Man's nature is not intrinsically corrupt, but it is weak; as a result, the emotions often gain supremacy over the reason. With profound penetration, Berdyaev writes,

> There are two different types of enjoyment — one reminds us of original sin and always contains poison; the other reminds us of paradise. When a man is enjoying the gratification of sexual passion or the pleasure of eating he ought to feel the presence of poison and be reminded of original sin. That is the nature of every enjoyment connected with lust. It always testifies to the poverty and not to the richness of our nature. But when we experience the delight of breathing the sea or mountain air or the fragrance of woods and fields, we recall paradise; there is no lust in this.
>
> We are comparing here pleasures that have a physiological character. But the same comparison may be drawn in the spiritual realm. When a man is enjoying the satisfaction of his greed or vanity he ought to feel the poison and be reminded of the original sin. But when he is enjoying a creative act that reveals truth or creates beauty or radiates love upon a fellow creature he recalls paradise. Every delight connected with lust is poi-

soned and reminiscent of original sin. Every delight free from lust and connected with a love of objective values is a remembrance or a foretaste of paradise and frees us from the bonds of sin. The sublimation or transfiguration of passions means that a passion is purified from lust and that a free creative element enters into it. This is a point of fundamental importance for ethics. Man must strive first and foremost to free himself from slavery. Every state incompatible with spiritual freedom and hostile to it is evil. But every lust (*concupiscentia*) is hostile to the freedom of the spirit and enslaves man. Lust is both insatiable and bound to pall. It cannot be satisfied, for it is the bad infinity of craving. There exists a different kind of craving that also extends into infinity, e.g., the hunger for absolute righteousness; those who hunger and thirst after righteousness are blessed because they are concerned with eternity and not with bad infinity. The divine reality that fills our life is the contrary of the boredom and emptiness born of the evil lust of life. Lust from its very nature is uncreative and opposed to creativeness. Creativeness is generous and sacrificial, it means giving one's powers, while lust wants everything for itself, is greedy, insatiable and vampirish. True love gives strength to the loved one, while love-lust vampirically absorbs another person's strength. Hence there is opposition both between lust and freedom, and between lust and creativeness. Lust is a perverted and inwardly weakened passion. Power is a creative force, but there is such a thing as the lust of power; love is a sacrificial force, but there is also the lust of love.[10]

Whatever be the primary reasons for the present overemphasis on sex, it must not be attributed to Freud himself. A distinction must in fairness be made between Freud and

Freudianism, a kind of pan-Sexism that reduces everything to sex in a way that Freud himself never intended. Those who have carried his theories of analysis to the extreme of interpreting everything in terms of sex have been subject to considerable satire; the most interesting example appeared in *G. K.'s Weekly*, which translated life into terms of beer instead of sex. It reads:

> It is now an established fact that all human motive and action is due to Beer; not merely among adults but also among children....
>
> The whole life of a child (of either sex) is actuated by Beer. The first action of which a child is capable is a lusty yell; we have established that this is no less than a cry for Beer, or at any rate for some kind of drink. The next action of the child is to drink. If it does not drink beer it is because its system is not yet capable of drinking beer. But behind the relish of milk is the desire for beer. These we call the primary instincts. The secondary instincts are to be found in the love of popping corks, of yellow-brown colours, of frothy substances (like soap), and so on. The child instinctively calls his father Papa (which represents the popping of the cork), and his mother Mamma (which gives the noise of the liquid being poured into a glass). All the gurgling noises of childhood go to prove the strength of the instinct....
>
> Most of our knowledge is based upon dreams, which we have taken as the most reliable evidence scientifically possible. We know (by means too long and elaborate to tell here) that even very young children dream about beer; nay, more, that they dream about nothing else. When a child dreams of a boat upon a lake, what is it but a symbol of beer? Of a shower of rain, a river, a sea? Everything yellow or brown is beer. Everything frothy

or sparkling is beer. Everything in something else is beer (a nut in its shell, for example, is obviously representative of beer in the bottle). Everything issuing from an aperture is beer. Everything that moves is beer, particularly quick-moving, jerky things, which are reminiscent of "hops." In fact, we may say that the child cannot dream of anything but beer. There is no dream possible but beer....

Here is an example. The patient was Miss X. She came to us in great trouble. "My nerves are all gone to pieces," she said. "I want you to help me." Professor Bosh questioned her, and kept her under observation. He discovered that before going to bed she was in the habit of brushing her hair. "The brush was of an amber color, and was transparent. The patient would raise it slowly to her lips, pause and then proceed to brush her hair. This was quite unconscious. In reply to my questions it transpired that several years before she had been forbidden by the family doctor to drink anything alcoholic. She had been in the habit of taking a glass of ale every night at supper." Professor Bosh explained this to her, and at once convinced her of its truth. She submitted herself to treatment, and was soon perfectly well and strong.[11]

Unlike the extreme Freudianism, Christianity is not so narrow-minded as to make sex the most important instinct of life or to attribute mental disorders exclusively to its repression. If the repression of its errant and unlawful impulses is the cause of mental abnormalities, why is it that those who are most abandoned to carnal license are the most abnormal, while those who believe in religion and morality are the most normal? Using a more comprehensive and saner outlook on life, Christianity traces, not one, but several roots of mental disorders in the nonphysical and moral realm. There is sex, to be sure; but there are also six other possible causes — pride, covetousness, anger, envy, gluttony, and sloth.

In order to understand the proper role of the sex instinct, consider the true nature of man. Every human is looking for perfection — constantly trying to transcend himself, to get out of himself, in some way to expand himself, to escape his self-limitations. There is a kind of holy impatience in us all. The "I," the "Me," in each of us feels limited; it craves for expansiveness; it finds the earth too small, even the stars too close; the possessed makes us hungry where most it satisfies. We want to be perfect; but we are only in a process of realization. Not being able to find peace within ourselves, we seek to atone for our limitations by extending ourselves in one of three directions — through the mind, through the body, or through things.

Self-preservation is one of the first laws of nature, and it implies a legitimate self-love; for if we did not love *ourselves,* we could not continue to live. Our Divine Lord reminded us to love our neighbors *as we love ourselves.* Self-love, knowing it cannot exist by itself any more than the stomach can exist without food, extends itself in one direction by the acquiring of knowledge; and the more we know of the truth, the more our personality is developed. The quest for perfection of the self reaches to the infinite. No one has ever said, "I know enough." That is why we hate to have secrets kept from us (men hate this just as much as women). We are incurably curious; we were made to know.

We escape the limitations of the body in another direction by the expansion of our flesh in the procreation of other personalities. Love always tends to an incarnation. In order that human life might be preserved and continued, God implanted two great appetites and pleasures in man. One is the pleasure of eating to preserve the corporal life of the individual;

the other is the pleasure of marriage to preserve the life of the race.

The third way of perfecting ourselves is through the ownership of things. Just as we are free on the inside because we can call our soul our own, so we want to be free on the outside by calling possessions our own. Personal or private ownership is natural to man; it is the economic guarantee of freedom, as the soul is its spiritual guarantee.

The Church teaches that the human person is constantly striving for perfection and is restless until it perfects its mind in knowledge, or generates its kind in marriage, or assures its economic security through things. Each of these urges and instincts and cravings is right and God-given. In each instance, the "I" is attempting to find another "I." Because the "I" loves itself, it also loves wisdom, it loves the flesh, and it loves property.

Where then does abnormality arise, if these pursuits are natural? How could they cause a psychosis or anxiety or a complex, any more than the eye does in seeing or the ear in hearing? If we were animals, these pursuits toward perfection would, indeed, never cause disturbance, for an animal's desire can be fully satisfied; but man's cannot. No animal is curious about chlorophyll when it sees a plant, nor does a squirrel have an anxiety complex about whether there will be a shortage of nuts ten years hence. But man's impulses and passions are subject to his will. Not being mechanically ordered as *means* to the salvation of his soul, he can misuse his passions, make them *ends* in themselves, try to find the absolute in their relative.

Self-love, which is good, can be perverted into self-adoration, in which one says, "I am my own law, my own truth, my own standard. Nobody can tell me anything. Whatever I call right *is* right; what I call wrong is wrong. Therefore, I am God." This is the sin of pride, the perversion of self-love into egotism. Such undue self-inflation is one of the principal causes of unhappiness; the more a balloon is inflated, the easier it is to puncture it. The egotist walks warily, in constant danger of having his false values destroyed.

The sex instinct, which is good, can also be perverted. In the days of pagan Rome some corrupt individuals attended banquets, gorged themselves with food, tickled their throats, disgorged the food, and then went back and ate more. This was wrong because, as reason told them, one eats to live and the pleasure must not be separated from its function. In like manner, when the fires of life are aroused deliberately, not to light new torches of life, but to scorch the flesh, there is the sin of lust. This *is* a perversion animals cannot commit because they cannot defunctionalize and artificially centralize their instincts.

Third, humankind's legitimate desire for self-expansion through ownership can be perverted into an inordinate passion for wealth, without regard for either its social use or the needs of the neighbor. This is the sin of avarice, in which a person does not possess a fortune, but a fortune possesses him.

Because the human will can pervert the good passions, instincts, cravings, and aspirations into pride, lust, and avarice, the Church enjoins mortification — through prayer, which humbles the proud soul, through fasting, which harnesses the errant impulses of the body, and through alms, which detach us from inordinate love of things. In the higher realm, the Church allows some chosen souls to take the vow of obedience to atone for the proud, the vow of chastity to redeem the licentious, and the vow of poverty to compensate for the greedy. These vows are taken, not because enjoyment of the mind, the flesh, or property is wrong, but because some members of society abuse them and pervert them. These holy souls make up for others' excesses by bending backward, as it were, in their own use. Thus is the right order of goods preserved in God's universe.

In the light of the above, there is no more towering non-sense than to say that the Church is opposed to sex. She is no more opposed to sex as such than she is opposed to eating a dinner, to going to school, or to owning a house. Nature is not corrupt. As Aristotle said, "Nature never tells a lie." It is humanity's false use of nature that darkens the face of the world. Nor does the Church, like a monomaniac, believe that sex is the only instinct a human has or that all other instincts are to be interpreted in terms of sex. Rather, with a deeper understanding of human nature, she says that the craving for perfection is basic and that sex is only one of the *three* ways in which a relative perfection is achieved in this life.

Where, then, did the sex fanatics get the idea that the Church is the enemy of sex? They got it from their inability to make a distinction — a distinction between *use* and *abuse*. Because the Church condemns the abuse of nature, sex fanatics think that the Church condemns nature itself. This is untrue. Far from slighting the value of the human body, the Church dignifies it. It is surely nobler to say, with the Christian, that the body is a Temple of God than to say, with some modern minds, that man is merely a beast. As Clement of Alexandria said, "He ought not to be ashamed to mention what God was not ashamed to create." There is no sin in the right use of the flesh; even without the Fall of Man, the human race would have been continued through procreation. And Saint Thomas tells us that there was more pleasure in marriage before the Fall than now, because of the greater harmony and peace in man's soul. Saint Augustine has said, "We should, therefore, wrong our Creator in imputing our vices to our flesh; the flesh is good, but to leave the Creator and to live according to this created good is mischief."[12]

The Church does, of course, speak of sin in the domain of sex, as it speaks of sin in the domain of property or of sin in the area of self-love. But the sin does not lie in the instinct or the passion itself. Our instincts and our passions are God-given; the sin lies in their perversion. Sin is not in hunger, but in gluttony. Sin is not in the seeking of economic security, but in avarice. Sin is not in drink, but in drunkenness. Sin is not in recreation, but in laziness. Sin is not in the love or the use of the flesh, but in lust, which is its perversion. Just as dirt is matter in the wrong place, so sex can be flesh in the wrong place.

An undue concentration upon a single one of life's activities tends to make a person abnormal through lopsided interest. This is especially true of an excessive preoccupation with the carnal. It tends to make what is physical psychic, by tracing back everything to a single instinct. Sex in other ages was physical; it resulted in new life. Today, because it often thwarts life, it is also psychic. Sex is *thought about* as a medium of pleasure to such a degree that it has become an obsession. Just as a singer could go crazy by concentrating on his thorax instead of his song and an orchestra conductor could become a neurotic by concentrating on his baton instead of his score, so humans today can go crazy thinking about sex instead of about life.

For it is the *isolation* of the sex factor from the totality of human life, the habit of regarding it as identical to the passion an elephant might feel, the ignoring of the body-soul tension in the human, which causes so many abnormalities and mental disorders. False isolation of the part from its whole is a common trait in contemporary thought. A person's life nowadays is divided into many compartments that remain ununited and unintegrated. A businessman's business has no connection with his life in the family — so little in fact that his wife (his "little wife") is kept ignorant of her husband's income. As there is no connection between a man's profession and the rest of his daily existence, neither is there a connection between his daily life and his religion. This chopping up of life into watertight compartments becomes more disastrous as occupation and work are related, less and less, to a strictly human ideal; mechanization plays a catastrophic role.

Serious effects result from this mechanization and the whole tendency to overspecialization in modern life. These two phenomena of our times are both related to the analytic habit of mind, imposed by the fashion of a predominantly scientific approach in the intellectual world. Everything is viewed in isolation by modern man, because this method is the legitimate procedure of science. But there are fields where a study of the unit torn from its context ceases to be adequate. The study of life itself has begun to suffer by an excessive use of analysis — hence the reaction of "holism" in psychology and biology.

The human sex drive is *at no moment* an instinct alone. Desire from its beginning is informed with spirit, and never is one experienced apart from the other. The psychic and the physical interplay. Just as the idealists, who deny the existence of matter, sin against the flesh, so the sensualists and carnalists sin against the spirit. But to betray either aspect is to invite revenge. "Our body is a part of the universal order created and preserved by God. Rightly viewed, it is itself a self-contained universe entrusted to us as a limited but sacred property. The most substantial sin is that which we commit against ourself and especially against our own body. The offense against our own body includes a sin against the Creator."[13]

Sex instinct in a pig and love in a person are not the same, precisely because love is found in the will, not in the glands — and will does not exist in a pig. Sexual desire in a person

is different from sex in a snake because, in the human being, it promises something it cannot completely supply. For
the spirit in man anticipates, which a snake does not: Man
always wants something more than he has. The very fact
that none of man's passions for knowledge, love, and security can be completely satisfied here below suggests that he
might have been made for something else.

The existence of shame (which exists nowhere except in
humans) again shows how this one instinct, above all others,
involves the soul. Shame draws a veil over the deepest mystery of life and preserves it from impatient use, holding it in
check until it can serve life as a whole and can thus satisfy
both body and soul. There would be no such disgust in man
were it not that everyone of us feels the body to have a peculiar sanctity, not only because of its potency to continue
the creative act of God, but also because of its possibility of
becoming a veritable Temple of God.

The person is in search of the absolute, *i.e.,* perfect happiness. To use sex as a substitute for the absolute is a vain
attempt to turn the copy into the original, to make the
shadow become the substance, and the conditioned, the absolute. The infinite cravings of a soul cannot be satisfied by
the flesh alone. Love, remember, is not in the instinct; it is
in the will. If love were purely organic, no more significant
than any other physical act, such as breathing or digesting,
it would not sometimes be surrounded by feelings of disgust.
But grown-up love is much more than these — it is not an
echo of a child's forbidden fantasy, as some would tell us.
Each soul feels a restlessness, a longing, an emptiness, a desire, which is a remembrance of something that has been
lost — our Paradise. We are all kings in exile. This emptiness
can be filled only with Divine Love — nothing else! Having
lost God (or having been robbed of Him by false teachers and
sex charlatans), the person tries to fill up the void by promis-

cuous "love affairs." But love, both human and Divine, will fly from him who thinks it is merely physiological: Only he can love nobly who lives a noble life.

It is wrong to say that the deep spiritual love of the saints for God is a sublimation of the sex instinct — as some perverse minds have actually suggested. This is like saying that love of country is derived from the elephant's love of the herd. The idea that religion had its origin in the sex instinct is almost too silly to be refuted, for the greatest religious influences in history have been the most detached from sex. The more a person lives in the presence of God, the more he or she develops a reflex against the wrong use of sex, as automatic as the way an eye blinks when the dust blows. On the other hand, the sex fanatics are not only nonreligious persons, but usually antireligious persons. It is curious to hear such people urge that we ought to repudiate Christian morality and develop a new ethics to suit the unethical lives of a few thousand individuals they have polled. Because statisticians can find 5000 living carnal lives, it is suggested that their ideal shall be made the universal ideal. An equal number of cases of lockjaw could be found in the United States; one wonders if lockjaw should therefore be made a physical standard of health? Sins do not become virtues by being widely practiced. Right is still right if *nobody* is right, and wrong is wrong if everybody is wrong. Some have contended that sex aberrations are as common as the common cold; but nobody has so far asked us to consider the cold normal and desirable.

On the positive side, it is the Christian position that the sex instinct is the *reflection* of love in the spiritual order. The sun comes first, then its reflection in the pool. The voice is not a sublimation of the echo, and neither is the belief in God a sublimation of a carnal instinct. All love and all perfection and all happiness are first in God, then in things. The closer creatures, such as angels and saints, come to God, the happier they are; the farther away they stay, the less they can reveal the works of Divinity.

There are five aspects of love by which the nature of man is uplifted and fulfilled: The love of man or woman for God; the love of man and woman for each other; the love of parents for children and of children for parents; the love of men and women for country or community; and the love of men and women for excellence in some creative activity, in art, in literature or philosophy. These are not five kinds or species of love which are given to ennoble men, but five aspects of love which is one, even when we think of it as flowing between God and man. In every little child lying in his mother's bosom, there is something of the Incarnation; the mystery of humanity becomes the revelation of Heaven; and in such incarnation of the Divine Love we can behold, born in every aspect of human love, the Word become Incarnate of Him in whose will is our peace.[14]

Since the stress on sex is due to a forgetfulness of the true nature of man as body and spirit, it follows that the release from anxieties, tensions, and unhappiness (created by identifying man with a beast) is dependent upon a restoration of the meaning of love. Love includes the flesh; but sex, understood as animal instinct, does not include love. Human love always implies Perfect Love.

There is a double love in each of us — a love that is self-realizing and looks to our own good, and a love that is self-effacing and looks to the good of another.[15] Both loves are included in the Divine Command, "Thou shalt love thy neighbor as thyself" (Matt. 22:39). The one love is self-assertive and possessive — it makes us eat, drink, and work to sustain our life. The other love is sacrificial or possessed and seeks not to own but to be owned, not to have but to be had. The first takes water that it may live. The other shares or even gives up the water that the neighbor may live.

Each love is right and good and is meant to act as a brake on the other. If self were entirely neglected, one would not only lose all self-respect, but one would be consumed, as a moth in the flame. No one of us wants this; we do not long to see our personalities extinguished or dissolved in some great Nirvana of unconsciousness. But selfless love is essential, too. If it is neglected, we have egotism, selfishness, conceit, snobbishness, and carnality.

To put this tension between the two loves into other words, there is in each heart a pull between the romance and the marriage, between the courtship and the union, the chase and the capture. Earthly love that is only the quest is incomplete; love that is only attainment is inert. If love is limited to possession, the beloved is absorbed and destroyed; if love is limited only to desire, it is a useless force that burns itself out as a spent star. This failure of either search or satisfaction to satisfy causes the mystery and sometimes the pain of love.

As pursuit alone, love is death by hunger; as satisfaction alone, love is death by satiety and its own "too much." If love could reach no higher than earth, it would be like the pendulum of a clock alternating and ticking away between chase to capture, capture to chase, endlessly. But our hearts crave something more. We long for an escape from this weary iteration of pursuit to capture; we do not wish in love to emulate the hunter who starts for new prey only because he has already killed the old.

And there is an escape. It lies in the eternal moment that combines both search and finding. In Heaven we shall capture Eternal Love, but an infinity of chase will not be enough to sound its depths. This is the Love in which you at last may have yourself and lose yourself in one and the same eternal now. Here the tension of romance and marriage is reconciled in an eternal instant of joy, an instant that would break the heart were it not that Love is life. Never to thirst would be inhuman, ever to thirst would be hell; but to drink and thirst in the same eternal now is to rise to the highest bliss of Love. This is the Love we "fall just short of in all love, the Beauty that leaves all other beauty pain, the unpossessed that makes possession vain." The closest we can come to such experience in our earthly imagination is to think of the most ecstatically happy moment of our lives — and then to live that moment eternalized. This kind of love would be speechless and ineffable; there could be no adequate expression of its ecstasies. That is why the Love of God is called the Holy Spirit, the Holy Breath — something that is too deep for words.

It takes not two, but three to make perfect Love, whether it be in the flesh (husband, wife, and child), or in the spirit (lover, beloved, and love), or in Divine Nature (Father, Son, and Holy Spirit). Sex is duality; Love is always triune.

It is this fullness of Love that every heart in the universe wants. Some suspect it not, because they have never lifted the blind of their dark hearts to let in the light of God; others have been robbed of the hope by those who cannot think of love in any other terms than the concourse of two monkeys; others draw back from it in foolish fear lest, having the Flames of Love Divine, they may lose the dying embers of their present perverted desires. But others see that, as the golden streaks across the waters of the lake are reflections of the moon above, so human love is but the crushed-out reflection of the Heart Divine. In God Alone is the consummation of all desires.

To the woman at the well who had five husbands and was living with a man who was not her husband, Our Lord said, "Whoever drinks of this water, shall thirst again" (John 4:13). There are no human wells deep enough to quench the insatiable thirst of the human soul. But this desire can be satisfied: "He that shall drink of the water that I will give him, shall not thirst forever; but the water that I will give him, shall become in him a fountain of water, springing up into life everlasting" (John 4:13, 14). Religion ennobles love, and those who rob man of God spoil his nature. Only a Divine religion can protect the spiritual against the physical or prevent the animal in us from conquering the mind, making man more brutal than the brute.

How life changes its meaning when we see the love of the flesh as the reflection of the Eternal Light shot through the prism of time! They who would separate the earthly sound from the heavenly harp can have no music; they who believe that love is only the body's breath soon find love breathes its last and they have made a covenant with death. But they who see in all earthly beauty the faint copy of Divine loveliness, they who see in fidelity to every vow, even when the other is untrue, a proof that God loves us who are so unlovable, they who, in the face of their trials, see that God's love ended in a cross, they who allow the river of their rapture to broaden out the blended channels of prayer and worship — these will, even on earth, learn that Love was made flesh and dwelled among us. Thus, Love becomes an ascension toward that blessed day when the limitless depths of our souls will be filled with the boundless giving, in one eternal now, where love is life's eternity and God is Love.

Notes

1. Emil Ludwig, *Dr. Freud,* p. 166, Hellman, Williams & Company. New York, 1947.

2. *The Condition of Man,* p. 364, Harcourt, Brace & Company, Inc., New York, 1944.

3. *The Nature and Destiny of Man,* Vol. 1, p. 121, Charles Scribner's Sons, New York.

4. Introduction, in Arthur Schopenhauer, *The Living Thoughts of Schopenhauer,* p. 28, New York, 1939.

5. Cultural anthropologists have pointed out that Freud's conceptions of the history of civilization are false and unfounded. The inventor of his favorite notion of "prelogic thought" (or archaic mentality), the late Levy-Bruhl, wrote a full recantation, only recently published. In his notebooks (Carnets, in *Revue philosophique,* 1947) he declared that there is no such thing as prelogic thought and that he had been utterly mistaken to interpret his data in such a manner. Second, the notion that schizophrenia is caused by mental factors operating according to Freudian mechanisms is tottering. This idea is particularly dear to one group of Freudians. R. G. Hoskins (*The Biology of Schizophrenia,* New York, 1946) of the Harvard Medical School has stressed the fact that there are so many indications of organic pathology in this disease that a purely mental origin is improbable.

6. T. S. Eliot, *Four Quartets,* No. 3, The Dry Salvages, V, p. 27, Harcourt, Brace & Company, Inc., New York, 1943.

7. *The Bow in the Clouds,* Sheed & Ward, Inc., London, 1931.

8. Pierre Henri Simon, *Marriage and Society,* in *Body and Spirit,* p. 112, Longmans, Green & Company, Inc., New York, 1939.

9. For a strictly empirical statement of the profound differences between animal and man, especially in regard to instincts, see K. Goldstein, *The Organism,* New York, 1939, and *Human Nature in the Light of Psychopathology* (William James Lectures), Cambridge, Mass., 1940.

The naturalistic fallacy of confusing love with the sexual urge has been forcibly criticized by M. Scheler, *Wesen und Formen der Sympathiegefuhle,* Bonn, 1922. Scheler pointed out that to identify all kinds of love with that of sex is possible only if the phenomenological differences are totally disregarded (such as those of parental, filial, sexual love, etc.). In one sense, all love is one, in so far as it (1) is directed toward a person; (2) always means transferring one's own person to that of the beloved; *non quaerit quae sua suni.* Within this frame, however. there are great differences and there is no possibility of "deriving" all forms of personal love from sexual love, even less from a mere biological sexual appetency. According to psychoanalytic doctrines, sexuality furnishes the exemplar or pattern on which all behavior, but particularly that of love, is fashioned. Sexuality, however, is not an exemplar, but the expression of a person's basic attitudes.

10. *The Destiny af Man,* p. 179, Charles Scribner's Sons, New York, 1937.

11. G. Walter Stonier, *Psycho-analysis, G.K.'s Weekly,* p. 74, Apr. 10, 1926.

12. There is a false "purity" current among the prudish, who want to be free of all contact with sex except when they can discover such a sin in another. "I am so glad that there are no impure words in your dictionary," remarked a lady to Dr. Samuel Johnson. "How do you know? Did you look for them?" was the doctor's biting reply. It is such people who create the impression that religion condemns and despises everything related to sex. In earlier days, the Church spoke even more freely on the subject than now. Saint Bernadino of Siena did not hesitate to speak out very bluntly in 1429, but the attitude changed after the Reformation.

13. Franz Werfel, *Between Heaven and Earth*, p. 121, Hutchinson & Company, Ltd., London.

14. W. F. Lofthouse, *The Family and the State*, p. 141, Epworth Press, London, 1944.

15. A profound treatment of this subject is to be found in M. C. D'Arcy, *The Mind and Heart of Love*, Faber & Faber, Ltd., London, 1946.

Chapter 9

REPRESSION AND
SELF-EXPRESSION

ABOUT SEVEN HUNDRED YEARS AGO, one of the most learned men who ever lived, Thomas Aquinas, wrote a treatise on the passions that to this day has never been surpassed. Treating of anxieties, he said, "Any idea which is hurtful to the mind does harm in just the proportion that it is repressed. The reason is: the mind is more intent on a repressed idea than if it were brought to the surface and allowed to escape."

This was not a completely new idea even when he wrote, for it was already implied in the Sacrament of Confession, which bares hidden anxieties, thus serving two purposes on the psychological level: It prevents their seeping into the unconscious and causing a complex, and it also weakens them because, when they are brought to the level of the will, they can be controlled or even conquered.

The nineteenth century (which was already four centuries removed from the Christian practice of confession and repentance) began to see the terrible effects of the general repression of anxieties, guilt, sin, and worries. But the new writers gave a slightly different twist to the old idea that repressions are dangerous. Because God, morality, and the possibility of personal guilt were all denied, the new philosophy affirmed that the repression of *passions and instincts* was wrong. (It was the repressed *idea* against which Thomas

Aquinas warned.) The new notion said that a person's id and his animal instincts ought to have free expression against the totems and taboos of the old superstitions of morality, God, religion. This psychology affirmed, "Be self-expressive. Religion and morality are destroying your personality." All restraint, authority, and discipline were viewed as harmful to the character. Such a philosophy could not stand up against sound reason.

If a person is really made better and saner because he gives way to his sexual instincts and is uninhibited by the Christian law of lifelong marriage, why should not a person be better because he gives way to other instincts, such as the hunting instinct? Why not organize a "kill your enemy" hunt, uninhibited by the moral taboo of a Fifth Commandment? If we were logical in allowing the same self-expression to the fear instinct as to the sex instinct, then we ought to praise a soldier who, in the midst of battle, deserts his post, just as some writers now praise a husband when he deserts his wife. If the sex instinct is not to be bound by moral taboos, why should the pugnacious instinct be bound? Why should not an aggression be allowed to assert itself by punishing the people who get ahead of us at a bargain counter — especially if they are smaller? If arrest followed this demonstration, why not plead that the civil law is only a moral taboo that originated among African headhunters and is, therefore, destructive of human personality, with no binding force in this enlightened twentieth century?

If the repression of the sex instinct is abnormal, why should not the repression of the hunger instinct be abnormal? Why not condemn dieting? No one has yet tried to convince the body cultists that a religious totem and taboo are responsible for a fourteen-day diet.

This theory of license is founded on the false assumption that *a psychological* complex can always be cured by giving

it a *physiological* outlet. This is as silly as saying that the way
to cure a worry about your debts is to drain the blood out of
your heart. The mental and the physical, the spiritual and the
carnal, are not on the same level. One might as well say that
the psychological urge some people have to kill others could
be cured by giving them a machine gun or that the mental
impulse to commit suicide could be cured by a plunge off the
Brooklyn Bridge. In regard to the sex instinct, self-expression
can hardly be the cure it is said to be — for those who are
most abandoned to the gratification of these instincts are not
only the most abnormal but also the most unhappy of people,
and they constitute the greatest menace to society.

The theory of license assumes that the so-called religious
"totems" and "taboos" have been responsible for repression
and are therefore the causes of mental disorders. But why, we
may ask, have these religious totems and taboos had such an
appeal if not because they already coincided with right reason
and the highest aspirations of the human race? Why should
moments of social degeneration and world chaos, such as
the fall of Rome and our own times, be also the periods of
greatest license and irreligiousness?

But there is a profounder objection to this program for
man. For if the free expression of a person's carnal instinct
against his moral instinct is right, then surely the repression
of the moral instinct must create a problem of still greater
repression. There is always going to be something repressed.
Giving the animal instincts free play causes a repression of
moral ideals. All that this false theory of license does is to
substitute one form of repression for another. The facts of
history and individual experience prove that nothing has so
much contributed to the development of mental disorders,
especially neuroses, as the repression of the moral sense by
those who wanted no higher ethics than that of the stud farm.

Finally, the theory is founded on a false idea of what

self-expression means. Everything *ought* to be self-expressed according to its nature. But the nature of a human being is not the same as the nature of a goat. Endowed with an immortal soul, as well as with a body, a person is most self-expressive, not when he follows his animal instincts, but when his rational, God-given nature is in command. When a person expresses himself contrary to his nature, he begets sin in his soul, evil tendencies in his bones, odd twists and abnormalities in his unconscious — to say nothing of remorse in his conscience. Such a person's whole being rebels against its misdirection by the evil will. A railroad train is most self-expressive when it follows the tracks laid down by the engineer; if its self-expression consisted in repudiating the tracks (because they were laid down by an engineer with a religious psychosis), it would discover it was no longer free to be a railroad train. If a triangle sought the power to express itself into four sides, it would discover it was no longer free to be a triangle. A boiler that rebels against the dogmatic limitation of having only a certain number of pounds pressure per square inch and thus explodes finds that its expression is nothing but self-destruction.

Dr. C. E. M. Joad has written that the theory of self-expression is so ridiculous that nobody really believes in it.

> What we do believe is that some forms of self-expression are good, others bad; that the expression of self in sympathy is good; in jealousy, bad; in kindness, good; in cruelty, bad; in helpfulness and service, good; in malice and self-aggrandizement, bad. However — and this also we know — in so far as what is expressed is bad, the more expression of it there is, the worse. For example, if I am good-tempered and kindly when sober, but am a congenital dipsomaniac with a tendency to wifebeating when drunk, it is obvious that the more I express

myself in terms of my sober traits and kindliness and good temper, and the less I express myself in terms of my congenitally drunken traits of rage and violence, the better.[1]

Very serious effects follow the abandonment of oneself to biological and animal instincts. It increases despair and morbidity; the individual becomes trapped in the license to which he or she submits. Freedom is destroyed when the victim becomes a slave to something external. Scripture tells us that the one who sins becomes a slave to sin. This kind of self-expression, instead of allowing a person to become self-possessed, ends in his losing control over the self and making it other-possessed, which is the new form of modern slavery. Finally, because it repudiates the moral sense, such self-expression lessens responsibility and thus leads to the destruction of the human character. As time passes, it brings sorrow and despair. For if abandonment to the passions and animal lust is the pathway to self-expression, then what consolation shall an individual seek in old age? Such a philosophy may satisfy young animals, but not old animals.

Actually, there are needed for humanity's development two kinds of activities or expressions: the immanent and the transcendent. One remains within the person; the other acts without. The false philosophy of self-expression admits only the second kind and results in a completely externalized human being. A true self-expression perfects the spirit first and then objectifies it, producing culture; culture always perishes when inwardness of the spirit is lost in the "activism" of externals. Slavery results — a new serfdom quite different from the slavery of earlier ages. For in the old variety, man was subject to an external force *against* his will; in the new slavery, man is subject to the external *through* his own egotistic, selfish will.

Marx and Freud were right in dealing with slavery as one of man's recurring problems, but neither of them understood its nature. Both of them took the inner slavery for granted; both rightly assumed that egotism is normal, one of them studying it *in* the collective field, the other in the individual. Such egotism is Fallen Man's flaw, recognized by everyone who assumes a Transcendent Source from which man comes and toward which he tends. Some day, some historian with profound insight will show us how external slavery is always the mass production of internal slavery — how man, in slavery to his own lower nature, has attempted to make his condition normal by enslaving others.

Debauchery is another effect of personal sin that seeks external expression, in this case by corrupting others. For the inwardly empty cannot bear their burden alone — they tend to empty society of whatever values it possesses. Solitariness of the soul creates its own atmosphere and makes a solitary world. Self-expression, understood as the expression of the animal self whose satisfactions are *external,* thus begets not only its own destruction but also the dissolution of peaceful society. The traditional restraints and moral sanctions of society come to be regarded more and more as worthless, outworn taboos or as cruel checks placed upon individual egotism, which now goes under the name of freedom. A stage is eventually reached where there is no acknowledged limit to self-expression. The most traitorous deeds are defended as civil rights; the defense of even the natural law is ridiculed as "medieval." This lawlessness, if widespread, creates such confusion in society that a tyrant soon arises to organize the chaos through force. Thus is fulfilled the dictum of Dostoevski that "unlimited freedom leads to unlimited tyranny."

This brings us to the contrasting Christian philosophy of self-expression. Christianity, like modern paganism, believes that repression is harmful, but it makes a necessary distinction. Christianity says that the repression of evil thoughts, desires, and acts — such as the urge to kill, despoil, calumniate, rob, injure, covet, hate — is good for the soul; it deplores the repression of guilt or sin through a denial of the need of confession. And it states that the repression of actual graces, inspirations to a good life, and the urge to sacrifice self for neighbor is bad for the soul.

Christianity does not believe that the repression of the sex instinct is good. But it does believe in repressing the *abuse* of these instincts, so as to prevent lust in the one case and gluttony in the other. The Church has never taught that a human being is made up principally of two levels, the conscious and the unconscious; she states that there are three levels, body, soul, and the desire of God. Man is not just a beast, subject to the claims of his animal instincts; he has also ethical and spiritual selves that demand expression according to their natures. But this is not always easy.

The Church states that there is not an *automatic* subordination of the human body to the soul and of the whole personality to God — an ideal of ordered living that constitutes, for the Christian, the essence of self-expression. Both man and nature appear to have departed in some way from their original pattern or essence. Something has happened to damage human nature, and all the evidence points to the fact that this came about because man himself in some way abused his freedom. Both the world and man seem to have fallen; they are on a lower level than they were destined to be, and the responsibility for this fall cannot be placed upon God. It must be man. Because of this fall, there is a bias toward evil in man; as a result, the body does not always submit itself to the soul, nor does the soul always look, for its commands, to God. Sometimes the body makes claims that are very imperative, although they are against the best interests of the soul. Sometimes the soul, in its turn, is willing to concede primacy to those libidos, on the grounds that the return will be much more immediate than the returns of the spirit.

Because there are three and not two elements involved in human personality, it follows that the Christian doctrine of self-abandonment is radically different from the philosophy of abandonment to the animal instincts. Those who believe in carnal self-realization "do not seem able to grasp the fact that to embrace any and every experience is the easiest thing in the world, whereas to refuse some experiences for the sake of possessing others is an infinitely harder but truer method of attaining self-realization. Moreover, it is fatal to talk smoothly of the necessity of self-realization without taking the slightest thought as to what sort of self is to be realized."[2]

Materialist psychology believes in a *passive* abandonment of the soul, in which the higher part of the personality gives free rein to the lower part and its spontaneous appetites. It falsely believes that, by living according to animal inheritance, personality will receive back from the mysterious animal forces those gifts of creativity that the sick soul has lost. The Christian, on the contrary, believes, not in a passive abandonment, but in an *active* abandonment that consists in an effort of self-control. The soul takes itself in hand, disciplines the lower errant passions to bend them to higher aims. Just as the farmer could not live unless he had domesticated the animals and made them subject to himself, so man cannot live with himself unless he trains the wild beasts that are within him, makes them subject to himself, and then, in turn, surrenders his whole personality to God.

Happiness consists in overcoming the bias to evil by realizing one's Divine vocation and by overcoming the urge of nature; and this is not achieved through the orgiastic release of primeval forces, but rather through an *askesis* that amounts almost to violence. This is what Our Blessed Lord had in mind when He said that the Kingdom of Heaven suffers violence and only the violent will bear it away. To the Christian, the way of perfection is the way of discipline, because he or she understands perfection as the satisfaction of personality in its highest reaches — namely, the attainment of life and truth and love, which is God. If a person passively abandons himself, he is doomed to death in his present condition. To recover health, he must take a bitter medicine and undergo a kind of operation. When Our Blessed Lord spoke of His doctrine as a yoke, He asked His followers to be pure in a world full of Freudians; to be poor in spirit in a world of competitive capitalism; to be meek amid the armament makers; to mourn among the pleasure seekers; to hunger and thirst after justice amid the pragmatists; to be merciful among those who would seek revenge. Anyone who does these things will be hated by a world that does not want God.

This Christian law of discipline is very different from both the Hindu and the Greek ways of perfection, which were based upon a kind of self-induced indifference. Generally, the Hindu was indifferent to personality, and the ancient Greek was indifferent to the world. The Christian rejects the idea that a person ought to work either for the extinction of his soul or for a complete detachment from the world order. His Church tells him that self-expression is inseparable from the salvation of the world and of the individual soul. That is why the essence of the Christian system is seen in Sacraments that utilize the disordered elements of the universe by sanctifying them, so that they are made to serve the purpose of the soul and the furtherance of human personality. By accepting the supreme worth of both the world and of humanity, the Church says the purpose of our saving ourselves is also that of saving the world.

A further forgotten point on the subject of Christian asceticism is that self-discipline, which is the condition of self-expression, is seen not as an end, but a means. The end of all self-discipline is love. Anyone, therefore, who makes the taming of animal impulses the end and prime purpose of his life — as some of the Oriental mystics do — achieves the negation of the flesh but not the affirmation of the spirit. Saint Paul told the Corinthians that, if a person should deliver his body to be burned, it would profit him nothing unless he had Divine Love. The Christian uses mortification to liberate himself from the slavery of his fallen nature, freeing himself to live in God's Love. Our Blessed Lord never said that carnal desires in themselves were evil. He said only that we must not permit them to burden the soul with such anxiety for their satisfaction that we lose the greater treasures. The end of Christian living is the attainment of love, and there is a double commandment touching this love: one, to love God; the other, to love neighbor. To realize either aspect, some asceticism is required. The only way we can help ourselves to love God is by conquering our selfishness, and the only way that we can ever conquer the evil in our neighbors is by making them feel the beneficent power of our love.

That love can be choked and nearly destroyed by other weeds besides lust. Worldliness is one of these. An almost forgotten truth, even among some practicing Christians, is that it is never the physical world, but only the spirit of the world, that is evil; therefore the soul must detach itself from the world. "Love not the world, nor the things which are in the world. If any man love the world, the charity of the Father is not in Him" (1 John 2:15). This world that Saint John castigates is not the world of our bread-and-butter existence, but rather that secular spirit that regards time and space as a closed system from which God is excluded. Politics and economics divorced from the moral law, education without religion — these are some of the manifestations of the worldly spirit, and all of them are harmful.

But nonattachment from the world, as an ideal worth seeking for itself, is not the answer. We cannot say, with Aldous Huxley, "The ideal man is the non-attached man. Non-attached to his bodily sensations and lusts. Non-attached to his cravings for power and possessions. Non-attached even to science and speculation and philanthropy."[3] The nonattachment of Buddhism or Taoism is not the Christian ideal; though it sounds very noble to say that they who possess are possessed, are slaves to the illusions of life. Nonattachment and unworldliness are vain unless they are regarded as secondary, as a mere means to attain to the primary goal, which is love of God and neighbor.

But this is not an age in which asceticism, as an end, offers so great a temptation to most people that they need this warning. Self-indulgence is an error many times commoner today. It is more fatal, too. There is nothing so dangerous for a civilization as softness, and there is nothing so destructive of personality as a want of discipline. Arnold Toynbee, the historian, tells us that, out of twenty-one civilizations which have vanished, sixteen collapsed because of decay within. Nations are not often murdered; they more often commit suicide. That is the sinister meaning of our present mood of selfishness and love of pleasure, our affirmation of our own egotism, our widespread refusal to discipline the self. Although two world wars have imposed upon us many sacrifices that we have accepted willingly, even these have not been sufficient to make us perform the greatest sacrifice of all — to give up the illusion that a person is most self-expressive when he allows the animal to gain mastery over the spirit.

We are scandalized at seeing what the release of the sub-human has done to the Fascists, Nazis, and Communists. Yet we have not learned that the same deleterious effects can be present in the individual who, starting with the philosophy that he is only a beast, immediately proceeds to act like one. To just the extent that a person is unmortified in his selfish passions, it becomes necessary for some external authority to control and subdue those passions. That is why the passing of morality and religion and asceticism from political life is inevitably followed by a police state, which attempts to organize the chaos produced by that selfishness. Law gives way to force; ethics is replaced by the secret police. "There is no correlation between the degree of comfort enjoyed and the achievement of civilization. On the contrary, absorption in ease is one of the most reliable signs of present or impending decay."[4]

The totalitarian regimes are symptomatic of a disease that has also attacked the men and women in countries that are free. It is the disease of disorder within humanity. Few realize the terrible dimensions of the present catastrophe; they are blinded by the fact that man has made great material progress. The truth of the matter is, however, that humanity has lost control over itself at the very moment when it has gained control over nature. Because humans have lost self-control and denied the spiritual purpose in life, they utilize for destructive ends the forces of nature that they have harnessed. Every gain in mastery of the forces of nature becomes a potential danger unless it is matched by an equal gain in man's mastery over his animal impulses.

To just the degree that a materialist psychologist interprets self-expression as the release of the animal instincts, he contributes to the world's present woe and disorder. Animal-guided humans cannot conduct a civilization. They are more at home in war than in peace. We of today can be united against a common enemy through hate; it takes spirit and a common purpose to bind us together when peace comes.

It used to be that wars were hard to wage, that peace came naturally with victory. Today the situation is reversed; the powers of destruction are greater than the powers of construction in the modern world.

Peace is a fruit of love, and love flowers in the person oriented toward God. The greatest privilege that can come to a person is to have his life God-directed; this follows when he has remotely paved the way by disciplined self-direction. God cares enough for us to regulate our lives — and this is the strongest proof of love that He could give to us. For it is a fact of human experience that we do not care very much about the details of other people's lives unless we love them. We are not deeply interested in hearing more of those individuals whom we meet in the subway and in the street and on the highway. But as soon as we begin to know and love any of them, then we become more and more interested in their lives; we have a greater care for them. As we bring them into the area of our love, both our interest and their happiness increases. It is like this when we bring ourselves into the area of God's love: there is an increasing Divine guidance of the details of our life, and we are ever being made more sure of the depth and reality of His Love. To the extent that we abandon our personality to Him, He will take possession of our will and work in us. We are no longer ruled by commands coming from the outside, as from a cruel master, but by almost imperceptible suggestions that rise up from within. We feel as if we had wanted all along to do those things He suggests to us; we are never conscious of being under command. Thus our service to Him becomes the highest form of liberty, for it is always easy to do something for the one we love.

And God, of course, wishes us to seek the happiness He can give if we will let Him. A mother who has a wayward daughter desires nothing more than to penetrate into her mind to inspire her will; her greatest sorrow is her inability to do this. The happiness of both is conditioned upon the daughter's allowing the mother's love to operate, for no parent can ever guide a child who wars against the parent's will. Neither can God guide us if we allow the animal in us to direct our will, demanding the satisfaction of each of its rebellious claims. As the whole order of the universe rests on the surrender of the chemicals to the plants, of the plants to the animals, of the animals to man, so the peace of man comes only in the surrender of self to God. Psychologists teaching that the needs of the id are more important than the ideals of the superego, that a discipline of sex ends in a tension and neurosis that can be released only by carnal abandonment — these individuals have increased the world's selfishness, egotism, and cruelty.

The principal cause of all unhappiness is unregulated desire — wanting more than is needed or wanting what is harmful to the spirit. The modern world is geared to increase our desires and our wants by its advertising, but it can never satisfy them. Our desires are infinite; the supply of any good on earth is finite. Hence our unhappiness and anxieties, our disappointments and our sadness. The only exit from this state is by control of the senses through mortification. This is what Our Lord meant when He said, "And if your hand, or your foot scandalize you, cut it off, and cast it from you. And if your eye scandalizes you, pluck it out, and cast it from you" (Matt. 18:8, 9). Because, in our modern civilization, the biological is divorced from the spiritual, because freedom is isolated from dependence on God like a pendulum cut off from a clock, because liberty is interpreted only as freedom *from* something and not as freedom *for* something, it is especially necessary to revive the Christian practice of self-discipline.

As Rom Landau rightly observes,

Nothing short of religion will inspire self-detachment. A man will refuse for the sake of himself as a finite human animal to undergo the discipline to which he will gladly submit, once he is brought into conscious relation with God. This is the *crux af the entire problem.* Separate a man from his spiritual nature, let him talk of himself merely as a physical organism, and his respect for himself will not be such as to induce him to make a sacrifice for anything that he considers essential to his material well-being or enjoyment. Once he faces God and becomes aware of the divine nature of his personality, he will recognize that more is involved than what constitutes his physical being. He will do for himself as related to God what he would not dream of doing otherwise.[5]

Christian self-discipline is really self-expression — expression of all that is highest and best in self; the farmer plows under the weeds for the completest expression of the corn's desire to grow. Self-control, through mortification or asceticism, is not the rejection of our instincts, passions, and emotions, nor is it thrusting these God-given impulses into unconsciousness, as the materialists accuse the Christians of doing. Our passions, instincts, and emotions are *good,* not evil; self-control means only curbing their inordinate excesses. To take a little wine for the sake of one's stomach, as Saint Paul told Timothy, is to obey an instinct; but to take so much of it as to forget that one has either a head or a stomach is to abuse wine as a creature of God.

Once the instincts and passions are subject to the will, they can be controlled and guided. The Church does not *repress* passions when it restrains their unlawful expression. It does not *deny* emotions, any more than it denies hunger; the Church only asks that, when a person sits at table, he shall not eat like a pig. Our Lord did not repress the intense emotional zeal of Paul; He merely redirected it from hate to love. Our Lord did not repress the biological vitalities of a Magdalene; He merely turned her passion from love of vice to love of virtue. Such a conversion of energies explains why the greatest sinners — like Augustine — sometimes make the greatest saints; it is not because they have been sinners that they love God with their special intensity, but because they have strong urges, violent passions, flowing emotions which, turned to holy purposes, now do as much good as they once did harm.

Strong passions are the precious raw material of sanctity. Individuals who have carried their sinning to extremes should not despair or say, "I am too great a sinner to change," or "God would not want me." God will take anyone who is willing to love, not with an occasional gesture, but with a "passionless passion," a "wild tranquillity." A sinner, unrepentant, cannot love God, any more than someone on dry land can swim; but as soon as a person takes his errant energies to God and asks for their redirection, he will become happy, as he was never happy before. It is not the wrong things one has already done that keep one from God; it is present persistence in that wrong.

Someone who turns back to God, as the Magdalene and Paul, welcomes the discipline that will enable him to change his former tendencies. Mortification is good, but only when it is done out of love of God. A "saint" who spends his or her life sizzling on hot coals or reclining on railroad spikes would never be canonized by the Church. Asceticism for asceticism's sake is actually a form of egotism, for self-discipline is only a *means,* the end of which is a greater love of God. Any form of asceticism that disrupted charity would be wrong — this was the mistake of the monk who decided to live only on crusts and upset the whole monastery, turning it into one vast crust hunt to satisfy his idiosyncrasies. Asceticism that makes us less agreeable to our neighbors does not please God.

Mortifications of the right sort perfect our human nature; the gardener cuts the green shoots from the root of the bush, not to kill the rose, but to make it bloom more beautifully. As the perfection of the rose and not the destruction of the bush is the purpose of pruning, so union with God is the purpose of self-discipline. Good deeds that are done for human ends, such as to perpetuate one's name, receive nothing but a human reward; only deeds of mortification, done out of Divine Love, perfect the soul. But they must be done from the right motive, and they must sacrifice the very things to which we wish to cling. Saint Paul reminds us powerfully that the most intense mortification done without love of God is useless: "And if I should distribute all my goods to feed the poor, and if I should deliver my body to be burned, and have not charity, it profits me nothing" (1 Cor. 13:3). Archbishop François Fénelon shows how reservations in our willingness to accept self-discipline impede spiritual progress.

> People often hover around such reservations, making believe not to see them for fear of self-reproach, guarding them as the apple of the eye. If you were to break down one of these reservations, you would be touched to the quick... a very sure proof of the presence of evil. The more you shrink from giving up on any such reserved point, the surer it is that it needs to be given up. If you were not fast bound by it, you would never make so many efforts to convince yourself that you were free. Why is it that the vessel does not make way? Is the wind wanting? Nowise; the spirit of Grace breathes on it, but the vessel is bound by invisible anchors in the depths of the sea. The fault is not God's; it is wholly

ours. If we will search thoroughly, we shall soon see the hidden bonds which detain us. That point in which we least mistrust ourselves is precisely that which needs most distrust.[6]

Mortification is based, not on hatred, but on preference. The mother sacrifices the bloom in her cheek to put it on the cheek of an infant daughter; the scholar surrenders any hope he held for the development of his muscles; the moral life demands our saying "No" to false ideals that glorify power and egotism. It is quite a wrong thing, therefore, to say that you "give up" something during Lent. Our Lord never asked us to give up anything; He asked us to exchange: "What exchange shall you give for your soul?" When someone is in love with God, he finds that there are some things he can get along without (his own pleasure), and something else he cannot get along without, namely, the peace of soul that comes from obeying God's Will. So he exchanges the one for the other, surrenders the lesser good to gain a Kingdom. He makes such a series of profitable exchanges every day he lives.

Love of God thus becomes the dominant passion of life; like every other worthwhile love, it demands and inspires sacrifice. But love of God and man, as an ideal, has lately been replaced by the new ideal of tolerance that inspires no sacrifices. Why should any human being in the world be merely tolerated? What human has ever made a sacrifice in the name of tolerance? It leads people, instead, to express their own egotism in a book or a lecture that patronizes the downtrodden group. One of the cruellest things that can happen to a human being is to be tolerated. Never once did Our Lord say, "Tolerate your enemies!" But He did say, "Love your enemies; do good to them that hate you" (Matt. 5:44). Such love can be achieved only if we deliberately curb our fallen nature's animosities.

Self-discipline does more than this for us, however; it gives our lives a steady goal. The form of self-discipline most valuable in helping us to know where we are going is meditation, which will finally give us self-control through self-realization. Most tragic of all modern souls are those self-imprisoned in their own minds; meditation alone can break that maddening self-centered circle with an invasion by the Divine.

There are many men and women today who never meditate or discipline themselves in any other way. They find that they are cloyed with what they thought would satisfy; they try to make up for each new disillusionment with a new attachment; they try to exorcise the old disgusts and shames with febrile new excitements. They change their partners in love, but their boredom and ennui remain. Their disorders become habit, and a seeming necessity; they allow open wounds in their souls because they deny that there are wounds, or even souls. The chains of their slavery to despair are forged; their past sufferings still persist in their remorse; their future is dark with fear; their pleasures are less keen than they used to be, their anxieties more permanent; their excitements follow more rapidly, and their conscience is less in repose; their minutes in sin become nights of fear. They are a burden to themselves, a bore to their friends, disgusted but never satiated, made more hungry but never satisfied; in the end they pay charlatans handsome fees to be told that there is no sin and that their sense of guilt is due to a father complex. But the moral cancer remains, even then; they feel it gnawing at their hearts.

What shall these poor, frustrated, psychotic, and neurotic millions in our midst do to escape a creeping insanity and a growing madness?. The only answer for them is to enter into themselves, to lift their eyes to the Divine Physician and cry, "Have mercy on me, O God!" If they only knew it, a single confession would rescue them by helping them to have their sins forgiven; it would also save them the small fortune spent in having their sins explained away.

God has promised us pardon if we are penitent, but not if we procrastinate. Sin will wear out mind, heart, and soul, but it will not wear itself out — it will have to be purged out. The secret of peace of soul is to combine detachment from evil with attachment to God, to abandon egotism as the ruling, determining element in living and to substitute Our Divine Lord as the regent of our actions. What is anti-God must be repressed; what is Godly must be expressed. Then one will no longer awaken with a dark brown taste in the mouth or a feeling of being run-down at the heels. Instead of greeting each day with the complaint, "Good God, morning!" one will say, from the happiness of a soul in love, "Good morning, God!"

Notes

1. *Decadence,* p. 213, Faber & Faber, Ltd., London, 1948.
2. L. S. Thornton, *Conduct and the Supernatural,* p. 289, Longmans, Green & Company, Inc., 1915.
3. *Ends and Means,* p. 3, Harper & Brothers, 1937.
4. Richard Weaver, *Ideas Have Consequences,* p. 116, University of Chicago Press, 1948.
5. *Sex, Life and Faith,* p. 305, Faber & Faber, Ltd., 1946.
6. *Spiritual Letters.*

Chapter 10

REMORSE AND PARDON

THE DENIAL OF GUILT or the effort to reduce ethics to psychiatry is as unsound and unscientific as the error of denying that there are genuinely mental troubles or the reduction of psychiatry to ethics and moral theology. In actual fact, no moral theologian denies the validity and necessity of psychiatry; but since many analysts do deny the realms of the moral, the Divine, and the supernatural, it is important to continue stressing the difference between the two.

Even when a client has his psychoanalyst's encouragement to laugh off the possibility of moral evil or a sense of guilt as the cause of his worries, his rejection of ethical standards is still a form of escapism. In such cases, it is vain for the frustrated soul to say that he will work the problem out "for himself." For the soul that relies upon itself is unrealistic. Cure is conditioned upon the realization of two basic facts: There is some evil in the soul; and the perfection and cure are not to be sought in the person himself. Just as medicine must come from outside of the body, so moral healing must come from outside of the soul. Yet many modern men and women run to the ends of the earth to escape the one source of health and recovery.

Escapists refuse to face the fact that their own lives are disordered; or else they try an "easy" way out of their misery that lands them into worse confusion. Some of the "easy" ways out are the escapism of scandalmongering, which seeks to find others who are worse than the self and thus make the self seem good by comparison; the escapism of ridicule, which makes fun of the virtuous and religious to avoid the reproach of their goodness; the escapism of noise, of drowning oneself in excitement, crowds, collective trances, so that the sweet, low voice of conscience, through which God speaks, is never heard; the escapism of Communism, an anarchical revolution by which one covers up one's own need of personal, inner, spiritual regeneration by revolutionizing everyone else. For by pointing out the wrongs of others, the Communist avoids the need of righting himself; by spreading the ideology of class conflict, he creates the illusion that the evil he hates is not within himself, but in the social system. The social conscience thus dispenses many people today from any compulsion to set right their individual consciences. There is also the escapism of calling religion "escapism": This atheistic riposte is the most wrongheaded of them all — to throw it at a distraught friend, as I've noted before, is like telling a man whose house is on fire that he is an "escapist" if he calls the fire department.

The real escapists follow many different routes, but none of them are humble enough to admit that there is some evil in them; all of them are too proud to admit that they need outside help to cure their misery. By denying guilt, they show that they are cowards; by denying any perfection outside themselves, they become snobs. The last, desperate stage of escapism is religious persecution; hatred of religion is projected self-hatred. It is not easy for normal persons to understand how goodness and truth can be hated, but they are. Truth can be hated, because it implies responsibility. Goodness is hated, because it is a reproach. If Our Blessed Lord had been tolerant and broad-minded, He would never have been crucified; it was the perfection of His virtue that constituted a judgment of the wicked.

But since those who persecute religion as a form of escapism must constantly think about God and His Church, it follows that they are often closer to conversion than the indifferent person of a Western Liberal Civilization, who does not trouble making up his mind on any ultimate question.

Escapism never succeeds. In every sinner whose frustrations and neuroses are due to a burdened conscience, there is a latent contradiction. The person is pulled in two directions. He is not so much at ease with sin as to be able to make it his definite vocation, nor, on the other hand, is he so much in love with God as to disavow his faults. The dualism arises from a desire of God, on the one hand, and a turning from God on the other. Such people have insufficient moral energy to be bad or to be good; they have not enough religion to find true peace of soul, yet quite enough of it to intensify their sense of frustration after they have sinned.

Those who live in this moral twilight between faith and lack of faith have rarely a clear notion of the purpose of life. Yet a person must have a goal before he can live. In making a journey, one first decides the destination and then the intermediate steps; this is what the Scholastics mean by, "The first in intention is the last in execution." The choice of Paris for a holiday is the first step in a long series of preparations for the trip, but Paris is the last place one reaches in the journey. People who lose sight of the purpose of living — namely, to attain perfect happiness — begin to concentrate on *means*. Like the fanatic, as once defined, they "redouble their efforts after they have lost sight of their goal." Their actions become staccato, jumpy, a crazy quilt of conflicting patterns. Possibility, in the sense of a progressive development and enrichment of personality, disappears. When possibility is lost, one of two things happens to a mind: Either it immerses itself in trivialities, with an accompanying cynicism, flippancy, and superficiality, or else it tries to avoid responsibility for the inanity and foolishness of its life by denying the existence of human freedom and responsibility and subscribing to determinism of the Darwinian, Freudian, or Marxian variety.

But there are some men and women who, admitting their sins and faults, are still unhappy. Where there is a genuine sense of guilt, release can come only from Divine Mercy confronting human misery. Unless we are ready to ask for the forgiveness of our sins by God, the examination of conscience may be only a vain form of introspection, which can make a soul worse if it ends in *remorse* instead of *sorrow*. For the two are quite distinct: Judas had remorse. Peter had sorrow. Judas "repented unto himself," as Scripture tells us; Peter, unto the Lord. As a psychic malady sometimes results from a failure to adjust self to the right environment, so a moral evil results from the failure of the soul to adjust itself to God. Despair is such a failure — Judas despaired, but Peter hoped. Despair comes from unrelatedness, from the refusal of a soul to turn to God. Such a soul opposes the order of nature.

When there are seven people in a room, few ever refer to the fact that there are fourteen arms present. But if we found a detached arm lying in a corner, it would create consternation; it is a problem only because it is detached. A soul isolated from God is like that arm. Its conscience (to take another example) is like a broken anklebone; it hurts because it is not where it ought to be. The final stage of this sadness resulting from a person's unrelatedness to God is a desire to die, combined with a fear of death — for "conscience doth make cowards of us all."

But if remorse is a sense of guilt unrelated to God, it is well to consider other states of mind and conscience from this single aspect. We find that there are several classes of souls, ranged according to the degree of their relatedness to God.

There are those who killed their conscience by sin and world-liness and who have steadfastly refused to cooperate with the Divine Action on the soul in order to amend their lives, confess their sins, and do penance; there are those who have awakened from a state of sin; there are those who followed conscience and the laws of God for a time and then turned away from God; and, finally, there are those who kept their baptismal innocence and never defiled their conscience. The second and the fourth classes are very dear to God. There are thus two ways of knowing how good God is: One is by never losing Him, and the other is by losing Him and find-ing Him again. Souls who have strayed and returned, Our Lord said, rejoice the Angels in Heaven more than the stead-fastly faithful. This is not difficult to understand; a mother with ten children rejoices more in the recovery of the single sick child than in the continued possession of health by the other nine.

For the sinner to be made well, then, confession and sor-row are required.[1] And the sorrow must have in it an appeal to God's mercy to distinguish it from remorse. Saint Paul makes the distinction in writing to the Corinthians: "For the sorrow that is according to God works penance, steadfast unto salvation; but the sorrow of the world works death" (2 Cor. 7:10). Remorse, or "the sorrow of the world," re-sults in worry, jealousy, envy, indignation; but sorrow related to God results in expiation and hope. Perfect sorrow comes from a sense of having offended God, Who is deserving of all our love; this sorrow or contrition, felt in confession, is never a vexing, fretful sadness that depresses, but it is a sadness from which great consolation springs. As Saint Au-gustine put it, "The penitent should ever grieve, and rejoice at his grief."

The experience a repentant sinner undergoes in receiving the Sacrament of pardon has been well described by Blessed

Angela of Foligno. She tells us of the time when she first took cognizance of her sins.

> I resolved to make my confession to him. I confessed my sins in full. I received absolution. I did not feel love, only bitterness, shame and sorrow. Then I looked for the first time at Divine Mercy; I made the acquaintance of that Mercy which had withdrawn me from hell, which gave me grace. An illumination made me see the measure of my sins. Thereupon, I understood that in offending the Creator, I had offended all creatures.... Through the Blessed Virgin Mary and all the saints, I invoked the mercy of God, and on my knees, I begged for life. Suddenly, I believed that I felt the pity of all creatures and of all saints. And then I received a gift; a great fire of love and the power to pray as I had never prayed... God wrote the Pater Noster in my heart with such an accentuation of His Goodness and of my unworthiness that I lack words to speak of it.

It is very difficult for the world to understand such sorrow as hers, but that is only because it does not have such love. The more one loves, the more one shrinks from hurting the beloved, and the more one grieves at having done so. But this grief should not make us dour and self-centered like those who say, "I can never forgive myself for that." That is hell — when the soul refuses to accept forgiveness for having wounded Love Divine.

The difference in standards between the pagan, old or new, and the believer, which results in remorse in one instance and sorrow in the other, is evidenced by the Lord's six statements beginning with, "But I tell you." These contradict six precepts of worldly wisdom, each beginning, "You have heard."

The Pagan Standard	**The Christian Standard**
Do not let him get away with it. Stir up class enmity in order to seize power.	You have heard that it was said to the men of old, You shall not kill; if a man kills, he must answer for it before the court of justice. But I tell you that any man who is angry with his brother must answer for it before the court of justice, and any man who says Raca to his brother must answer for it before the Council; and any man who says to his brother, You fool, must answer for it in hell fire (Matt. 5:21, 22).
Be self-expressive. Repression of sex instincts causes frustration. Liberty means the right to do whatever you please in the realm of the flesh.	But I tell you that he who casts his eyes on a woman so as to lust after her has already committed adultery with her in his heart. If your right eye is the occasion of your falling into sin, pluck it out and cast it away from you; better to lose one of your limbs than to have thy whole body cast into hell (Matt. 5:28, 29).
Get a divorce! Marry again.	But I tell you that the man who puts away his wife (setting aside the matter of unfaithfulness) makes an adulteress of her, and whoever marries her after she has been put away, commits adultery (Matt. 5:32).
Take matters into your own hands. Say: I'll be damned if I will do it.	But I tell you that you should not bind yourselves by any oath at all; not by Heaven, for that is God's throne; nor by earth, for earth is the footstool of his feet; nor by Jerusalem, for it is the city of the great king. And you shall

The Pagan Standard	**The Christian Standard**
	not swear by your own head, for you have no power to turn a single hair of it white or black. Let your word be Yes for Yes, and No for No; whatever goes beyond this, comes of evil (Matt. 5:34–37).
Hit him back. Get even with him. Forgiveness is weakness.	But I tell you that you should not offer resistance to injury; if a man strikes you on your right cheek, turn the other cheek also towards him; if he is ready to go to law with you over your coat, let him have it and thy cloak with it; if he compels you to attend him on a mile's journey, go two miles with him of your own accord. Give to him who asks, and if a man would borrow from you, do not turn away (Matt. 5:39–42).
Hate him if he hates you. Sue him! Kill him!	But I tell you, love your enemies, do good to those who hate you, pray for those who persecute and insult you, that so you may be true sons of your Father in Heaven, who makes his sun shine on the evil and equally on the good, his rain fall on the just and equally on the unjust. If you love those who love you, what title have you to a reward? Will not the publicans do as much? If you greet none but your brethren, what are you doing more than others? Will not the very heathen do as much? But you are to be perfect, as your heavenly Father is perfect (Matt. 5:44–48).

Since the Christian is trying to do something very difficult in aspiring to follow Our Lord's precepts, he sometimes fails. His sorrow is greater than the pagan's remorse, for it is the result of his having offered an affront to One he loves.

Deep sorrow does not come because one has violated a law, but only if one knows one has broken off the relationship with Divine Love. But there is yet another element required for regeneration, the element of repentance and reparation. Repentance is rather a dry-eyed affair; tears flow in sorrow, but sweat pours out in repentance. It is not enough to tell God we are sorry and then forget all about it. If we broke a neighbor's window, we would not only apologize but also would go to the trouble of putting in a new pane. Since all sin disturbs the equilibrium and balance of justice and love, there must be a restoration involving toil and effort.

To see why this must be, suppose that every time a person did wrong, he was told to drive a nail into the wall of his living room, and that every time he was forgiven, he was told to pull it out. The holes would still remain after the forgiveness. Thus every sin (whether actual or original) after being forgiven leaves "holes," or "wounds," in our human nature, and the filling up of these holes is done by penance; a thief who steals a watch can be forgiven for the theft, but only if he returns the watch.

The difference between forgiveness and reparation is indicated in Sacred Scripture. When Moses sinned by doubting, God forgave him — but God still imposed a penance on Moses. "You shall not pass this Jordan" (Deut. 3:27). David repented for his adultery, and Nathan the prophet absolved him: "The Lord has taken away your sin: you shall not die" (2 Kings 12:13). But God demanded satisfaction, "The child that is born to you, shall surely die" (2 Kings 12:14). It is the same today: God's pardon in the Sacrament restores us to

His Friendship, but the debt to Divine Justice remains, either in time or in eternity.

The temporal expiation for many sins is necessarily considerable, and it requires considerable self-discipline on the part of the penitent. Faith in Christ's merits alone is not adequate for the remission of sins; as a matter of fact, faith without penance is always insufficient.

> Christ's infinite merits and satisfactions are enough and yet not enough, because God will not treat us as robots or automatons. There are those who often accuse us of attributing magical effects to the Sacraments. We retort that they are the culprits, who attribute magic to Redemption, whereas we assert that there is magic neither in the Sacraments nor in Redemption. God respects our free-will, and without the cooperation of our free-will will do nothing. His operation is dependent on our cooperation, just as the electric current is dependent on the lamp for the production of light. Confession has the innate power to remove all traces of sin, but, before it can do so, there must be perfect cooperation, i.e., perfect rectification of the will. Free-will is the core of the difficulty.

> An illustration may help to clarify the issue. Suppose two men had a quarrel, and one of them got into an uncontrollable rage and struck his companion so hard that he damaged his own hand and wrist. Afterwards, the aggressor apologized and his apology was accepted. Would you call that the end of the incident? "No," you would say, "what about the hand?" Acceptance of the apology would not heal the hand.

> So it is with us. By sin we damage our will; and the damage is not necessarily repaired by God's decree of pardon. Sometimes when we sin we turn to the crea-

ture with great intensity. Completely to rectify our will, we must turn back to God with equal intensity; that we frequently fail to do, with the result that our will remains scarred and out-of-the-straight. The will must be rectified before we can be fit for heaven.

If we turn back to God with an intensity equal to or greater than our intensity in sin, Confession takes away both the guilt of sin and the temporal punishment due to sin.

If we turn to God with less, though with sufficient intensity, the will still remains damaged, and other good works will be required to complete its rectification.

Here we have the explanation of the heavy penances imposed in the early Church. The early Christians did not doubt the efficacy of the Sacrament of Penance, but the adequacy of their own repentance. This is the explanation, too, of Christ's own insistence on penance.[2]

Or consider sin as a journey away from God. Imagine that *A* is a minor son, bound to respect his father's wishes. He is in Chicago. His father, *B,* tells him to go to the left on the map — to San Francisco. But instead *A* goes to the right, to New York. When *A* gets to New York, he telephones *B* and says, "Forgive me, will you, please? I am sorry for having offended you, who are deserving of my love." *B* forgives *A;* but look where *A* is! He is about nine hundred miles from his starting point, Chicago. In order to begin to do *B's* will, *A* has to go back to Chicago before he can go to San Francisco; or you could say that the nine hundred miles *A* traveled in sin must be traveled back in penance. *A* cannot begin to be good until he has retraced his evil ways.

But, like all examples, this one limps. For the fact is that *A* need not *walk* back those 900 miles; when *A* starts, he can call upon the Church to assist him with an airplane full of the merits of our Lord, of the Blessed Mother, and the Saints. The plane flies him back the rest of the way. Such a remission in whole or in part of the punishment due to *A's* sins is effected through indulgences. Through them, the Church gives her penitents a fresh start. And the Church has a tremendous spiritual capital, gained through centuries of penance, persecution, and martyrdom; many of her children prayed, suffered, and merited more than they needed for their own individual salvation. The Church took these superabundant merits and put them into the spiritual treasury, out of which repentant sinners can draw in times of spiritual depression. Or this spiritual capital may be likened to a blood bank; whenever any of her members are suffering from spiritual anemia or the deep wounds of sin, the Church gives them a blood transfusion. She can never do it for us if we are spiritually dead in sin; a transfusion will not avail a corpse. So to obtain the indulgences or remission of the penalties of sin, the recipient must be in a state of grace, must have the intention of gaining the indulgences, and must perform the prescribed works.

The sinner will willingly do penance: He knows that all sins cost the God-man something — His Cross — and so must cost us something; moreover, he does not want to be "let off," but rather to "make up" for his sins. In the Christian ages, people who died continued their repentance, even after death, by leaving money to or endowing hospitals, churches, and schools in Christ's name. (The modern person more often endows a scientific laboratory in his own name.)

Penance is a recognition that we have a "past." It is not morbid to recognize this fact; rather, to pretend that it does not exist is morbid. The past will affect our future. We are not only what we eat; we are also what our sins have made us. If we do not make amends for our past, we are postponing and increasing our eternal punishment; the only reason that time is given to us is in order that we may do penance. The true lover of God, conscious of having wounded Love, will voluntarily renounce his privileges and conduct himself in such a way as to be identified with the Christ Who bears five hideous scars on hands and feet and side.

In this world most of us mind pain more than we do sin; in fact, we often believe pain to be the greater evil. Penance helps us to set these disorders in their right perspective; when a man finds joy in penance, he realizes that no other evil can affect him more than sin. Unless there is love, sacrifice and penance will be felt as an evil, but not when love is there. We understand, when we accept penance, that the very selfishness that caused our sin makes some such sacrifice necessary as a condition of taming the errant impulses that caused the trouble. And when the full light of Christ's Love shines in a soul, it begins to incorporate, not only penances imposed by the Church, but all the trials of life into the great work of Redemption. Instead of breaking into bitter complaint about the reverses of fortune and the trials of life, it receives them in a spirit of resignation as the just wages of sin; through this patient acceptance, atonement is made for many sins.

There are *three* general ways of doing penances: prayers, alms, and fasting. In prayer, we beg God's mercy on our souls. By alms, we give back to God some of the gifts He gave to us, that we may justify our possessions. "Redeem you your sins with alms" (Dan. 4:24). By fasting, we mortify the root of all cravings of a sensual character. The increasing comforts of modern life afford many occasions for mortification. If a person cannot punish himself in respect to food, other pleasures within his reach — artistic, conventional, mechanical, and social — will supply many an occasion for actual fasting.

But penances are not done by ourselves alone; the penitent is helped by others who are in the Body of Christ. This could not be if we were isolated individuals, but it can come about if we belong to one Mystical Body where all are one because governed by one Head, vivified by one Soul, and professing the same Faith. Just as it is possible to graft skin from one part of the body to the other, and just as it is possible to transfuse blood from one member of society to another, so, in the spiritual organism of the Church, it is possible to graft prayer and to transfuse sacrifices. This Christian truth in its fullness is known as the Communion of Saints. Just as we are all bound up in the guilt of one another's faults, so we can be bound up in one another's reparation. Such a miracle takes place in the reversibility of merits and the interchange of advantages. That is why we ask our friends to pray for us, why we pray in the context of "*Our* Father." We have spiritual need of one another. "And the eye cannot say to the hand: I need not thy help; nor again the head to the feet: I have no need of you. Yea, much more those that seem to be the more feeble members of the body, are more necessary" (1 Cor. 12:21, 22).

Few consolations are greater than the knowledge that we are bound up in a great corporation of prayers and sacrifices. The Communion of Saints is the great discovery of those who, as adults, find the fullness of faith. They discover that for years there have been dozens, in some instances hundreds, of souls praying especially for them — storming heaven with the plea that a little act of humility by the convert might open a crack in his armor to let in God's grace and truth. Every soul in the world has a price tag on it, and since many cannot or will not pay the price themselves, others must do it for them. There is probably no other way to account for the conversion of some souls than the fact that in this world, as in the next, their parents, relatives, or friends interceded to God and won for them the prize of everlasting life.

Why are there monasteries and convents? Why do so many

young souls leave the lights and glamour of the world for the shades and shadows of the Cross where saints are made? The modern world so little understands their mission that, as soon as a newspaperman hears of a handsome young woman entering a cloister, he telephones the parents to ask, "Was she disappointed in love?" The answer, of course, is, "Yes, with the love of the world. She has fallen in love with God." These hidden dynamos of prayer, the cloistered men and women, are doing more for our country than all its politicians, its labor leaders, its army and navy put together; they are atoning for sins of us all. They are averting the just wrath of God, repairing the broken fences of those who sin and pray not, rebel and atone not. As ten just men would have saved Sodom and Gomorrah, so ten just saints can save a nation now. But so long as a citizenry is more impressed by what its cabinet does than by its chosen souls who are doing penance, the rebirth of the nation has not yet begun. The cloistered are the purest of patriots. They have not become less interested in the world since leaving it; indeed, they have become more interested in the world than ever before. But they are not concerned with whether it will buy and sell more; they care — and desperately care — whether it will be more virtuous and love God more.

With such noble men and women helping here and now, there and formerly, the rest do little enough penance for our individual sins. But, even so, many of the frustrated modern men and women look around wistfully for some easier way — for a religion which will give the emotional lift without the penitential drag, for some cult that is elevating but not too demanding. Having many passions to be mortified, many bad habits to correct, many egotisms to surrender, they want a streamlined cross. They seek a religion to give them a glow — but no blow. Some repudiate all religion, saying, "What can the Church give me?" At that stage of pride, the

Church can give nothing, but it can take something away —
one's sins. And that is gift enough, as a start.

Notes

1. A very readable and interesting treatment of confession is to be
found in *Pardon and Peace* by Alfred Wilson, C.P. (Sheed & Ward, Inc.,
London, 1947). A doctrinal approach is given by John Carmel Hienan in
his *Priest and Penitent* (Sheed & Ward, Inc., London, 1938).

2. Alfred Wilson, C.P. *Pardon and Peace,* p. 209, Sheed & Ward,
Inc., London, 1947.

Chapter 11

FEAR OF DEATH

An overemphasis on temporal security is a compensation for a loss of the sense of eternal security. When the soul becomes poor through the loss of its wealth, which is virtue, its owner seeks luxury and riches to atone for his inner nakedness. The richer the soul, the less store it sets on the material. It is not poverty that makes people quarrelsome and unhappy, as some claim; it is an overfondness for the things that money buys. Poor monks are usually friendlier and far happier than millionaires. And it is also an error to say that, if economic conditions were good, there would be no opponents of capitalism. Those who make this claim forget that: (1) Poor economic conditions are only an *occasion* for embracing alternative ideologies, not a cause; in some instances, economic trials are, instead, an occasion for renewed spiritual living. (2) Economic conditions were excellent in the Garden of Eden, but the first infiltrator got in and made a shambles of it. (3) What makes an unstable society is not the fact that people do not have enough but that they always want more. There is no limit to human demands, once the earth is made the be-all and end-all of living; soon people are willing to use every means available to possess as much of it as they can win. The real cause of such unbounded lust for what is often called "security" is fear of the eternal void within. Never before in history was the Gospel warning about God and Mammon as clearly fulfilled as today — for the soul that has lost its God must worship Mammon.

From this clutching at goods results a fear of death, a dread that we may lose whatever we have accumulated, that our temporal security will vanish into eternal insecurity. This fear of death, suffered by the modern pagan, differs from the fear of death of the faithful in several ways. The pagan fears the loss of his body and his wealth; the faithful fears the loss of his soul. The believer fears God with a filial fear such as a devoted child has toward a loving parent; the pagan fears, not God, but his fellow human beings, who seem to threaten him. Hence the increase in cynicism, suspicion, irreverence, strife, and war; the neighbor must be killed, by word if not by sword, because he is an enemy to be dreaded. The modern pagan, in refusing to continue life by the procreation of birth, becomes the sower of death. Denying the immortality of his own soul, he refuses immortality to the race by stifling his reproductive function, and thus he doubly courts the fear of death. Freud has said that Love and Death are related — which indeed they are, but not in the way Freud imagined. Love, understood as sex alone, does bring death when it sacrifices the race for the pleasure of the person. Love, understood not as glandular but as intellectual and volitional, also involves death, for it seeks to die that the beloved may live; this love, however, conquers death, through a resurrection. But to an unbeliever death, instead of being an empirical fact, has become a metaphysical anxiety. As Franz Werfel profoundly remarked on the subject: "The sceptic believes in nothing *more* than death; the believer believes in nothing *less*. Since the world to him is a creation of spirit and love, he cannot be threatened by eternal destruction in his essential being as a creature of the world."[1]

The world fears the very things Our Lord told us not to fear. He said we were not to fear dying, nor to fear being "called on the carpet" for our faith, nor to fear economic insecurity, nor to fear the future.

Therefore I say to you, be not solicitous for your life, what you shall eat, nor for your body, what you shall put on. Is not life more than the meat: and the body more than the raiment? Behold the birds of the air, for they neither sow, nor do they reap, nor gather into barns: and your heavenly Father feeds them. Are not you of much more value than they? And which of you by taking thought, can add to his stature one cubit? And for raiment why are you solicitous? Consider the lilies of the field, how they grow: they labour not, neither do they spin. But I say to you, that not even Solomon in all his glory was arrayed as one of these. And if the grass of the field, which is today, and tomorrow is cast into the oven, God so clothes: how much more you, O ye of little faith? Be not solicitous therefore, saying, What shall we eat: or what shall we drink, or wherewith shall we be clothed? For after all these things do the heathens seek. For your Father knows that you have need of all these things. Seek ye therefore first the kingdom of God, and his justice, and all these things shall be added unto you. Be not therefore solicitous for tomorrow; for the morrow will be solicitous for itself. Sufficient for the day is the evil thereof (Matt. 6:25–34).

But Our Lord told us what we *were* to fear — the consequences of judgment if we did not live right, blaspheming against the Holy Spirit, miserliness, and the denial of our faith.

The modern man has completely reversed this order of things to be feared. He takes lightly those things that the Savior warned us to fear; but he trembles at those things that the Savior bade us not to fear. Sometimes his unhealthy fear is hidden under a cover of silence: This is particularly true of the fact of death. The modern man seeks to forget about death altogether or — if he cannot do that — to conceal it, to render it unobtrusive, to disguise it. He feels awkward in the presence of death, does not know how to console or what to say. Everything in his attitude contradicts the Christian injunction, "Remember thy last end." For he regards all discussion of death as morbid; yet he will laugh at a comedy in which a dozen people are killed and will stay awake half the night reading a detective story about a murder. This, too, is *death,* and it enthralls him; but he concentrates upon the circumstances by which death comes, rather than upon the eternal issues of death, which alone are all-important. This modern insensitiveness to death is an insensitiveness to personality, to the moral order, and to destiny.

Many factors today build an unnatural attitude to death. Vain indeed are the pagan's attempts to turn death into comedy or to obscure its meaning by laughter, for when death is a personal threat, modern man is afraid to look upon its face. Physicians no longer warn their patients of the imminence of death; they act as if there were no preparation needed for eternity. Even the family of the imperiled patient plays a part in the great game of self-deception. Today's morticians make death look like life; they pretend that all that it involves is a little sleep, after which everyone will wake up on an eternal shore that has no passport regulations. The cult of staying young contributes to the macabre pretense that death will never come — first it denies the seven ages of man of which Shakespeare spoke, then it turns people's minds away from the fact of judgment that confronts them at the moment of death. Modern totalitarianism, with its herd mentality, absorbs persons into a collectivity and leads them to believe that they live in the mass, that they are important only as builders of a better future for the race; personal immortality becomes group immortality — which is no immortality, for even the group, too, will perish in time. Moreover, the moral mediocrity of any earthly Utopia ever planned is shocking to the individual's highest moral ideals; reasonable people cannot die cheerfully in the belief that such a banality will come about some day. Furthermore, every person must die before the Utopia he envisions is attained, and the only consolation this philosophy offers him is that his great-grandchildren will dance on his grave. All totalitarian schemes, however, hold out this hope; they place the Garden of Eden in the future. Their very denial of tradition, their passion to scrap everything that belongs to the memory of the human race, is another attempt to escape from the reality of death.

Those who try to ignore death sometimes say that it is a fear of dying that makes people religious. Certainly this fear has something to do with faith. It is one of the factors of religion because it brings us face-to-face with the mystery at the heart of life — Why? Whither? Wherefore? Ignore it, deny it, laugh at it, but each life runs up a bill that some day must be met, and with strict justice. As the merchant in the evening pulls out from his cash register the slip on which is written the debits and credits of the day, so, too, an hour will come when life's business is done, when the Great Judge will pull out conscience, the record of our rights and wrongs: "It is appointed unto all men once to die, and after that the judgment." It was the Devil who said, "You will not die." To rouse people out of the spirit of that lie, Christianity has enjoined them to ask themselves, "For what are you living today? It is for that that you will die tomorrow." It tells them, "Where the tree falls, there it lies," and "Watch and pray, for you know not the hour nor the day."

It is no answer to the fact of death to say that life is like a match that has been struck, which will burn for a moment and then cease to exist. If our life were like a match, death would have no terrors for us, as it has none for animals. But even the analogy of the match does not provide a case for human mortality; for although the match is blown out, its light still travels through space at the rate of 186,000 miles a second and survives somewhere in the universe. Nor can we show the transience of human life by saying that we are like the fruit on a tree, which clings and ripens and then falls and dies; for while the fruit clings to the skin, and the skin to the pulp, and the pulp to the seed, it nevertheless remains true that, although the ripe fruit falls and the birds peck at it for a time, there is still at the heart of it a seed that will live for another generation and provide its immortality.

Yet death is a fact. Animals die, and so do humans, but the difference is that humans *know* they *must* die. By that very fact, we surmount death, we get above it, we transcend it, look at it, survey it, and thus stand *outside* it. This very act is a dim foreshadowing of immortality. Our mortality is frightening to us largely because we can contemplate *immortality,* and we have a dim suspicion that we have lost the immortality that once belonged to us. We ought to have it; yet we have it not. Something has interfered. We are not all we ought to be. If death were merely a physical *must,* we would not fear it. Our fear comes from the moral fact that we know we *ought* not to die. We fear death because it was not part of the original plan laid down for us. And we also fear it because we have made so poor a use of our years of life. When the sense of sin is keen, this fear of facing our own failures may become paradoxically acute, so that the individual wants to lose himself in order not to have to live with himself. This is suicide and nihilism.

Death is a source of meditation on many of the great truths. It is a sign of evil in the world, for, to the Christian, death belongs not only to the biological order but also to the moral and spiritual realms. The first record of death that we have in the Scriptures associates it with sin and a rebellion against Love. Death makes its first appearance in this world as punishment. And death is, from the first, twofold; for a distinction must be made between the death of the body and the death of the soul.

As Saint John tells us in the Apocalypse, "You call yourselves living, and yet you are dead." Just as the life of the body is the soul, so the life of the soul is the grace of God; when the soul leaves the body, the body is dead, and when grace leaves a soul, that soul is dead. It was in virtue of this distinction that Our Blessed Savior told us not to fear those who kill the body but rather to fear those who would kill the soul. The correlation between death and sin is made very clear in Saint Paul's words, "The wages of sin is death." Every city is full of dead souls in live bodies as well as live bodies and live souls; the double death is a death of both body and soul.

Although Christianity sees in death a tragedy and a penalty, it nevertheless gives humanity its victory over it. The Lord of Life Himself descended to taste that death and to conquer it by resurrection from the dead. He thereby overcame death at its most devilish and destructive. The worst thing that evil can do is, not to bomb children, but to kill Divine Life; having done that, and been defeated in the moment of its greatest show of strength, it never could be victorious again.

Death has other meanings. It offers an affirmation of the purpose of life in an otherwise meaningless existence, for the world could endlessly carry on its Godless plan if there were no death. What death is to an individual, catastrophe is to a civilization — the end of its wickedness. Death is a negative testimony to God's power in a meaningless world; by it God brings the meaningless to naught. Once evil has come into the world, death is seen as a kind of blessing, for if there were no death, evil could go on forever. That is why God stationed an angel with a flaming sword at the Gate of Paradise, lest fallen man, eating of the tree of immortality, should immortalize his evil. But, because of death, evil cannot carry on its wickedness indefinitely. If there were no catastrophe such as the Apocalypse reveals at the end of the world, the universe would mark the triumph of meaninglessness; but the catastrophe is a reminder that God will not allow unrighteousness to become eternal. There is a day of judgment; and judgment means that evil is self-defeating.

The meaning of life can become apparent only in judgment and valuation. Personal judgment at the moment of death is a revelation of the meaning of personal life, and the cosmic judgment at the end of time is a revelation of the meaning of social values. All the catastrophes, wars, revolutions and toppling civilizations are reminders that our ideas have been found wanting, our bad dreams have been realized. If these thoughts of ours had been true and sound, they would not need to be destroyed, for truth is eternal; death comes only to life that has not fulfilled its inner meaning.

The revelation of the coming of the anti-Christ means that humanity has refused to accept eternal values, for death is not the triumph of death, but the triumph of meaning. Jerusalem has passed away because it did not know the time of its visitation. That same statement holds true for every other civilization. And so, by making an end to evil, God affirms the power of love over the power of chaos. This is the significance of His answer to Pilate, who said, "Know you not that I have the power to condemn you?" but Our Lord answered, "You would not have the power unless it were given to you from above." There is only one passage in Sacred Scripture where God is said to laugh; that is in the psalm, "He that sits in the heavens shall laugh and hold them in derision." The theology of this laughter is this: Incongruity inspires laughter. A street cleaner in a silk hat is a laughable and incongruous sight; God's laughter is likewise provoked by the incongruity of an earthly dictator thinking that he has become a god or that his evil is eternal. Death is God's necessary gift to a universe in which evil has been let loose.

But if death were irremediable, the universe could not be justified. It would be a closed system. The Resurrection is also necessary — it not only gives victory over death, but it wipes away evil or corruption. *Mortem moriendo destruxit.* Since the Resurrection and Pentecost, humanity can restore itself to Divine Love through the application of Christ's Redemption through the Sacraments. We do not recover immortality of body until the final resurrection. Nonetheless, all of us share a profound intuition that our deaths can serve a triumphant purpose. Why is a person less willing to die in a train wreck or an automobile accident than he is to be killed on a battlefield or as a martyr to his faith? Is it not because death is less terrifying and more meaningful as soon as we rise above the level of the commonplace and lift ourselves into the realm of eternal values where, alone, death has meaning?

Death is the end of evil; we see this revealed in the faces of the dead, which are often more harmonious than they were in life, as the sleeping face is more restful than the waking. Ugly feelings and hates, eccentricities and discords, disappear in the presence of the dead, so that we even say, "*Of* the dead say nothing but good." In the presence of the dead, we give praise and adulation; we resurrect the good things and the charities, kindnesses, and humor of our friend. The best qualities are what are recalled posthumously, making us wonder whether death itself may not be a thrusting to the fore of the good that we have done, a disprizing of the evil. Not that both of them will not be recalled — they will. But as life revealed the debit side of our character, so death, too, will show forth the credit side. Death is thus bound up with goodness.

And death is also bound up with love, or, rather, love is always bound up with death. Whoever accepts love, accepts sacrifice. We give the ring of gold, instead of the ring of tin, as a symbol of sacrifice, and sacrifice is a lesser form of death. Surpassing all minor sacrifices is the complete love that is willing to accept death for the beloved, as a soldier dies for his country. Whoever attaches too much value to life and runs away from death also runs away from perfect love: "Greater love than this no man has, that a man lay down his life for his friend." The acceptance of death is thus a manifestation of our love of God.

Death will individualize and personalize all of us. Because it separates the soul from the body, it finds out each and every one in its search; it will reveal the *real me* as against the *surface me*. The soul will stand naked before God, seen at last as it truly is. And if a soul is not then clothed with virtue, it will feel ashamed, as Adam and Eve were, when they had sinned and hid from God; for it was only *after* their sin that they felt naked and ashamed. This relationship between nakedness of the soul and sin is always a close one — at the judgment of our souls, in Eden, and in this life, where, the less grace men and women have in their souls, the more gaudily they dress, in a kind of compensation, as we noted earlier.

The separation of the soul from the body after death will bring another change; it will do away with the special advantages that some of us enjoyed in this life, for the body in relationship to the soul might be likened to a person driving an automobile. One person drives through life in a broken-down jalopy, another in a 20-horsepower motor, another in a 50-horsepower motor, and still another in a 200-horsepower motor, but when there is a traffic violation of the law, no one is judged by the kind of car he is driving but by whether or not he broke the law. In the same manner, at the moment of death, when the soul leaves the body, we shall be judged not by the earthly advantages that we had — beauty or talent, or the wealth that accompanied the body, or the social advantages — but only by the degree to which we responded to Divine Love. As Dives was separated from his five brothers by death, so each of us will be separated from the group and from the crowd. Then each and every one must step forward, alone, out of the ranks. There will be no attorneys there to plead our case, no alienists to argue that we were not in our right minds when we did wrong. There will be only one voice: It will be the voice of conscience that will reveal us as we really are.

Lord, I lie open to your scrutiny; you know me, know when I sit down and when I rise up again, can read my thoughts from far away. Wake I or sleep I, you can tell; no movement of mine but you are watching it. Before ever the words are framed on my lips, all my thought is known to you; rearguard and vanguard, you do encompass me; your hand still laid upon me. Such wisdom as yours is far beyond my reach, no thought of mine can attain it. Where can I go, then, to take refuge from your spirit, to hide from your view? If I should climb up to heaven, you are there; if I sink down to the world beneath, you are present still. If I could wing my way eastwards, or find a dwelling beyond the western sea, still would I find you beckoning to me, your right hand upholding me. Or perhaps I would think to bury myself in darkness; night should surround me, friendlier than day; but no, darkness is no hiding-place from you, with you the night shines clear as day itself; light and dark are one.

Yours are my inmost thoughts. Did you not form me in my mother's womb? I praise you for my wondrous fashioning, for all the wonders of your creation. Of my soul you have full knowledge, and this mortal frame has no mysteries for you, who did contrive it in secret, devise its pattern, there in the dark recesses of the earth. All my acts your eyes have seen, all are set down already in your record; my days were numbered before ever they came to be. A riddle, my God, your dealings with me, so vast their scope. (Ps. 139:1–17).

Death will thus manifest that uniqueness of each personality, which, as the Scholastics said, is *incommunicable*. Pascal wrote, "Nothing is so important to man as his own state, nothing so formidable to him as eternity." Death confronts self with self in its great moment of mental awakening in the morning of the afterlife. In that tearing away of all illusionment, the soul will see itself as it really is. It still drags a train of experiences behind it; it has the memory, that storehouse of habits good and bad, of prayers said, of kindnesses to the poor, as well as the refusal of grace, the sins of avarice, of lust, and of pride.

Since we are faced with this inevitable event, how shall we meet it? The pagan and the Christian have different ways of answering. The pagan as he lives moves progressively closer to death; the Christian moves backward from it. The pagan tries to ignore death, but each tick of the clock brings him nearer to it through fear and anxiety. The Christian begins his life by contemplating his death; knowing that he will die, he plans his life accordingly, in order to enjoy eternal life. There are two stages in the pagan's experience: human life and human death. In the Christian's, there are three: human life, human death, which is a gate to the third stage — Divine life. Christianity has always recommended the contemplation of death as an encouragement to lead a good life; and this is actually effective, for although we cannot go backward in time, we can go forward in time. We can therefore say to ourselves, "What I am living for today is that which I shall die for tomorrow."

The Christian principle for conquering death is twofold:
(1) Think about death. (2) Rehearse for it by mortification
now. The purpose of contemplation is to conquer the dread
and compulsion of death by voluntarily facing it. Through
anticipating the final end, we may contemplate new begin-
nings. Our Blessed Lord lived from the end of life backward:
"I came to give My life for the redemption of the world." The
Lamb is pictured as "slain from the beginning of the world."

The perspective on death robs us of our shoddy views of
living. If we think about death, we shake ourselves out of
our fantasy that the universe is not a moral one. In treating
schizophrenia, a violent electric shock is sometimes applied
to the head of the patient; the schizophrenic is so alarmed,
so threatened, that in order to escape what seems like dissolution the mind puts off its fantasy and the patient is thrust
back into the real world. Meditation on death has something
of that effect on the spiritual system. It breaks the spell that
made us think that pleasure is everything, that we ought to
go on making more money or building more buildings, that
religion is for the feebleminded, and other such illusions.

When we contemplate the death of self, the citadel of self
is bound to be attacked. We glimpse our own inner being
and its poverty. Each of us comes into life with fists closed,
set for aggressiveness and acquisition, but when we abandon life, our hands are open; there is nothing on earth that
we need, nothing the soul can take with it that could not
be taken away after any shipwreck — its own works. *Opera
enim illorum sequuntur illos.* Because meditation on our final
end takes the mind off the present self, it destroys excessive
egocentricity and lessens our fears and anxieties. For fears
diminish as we cease to think of ourselves in our immediate
aspect and adjust our minds, instead, to the larger landscape
of eternity.

Death can be robbed of its greatest fearfulness if we practice for it. Christianity recommends mortification, penance, and detachment as a rehearsal for the great event. For every death should be a great masterpiece, and, like all master-pieces, it cannot be completed in a day. A sculptor who wishes to carve a figure out of a block uses his chisel, first cutting away great chunks of marble, then smaller pieces, un-til he finally reaches a point where only a brush of hand is needed to reveal the figure. In the same way, the soul has to undergo tremendous mortifications at first, and then more re-fined detachments, until finally its Divine image is revealed. Because mortification is recognized as a practice of death, there is fittingly inscribed on the tomb of Don Scotus, *Bis Mortuus; Semel Sepultus* (twice died, but buried only once). When we die to something, something comes alive within us. If we die to self, charity comes alive; if we die to pride, service comes alive; if we die to lust, reverence for personality comes alive; if we die to anger, love comes alive.

The basic spiritual principle is this: Death must be con-quered in every thought and word and deed by an affirmation of the eternal. Spiritual writers advise us that everything should be done as if one were going to die in the next mo-ment. If we treat the living as though they were dying, too, then the good in them will come to the surface. Treat the dead as still alive, and our prayers will follow them; thus a belief in the state of purgation after death allows us to atone for our want of love while our friends were still on earth. The failure to help their bodies then can be balanced now by our spiritual assistance to their souls through prayer.

Death is meant to be our true birth, our beginning. Chris-tianity, in contrast to paganism, always blesses her children's spiritual birth into eternity. In the liturgy, the day on which a saint dies is called his *natilitia,* or birthday. The world cel-ebrates a birthday on the day a person is born to physical life; the Church celebrates it when a person is born to eternal life. There are only three exceptions to this, and they were made for very good reasons: The only physical birthdays in the liturgy are those of Our Divine Lord (December 25), of the Blessed Mother (September 8), and of Saint John the Baptist (June 24). This is because each of these births marked a special infusion of Divine Life into the world: Our Lord *is* Eternal Life; the Blessed Mother, through Her Immaculate Conception, participated in that Eternal Life from the first moment of Her Conception; and Saint John the Baptist was sanctified in his mother's womb when he was visited by His Lord, still tabernacled within the Blessed Mother. These three exceptions rather prove than contradict the rule that life comes through death, spirituality through mortification, and the saving of the soul in eternity through the losing of it in time.

For when a soul has proved that it loved God above all things, and proved it by detachment from all that stood in the way of its fullhearted love, it is prepared to stand before Love; then it will, in the language of Newman, feel the pain of never having loved enough.

> And when — if such thy lot — thou seest thy Joy
> The sight of Him will kindle in thy heart
> All tender, gracious, reverential thoughts.
> Thou wilt be sick with love, and yearn for Him...
> There is pleading in His pensive eyes —
> Will pierce thee to the quick and trouble thee.
> And thou wilt hate and loathe thyself; for though
> Now sinless, thou wilt feel that thou hast sinned
> As never thou didst feel; and wilt desire
> To slink away and hide thee from His sight;
> And yet will have a longing aye to dwell
> Within the beauty of His countenance.
> And these two pains, so counter and so keen —

The longing for Him, when thou seest Him not;
The shame of self at thought of seeing Him —
Will be thy veriest, sharpest Purgatory.

Notes

1. *Between Heaven and Earth,* p. 192.

Chapter 12

THE PSYCHOLOGY OF CONVERSION

A S ONE GOES UP the hierarchy of nature, one finds an increasing capacity for adaptation. H_2O is capable of assuming the three forms of ice, water, and steam; plants have adaptability only to seasons and local conditions; animals have additional powers of moving from place to place, but each one of them still remains more or less fixed in type. Man has the greatest capacity for change of all, because he who is born of the flesh can also be born of the spirit; he who is only a creature can become a child of God. Man alone is convertible. He alone can become something he is not. Conversion does not mean a further development in the natural order, but a generation into a supernatural order. The body is alive because of the soul, but the soul is dead when it has not that higher life that God alone can give. "Unless one is born again, he cannot see the kingdom of God" (John 3:3).

Just as plants and animals die when they are out of touch with their proper environment, so, too, souls die if they fail to live in union with God, Who alone can make them realize the fullness of their personalities. The great pity of life is that so many minds fail to make an acquaintance with the whole of their environment. There are some who can enjoy the barking of a saxophone but have no appreciation for the overture of a Beethoven. There are others who discover the world of science, but have not mental telescopes strong enough to discover the world of poetry. There are people satisfied to conquer a world of business, without the desire to conquer the world of philosophy. There are many who enter into contact with the world of credit but fail to enter into contact with the world of faith. Such minds are content to know a part of their environment but not the whole. They are very much like the deaf, who are dead to the great environment of sound — to children's laughter, the voice of a friend, the song of a bird, the sweet flow of poetry, the thrill of music, the sigh of the winds, and the sadness of a waterfall. Though sound and harmony constitute one of the greatest pleasures of this world, the deaf know of the world of sound as a vast and undiscovered realm. And the blind are dead to the great environment of beauty — to the gesture of a friend, the flash of an eye, the earnestness of a visage, the beauty of a rainbow, the twinkle of a star, and the fall of a meteor. Visual beauty is one of the sources of life's pleasures, but there are some as dead to it as if they had never been born.

Over and above the world of sounds and visible things, over and above the world even of science and philosophy, there is that still greater environment of life: the truth, love, and beauty of God, Who alone can satisfy the infinite aspirations of humanity. One of the sad and regrettable things today is that there are some people in this world who are dead, not only to the world of poetry, music, philosophy, but to the life and love of God. They form a class we may call the "Deity-blind." Such people are often alive to the temporal environment: Their words are correct; their sense of propriety shows in the embellishment of their homes and their choice of amusements; they are worldly; they are rich; they are sophisticated; they are successful; they are at ease; they are honored; they have eyes, but they are blind — blind to the beautiful environment of God and the Incarnate life of Christ.

But no one is at peace until he is in proper relation to

Divinity. Acquiring this might be called "Deo-version," or a turning to God. This kind of conversion means a substitution of Christ consciousness for ego consciousness; a transformation of the personality through the love of God in Christ; a surrender of the will so as to obey Christ above all things and at all costs. True conversion has nothing to do with emotional "uplift" or with a moral veneer of social action; it is a hard game, an arduous battle, a travail of soul from which emerges a new dedication of self. The Christ mind must become the soul of our thinking, the Christ vision the eyes of our seeing, the Christ truth must be in our mouths for speaking, and the Christ love in our hearts for loving.

We shall limit ourselves here to discussing the *psychology* of conversion, to describing the antecedents of conversion, as they manifest themselves in the soul. Generally these are twofold: a sense of conflict or crisis; and a strong desire to be united with God.

Every conversion starts with a crisis: with a moment or a situation involving some kind of suffering, physical, moral, or spiritual; with a dialectic, a tension, a pull, a duality, or a conflict. This crisis is accompanied, on the one hand, by a profound sense of one's own helplessness and, on the other hand, by an equally certain conviction that God alone can supply what the individual lacks. If there were *only* a sense of helplessness, there would be despair, pessimism, and eventual suicide. This is, indeed, the condition of the post-Christian pagan: He feels the total inadequacy of his own inner resources against the overwhelming odds of a cruel universe and thus falls into despair. He has one-half of the necessary condition for conversion — namely, a sense of crisis — but he fails to link up his powerlessness with the Divine Power, Who sustains and nourishes the soul. But when this is done, paganism vanishes and gives place to what might be called creative despair: "despair," because one realizes one's own spiritual disease; "creative," because one knows that only a Divine Physician outside oneself can bring healing to one's wings. This despair does not usually arise from a sense of one's stupidity or ignorance or mistakes, but because of one's inadequacy, one's sense of dependence, or even one's admission of guilt.

The soul becomes the battlefield of a civil war during a conversion. It is not enough that there be a conflict between consciousness and unconsciousness or self and environment, for such tensions can be simple psychological phenomena without profound significance for the soul. So long as the conflict is only psychological, so long as it is capable of being manipulated by the mind itself or by another human mind, there may result an integration or sublimation, or so-called "peace of mind," but there is no Deo-version, or peace of soul. The tension or conflict is never very acute when the dueling forces are contained within the mind itself; conversion is not autosuggestion, but a flash of lightning from without. There is a great tension only when the self is confronted with the nonself, when the within is challenged by the without, when the helplessness of the ego is confronted with the adequacy of the Divine.

Not until the tug of war begins, with the soul on one end of the rope and God on the other, does true duality appear as the condition of conversion. This crisis in the soul is the miniature and cameo of the great historical crisis of the City of God and the City of Man. There must be in the soul the conviction that one is in the grip of and swayed by a higher control than one's own will; that, opposing the ego, there is a Presence before Whom one feels happy in doing good and before Whom one shrinks away for having done evil. It is relatively unimportant whether this crisis, which results in a feeling of duality, be sudden or gradual. What matters is struggle between the soul and God, with the all-powerful

God never destroying human freedom. This is the greatest drama of existence.

Such a tension between God and the soul is clearly seen in the conversion of Saint Paul, when the glorified Christ appeared to him with the challenge "Why do you persecute me?" (Acts 22:7). In modern souls, this tension appears as an anxiety, not of the psychological, but of the metaphysical order, wherein the soul lives, as Pierre Rousselot said, "on the thread of disquietude." In other generations, the mind had problems; today's mind *is* a problem. The mystery has moved from the universe to the soul, from the universal to the particular. Perhaps that is the reason why novelists and poets, more often than philosophers, are now accepted as guides by the frustrated mind. But there is no lack of modern philosophers who try to analyze this tension in an abstract fashion. Some of them describe the soul in anguish over its own contingency, shrinking back frightened at the sight of its nothingness, and at the next moment looking forward with a sweet nostalgia for the infinite. Others, sensing an ethical pathos in this search, strive to find the absolute, a Friend of Righteousness whence all earthly justice is derived. Others, like Kierkegaard, analyzing despair, declare that it would be impossible to man if he had no intuition of the eternal. "That self which he despairingly wills to be, is a self which he is not; what he really wills (in despair) is to tear himself away from the Power which constituted it." Others study the tension in terms of finite satisfaction and infinite longing, of disappointment with what one has and a yearning for what one has not, with a dim knowledge that we should not want the infinite if we were not made for it or if we did not come from it. But disquietude results when the desire of God is caged in a restricted mortal frame, and this unrest impels man to a renewed passion for transcendence, light, and power. Pascal describes it thus: "My mind is disquieted. I am disquieted is better. Description

of man; dependency, desire of independence, need. Condition
of man; inconstancy, weariness, unrest."

Involved in the struggle is the impression that one is being
sought by Someone — by the "Hound of Heaven" in Thompson's language — who will not leave us alone. The tragedy
is that many souls, feeling this anxiety, seek to have it explained away, instead of following it to where, at the end of
the trail, it is seen as God and actual grace working on the
soul. The voice of God causes discontent within the soul in
order that the soul may search further and be saved. It em-
barrasses the soul, for it shows us the truth, tears off all the
masks and masquerades of hypocrisy. But it consoles the soul,
too, by effecting a harmony with self, with others, and with
God. It is for man to decide — to accept or reject the voice he
hears. Saint Augustine tells how, after hearing the story of a
conversion, he turned his back on an actual grace.

> Such was the story of Pontitianus; but thou, O Lord,
> while he was speaking, didst turn me round towards
> myself, taking me from behind my back where I had
> placed me, unwilling to observe myself; and setting me
> before my face, that I might see how foul I was, how
> crooked and defiled, bespotted and ulcerous. And I be-
> held and stood aghast; and whither to flee from myself
> I found not. And if I sought to turn mine eye from off
> myself, he went on with his relation, and Thou again
> didst set me over against myself, and thrust me before
> my eyes, that I might find out mine iniquity, and hate it.
> I had known it, but made as though I saw it not, winked
> at it, and forgot it.[1]

In this crisis, one becomes conscious that he has become a
stage wherein two great powers are waging war; his soul itself is with one power one moment and the other power at
another moment. There is a whisper that solicits one to the

mountain peaks, and there is a voice that summons one down to the valleys. There is a fear of what may lie ahead in the future, and a dread of continuing on as at present. The spirit calls to renouncement of old habits, but the flesh is reluctant to break the chains. Once these two currents of inner frustration and Divine Mercy meet, so that the soul realizes that God alone can provide what it lacks, then the crisis reaches a point where a decision must be made. In this sense, the crisis is crucial — it involves a cross. The crisis itself can take a thousand different forms, varying from souls that are good to those that are sinful. But in both these extremes there is a common recognition that the conflicts and frustrations cannot be overcome by one's own energy. The common forms of crisis are the moral, the spiritual, and the physical.

The crisis is moral when there is an awareness of sin and guilt, existing not only as a historical phenomenon that affects social and international life but as something inwardly experienced *as a broken relationship*. Those who hold the opinion that the only guilt is the admission of guilt and that the only sin is the belief in sin render themselves incapable of conversion. Since they acknowledge nothing in their universe except their ego, then they cannot admit an outside Power from whom the saving experience will come. There can be no crisis so long as the soul thinks of itself as disturbed because of having violated some vague cosmic law or because it is out of tune with the universe. A crisis demands two persons: the human person and the Person of God. Then the remorse for its sins tortures the soul and makes it yearn for a peace that it cannot gain of itself. Thus, by a peculiar paradox, sin becomes the occasion of a loneliness and a void that God alone can relieve. This emptiness is not that of a bottomless pit; it is the emptiness of a nest that can be filled only by the Eagle descending from the heights above. A soul in such a crisis seeks God after a series of disgusts as, like the Prodigal, it turns from husks to the Bread of Life. Such a crisis involves sadness, because one has fallen from the ideal; but it is mixed with hope, because the original pattern can be recovered.

Up to this point, the soul had covered up its sins; now it discovers them in order to repudiate them. What is owned can be disowned; what is perceived as an obstacle can now be surmounted. The crisis reaches its peak when the soul becomes less interested in stirring up external revolutions and more interested in the internal revolution of its own spirit; when it swings swords, not outward but inward, to cut out its baser passions; when it complains less about the lying of the world and begins to work on making itself something less a liar than before. The moral sphere has two ethical poles: one, the immanent sense of evil or failure; the other, the transcendent power of God's Mercy. The abyss of powerlessness cries out to the abyss of salvation, for *copiosa apud eum redemptio.* The Cross is now seen in a new light. At one moment it bespeaks the depth of human iniquity that, in essence, would slay God; at another moment it reveals the defeat of evil in its strongest moment, vanquished not only by the prayers for forgiveness from the Cross but by the triumph of the Resurrection. But this cascade of Divine Power cannot operate on a person so long as he lives under the illusion either that he is an angel or that sin is not his fault. He must first admit the fact of personal guilt; then — though the consciousness of having been a sinner does not vanish — the consciousness of being in a state of sin is relieved. This is probably the experience to which Charles Péguy referred when he said, "I am a sinner, a good sinner."

God becomes a possibility to the despairing soul only as it begins to see that it can do "all things in Him Who strengthens me." The naturally good man of Rousseau and Liberalism, the harmless egotist of Adam Smith, and the prudently selfish man of John Stuart Mill do not feel these moral tensions, particularly when their lives are cushioned in comfort. It has taken a century for followers of these false optimists to sense that their inner vacancy results from a freedom yearning for the infinite, yoked to a finiteness whose essence is disgust. A new self is needed, and man cannot renovate himself. No vague humanism, no busy dedication to social causes, can root out the sense of guilt — because guilt implies a *personal* relationship with God. And a personal relationship implies love. For us to become truly moral, there must be a surrender to an all-loving Christ Who can do what no human can do. And then the pain passes away: Though the emptiness of soul that sin has given us sees itself confronted by Christ, the emphasis is immediately shifted from our sin to His mercy, from self to the Cross. Once the will to sin is abandoned, then the soul sees that it has become acceptable to the Savior — not because it was good, but because the Savior is Good. In other religions, one must be purified before one can knock at the door; in Christianity, one knocks on the door as a sinner, and He Who answers to us heals. The moral crisis is ended when Christ confronts the soul, not as law but as Mercy, and when the soul accepts the invitation, "Come to me, all you that labor, and are burdened, and I will refresh you" (Matt. 11:28).

The crisis of conversion is sometimes spiritual rather than moral. This is frequent among those who have been seeking perfection but are not yet possessed of the fullness of the Faith and Sacraments. Some such souls have led a good life on the *natural* plane; they have been generous to the poor and kind to their neighbors and have furthered at least a vague fellowship with all peoples. Other souls have already had a smattering of the supernatural life; they lead as Christ-like a life as they know how, living up to faith in Him as they see His light. The crisis begins in those souls at the moment when they either recognize that they have tremendous potentialities that have not been exercised or else begin to yearn for a religious life that will make greater demands on them. Up to this moment of crisis, they have lived on the surface of their souls. The tension deepens as they realize that, like a plant, they have roots that need greater spiritual depths and branches meant for communion with the heavens above. The growing sense of dissatisfaction with their own ordinariness is accompanied by a passionate craving for surrender, sacrifice, and abandonment to God's Holy Will. Such a shift from mediocrity to love may be occasioned through the example of a saint, the inspiration of a spiritual book, the desire to escape from mere symbols to Divine Reality. However it comes, there is a duality present from the moment the soul hears Christ saying, "Be you therefore perfect, as also your heavenly Father is perfect" (Matt. 5:48).

Conversion from mediocrity to a full surrender is no easier than the conversion from sin to charity; in either case, there is the plucking out of an eye and the cutting off of an arm. It seems to the convert that he is asked to give up everything — not only all he has, but even control over his mind — but this is because he does not yet understand the joyous freedom of union with *God*. Pleasures of the flesh are always greater in anticipation than in realization, but the joys of the spirit are always greater in realization than in anticipation.

Not everyone accepts the demands made during a spiritual crisis. The rich young man, who had kept the commandments from his youth, went away sad when Our Lord asked him to give to the poor and follow Him. His crisis passed as he chose an ordinary good life, instead of the spiritual life. The crisis had a different ending in another rich man, Matthew, who left his cashier's desk to become an Apostle. Probably none of the Apostles called by Our Lord said, "Now, I must begin to be good"; they said, instead, "Now, I must begin to do His Will." Up to the time of a true conversion a soul has its own standards of goodness. After being confronted with the Grace of God, it seeks nothing else but correspondence to His Will. Such a soul is as relentless in its love as the Divine Love is relentless.

The spiritual crisis is very general, for in every soul is some reflection of the universal yearning for perfection. After conversion there is a supernatural love of God, but even before conversion there is a natural love of God. The difference between the two has been explained by Saint Thomas: "Nature loves God above all things as He is the beginning and end of natural good, but charity [loves Him] in so far as He is the object of beatitude and as a man has a certain fellowship with God."[2] Every person who loves, *naturally* loves God more than himself. This love is not conscious in many souls, and in others its practical effects are limited by concupiscence; but it is hidden in every pursuit of happiness, in every desire for an ideal large enough to satisfy all our longings. The individual may misname this Infinite which he seeks; he may identify it with wealth or flesh or power; but the motive force that drives him on is still his search for unending happiness. Even when a person settles for less and imagines it to be his Infinite, nevertheless the Supreme Good is even more desired; so that God is loved either consciously or unconsciously, by every being capable of love. But the desire to possess God in love would be an inefficacious desire, if God did not elevate human nature. When this happens, when the soul passes from a natural to a supernatural love of God, a conversion has occurred.

The spiritual desire for the Infinite can also be directed to God as Divine Truth. The human intellect, conscious of the fact that it does not know all, can become docile in the face of the Divinity and begin to crave a light that only God can give. Disappointed in their broad-mindedness, which tried no truth with fire, some start a search for that Divine Truth that admits no compromise. Christopher Hollis, explaining his conversion, said,

> When I looked at the New Testament, I did not find there any record of Christ talking as a friend talked; I did not find Him saying: "These are a few observations that have occurred to me. I should be very grateful if you would go away and think them over and see if you can find anything in them." I did find Him teaching with authority, hurling dogmas at the heads of His audience, commanding His audience to accept His teaching and holding out to them the appalling threat of eternal damnation if they refused to accept. When I was at school, among my schoolfellows were a Presbyterian and a Methodist. One term the Presbyterian came back and said that during the holiday his parents had read the New Testament and as a result, they had become Catholics. The Methodist thought this was a very funny story. I did not see at the time why it was so particularly funny and when some years later, I came to read the New Testament myself, I found it was even less funny than I had imagined.[3]

Chesterton, too, was solicited toward conversion by the desire for infinite knowledge, and he explained himself in this way: "I am the man who, with the utmost daring, discovered what was discovered before."

It is possible that the decline of reason in the modern world may drive more and more souls to investigate the disparity between what *they* know and what is knowable. Only by seeking for what is above the human can the human mind preserve its dignity: Either its reason mounts to Wisdom, or its emotions enchain reason and man becomes a beast. As carnality and comfort become the common goal of modern life, those with intelligence will fight harder than ever for the deliverance of their reason and will finally come to see that, without a *Divine Logos* behind the universe, there would never be reason in the universe. Pascal's belief that there are only two kinds of reasonable people may indeed be true — those who love God with all their hearts because they have found Him, and those who search for God with all their hearts, because they have not found Him.

Today there is in the world a vast army of good souls who have not yet entered into the fullness of the crisis; they are thirsty, but they fear to ask Him for a drink lest He pour it from a chalice. They are cold, but they fear drawing near His fires, lest those flames cleanse as they illumine them; they know that they are locked in the sepulchers of their own pettiness, but they fear that their Resurrection, like His, will bear the scars of battle. There are many who would like to stretch a finger to Our Lord; they shrink back lest He should seize their hands and woo their hearts. But they are not far from the Kingdom of God. Already, they have the desire; they need only the courage with which to pass through the crisis in which, through an apparent surrender, they will find themselves victors in the captivity of Divinity.

But there is a third type of conversion caused by a physical event. The crisis is physical when it comes through some unexpected catastrophe such as the death of a loved one, a business failure, disease, or some suffering that forces one to ask, "What is the purpose of life? Why am I here? Where am I going?" So long as there were prosperity and good health, these questions were never in the foreground; the soul with only external interests does not concern itself with God, any more than the rich man whose barns were full. But when the barns are burned, the soul is suddenly forced to look inside itself, to examine the roots of its being, and to peer into the abyss of its spirit. This excursion is not the delightful voyage of a summer day, but a tragic inquiry into the possibility that we have neglected to seek for the best wealth, treasures that rust does not consume, moths eat, or thieves break through and steal — treasures that only God can give when hearts are emptier than any purse. All crises, even those of material disaster, force the soul inward, as the blood is driven back to the heart during some sicknesses or as a city under attack moves to its inner defenses.

It would be well today for all of us to face the possibility of a very great catastrophe. Whether the catastrophe will come as a result of atomic warfare or world revolution or as a cosmic upheaval matters little; the form of it is only a detail. But what does matter is this possibility for disaster of which we do know. A tragedy of catastrophic proportions would reveal to a skeptical world that the universe is moral and that God's laws cannot be broken with impunity. Just as failure to eat causes a headache, a judgment on a violation of a law of nature, great crises in history are judgments on the way people think, will, love, and act. Periods of delirium and the times of tragedy following a schism of the soul from God sometimes do for a whole people what sickness or personal disaster does for a sinful individual.

Illness, especially, may be a blessed forerunner of the individual's conversion. Not only does it prevent him from realizing his desires; it even reduces his capacity for sin, his opportunities for vice. In that enforced detachment from evil, which is a Mercy of God, he has time to enter into himself, to appraise his life, to interpret it in terms of large reality. He considers God, and, at that moment, there is a sense of duality, a confronting of personality with Divinity, a comparison of the facts of his life with the ideal from which he fell. The soul is forced to look inside itself, to inquire whether there is not more peace in this suffering than in sinning. Once a sick person, in his passivity, begins to ask, "What is the purpose of my life? Why am I here?" the crisis has already begun. Conversion becomes possible the very moment a person ceases to blame God or life for his troubles and begins to blame himself; by doing so, he becomes able to distinguish between his sinful barnacles and the ship of his soul. A crack has appeared in the armor of his egotism; now the sunlight of God's grace can pour in. But until that happens, catastrophes can teach us nothing but despair.

We see this in the intellectual history of the proud man of the twentieth century; his abandonment of the philosophy of evolution and inevitable progress was succeeded by the philosophy of despair, defeat, and fear. Two generations ago, he was about to be a god; today, that god is being psychoanalyzed to find out why he feels "like the devil." Leon Bloy, who came to Christ through a consciousness of catastrophe and crisis, asks, as do many historians, "Are we not at the end of everything and is not the palpable confusion of modern times the symptom of some immense supernatural disturbance which at last will set us free?" The world may have departed so far from God and the path to its own peace that a tragedy would be the greatest mercy. The worst thing God could do to us would be to let us alone in our present chaos and defilement. Two world wars have not made the world better, but worse. And one wonders if the next catastrophe will be a war in the same sense of the last two or rather some calamity more surely calculated to produce repentance in man.

When a soul in sin, under the impetus of grace, turns to God, there is penance; but when a soul in sin refuses to change, God sends chastisement. This chastisement need not be external, and certainly it is never arbitrary; it comes as an inevitable result of breaking God's moral law. But the entrenched forces of the modern world are irrational; people nowadays do not always interpret disasters as the moral events they are. When calamity strikes the flint of human hearts, sparks of sacred fire are kindled and people will normally begin to make an estimate of their true worth. In previous ages this was usual: The disordered individual could find his way back to peace because he lived in an objective world inspired by Christian order. But the frustrated individual of today, having lost his faith in God, living, as he does, in a disordered, chaotic world, has no beacon to guide him. In times of trouble he sometimes turns in upon himself, like a serpent devouring his own tail. Given such a man, who worships the false trinity of (1) his own pride, which acknowledges no law; (2) his own sensuality, which makes earthly comfort its goal; (3) his license, which interprets liberty as the absence of all restraint and law — then a cancer is created that is impossible to cure except through an operation or calamity unmistakable as God's action in history. It is always through sweat and blood and tears that the soul is purged of its animal egotism and laid open to the Spirit.

It would be wrong to imagine that historical catastrophes are necessary because there is one side of the world where people are good and another side where they are wicked. When a germ gets into the bloodstream, it does not isolate itself in the right arm and spare the left; it is the whole body that is stricken. So with humanity. Being one body, everyone who belongs to our race is sinful to some degree. It is *our* wicked world, not *theirs*. It is not one group alone who are the cause of the world's ills. All of us stand in need of redemption. The more Christian a soul is, the more it sees itself responsible for its neighbor's sins; such a man or woman seeks to take that sin upon himself as if it were his own — as Christ, the Innocent, took upon Himself the guilt of the whole world. As the truest sympathy for those who mourn is to weep, so the true love for the guilty is to atone for their guilt. The burden of the world's regeneration is therefore laid on the one who knows Christ and hears His Voice in the Church and incorporates himself in His Body and Blood in the Eucharist. A sense of our solidarity in evil can then become a solidarity in goodness.

But there is no mathematical equality — no tit for tat — in the work of redemption. Ten just men could have saved Sodom and Gomorrah. In the Divine reckoning, it is Carmelite nuns and Trappist monks who are doing more to save the world than the politicians and the generals. The alien spirit that preempts civilization can be driven out only by prayers and fasting.

In the face of evil there are three kinds of souls. There are those who do evil and deny that there is evil or call it good. "Yea, the hour comes, that whosoever kills you, will think that he does a service to God" (John 16:2). There are also those who see evil in others, but not in themselves, and who flatter their own "virtue" by criticizing the sinful. "You hypocrite, cast out first the beam out of your own eye, and then you shall see to cast out the mote out of your brother's eye" (Matt. 7: 5). Finally, there are those who carry the burden of another's woe and sin as their own.

We are being taught in this century that the divisions that sever some people from others are very frail. Physical calamity breaks down these barriers. Modern warfare destroys the boundary line of combatant and civilian — not that it should do so, but, at least, its violations reveal that in a crisis the peril is not mine nor thine, but ours. When enough devout souls transfer this oneness of humanity from the physical to the moral and spiritual order, the world will be reborn.

Catastrophe can be to a world that has forgotten God what a sickness can be to a sinner; in the midst of it millions might be brought not to a voluntary, but to an enforced, crisis. Such a calamity would put an end to Godlessness and make vast numbers of people, who might otherwise lose their souls, turn to God. After a succession of hot, sultry days in the summer, we sense that there must be a storm before the cool days come back again. Similarly, in these days of confusion, there is an intuition of impending catastrophe, a feeling that some immense preternatural disturbance must bring the evil of the world to ruins before we can be set free again. As De Goncourt told Berthelot, who had boasted of the future destructiveness of war through the science of physics: "I think that when that day comes God, as a night-watchman, will come down from Heaven, rattling His keys, saying: 'Gentlemen! It is closing time.'" If that happens, we shall have to start all over again. It is not a question of the end of the world, but the end of an era — a manifestation of the sublime truth that the denial of Christian morality and truth brings us all to the edge of catastrophe, to the very rim of dissolution.

It has been said, "In time of peace, prepare for war." But we had better revise this and say, "In times of turmoil and dissolution, prepare to meet God!" When disaster comes and treasures are dissolved as an "unsubstantial pageant," the soul is more apt to turn to God in fear and in desperation. Here the tension is not between the sinner and the Christ of Mercy, nor between the aspiring soul and Christ the Holy One of God, but between the broken man and Christ the Judge. There will be some, even in crisis, who will rise against God, for the sins of blasphemy, as the Apocalypse tells us, will multiply with the pouring out of the vials of wrath. But the vast majority of people will, for the first time, realize that God's Judgment deals a sterner blow the farther we depart from His paths.

This kind of conversion can also occur among those who already have the faith. Christians will become real Christians, with less façade and more foundation. Catastrophe will divide them from the world, force them to declare their basic loyalties; it will revive shepherds who shepherd rather than administrate, reverse the proportion of saints and scholars in favor of saints, create more reapers for the harvest, more pillars of fire for the lukewarm; it will make the rich see that real wealth is in the service of the needy; and, above all else, it will make the glory of Christ's Cross shine out in a love that humans have for one another as true and loyal sons and daughters of God and devoted children of the Mother with an Immaculate Heart.

The crisis is upon us all, whatever our condition and whoever we be. But the crisis will not be conscious or effective so long as it is unaccompanied by desire. Now, desire implies *possibility:* "Nothing is impossible with *God.*" If there is no God, then nothing is possible. The desire for God is to the soul what breathing is to the body — breathing brings into our beings the possibility of physical life from the outside, as prayer, which is the highest expression of desire, brings into our souls the possibility of participation in God. This desire is not wholly the soul's own, for it feels itself to some degree under a sweet compulsion; God is pressing the soul, all the while it seems to be pressing Him. Later on, the soul will understand that even the desire for God came from God and that the fires that burned within itself were kindled from the hearth of God.

Conversion does not automatically follow on this longing; unless the desire for God is stronger than old habits and passions, the crisis of desire can end in frustration. The grace of conversion can pass — then one has missed the boat, has missed the Bark of Peter. The desire was there; but, because it was not prized highly, the ideal of Christ was given up, and the carnal and the worldly remained.

There has never been a convert who lacked desire — desire for God and also the desire to become a different person from any he has been before. When Ernest Psichari, the grandson of Renan, left his haunts of sin in France to go to the desert to find God, he said, "I have no stronger desire, no

firmer purpose. than to go across the world to conquer myself by force. I will not cross the land of all virtues as a mere
tourist.... God will enter under our roof when He wills."
Grace — the "entering" — is God's part; cultivating and harboring the desire for grace is our God-given part: "Ask, and
it shall be given you; seek, and you shall find; knock, and it
shall be opened to you" (Matt. 7:7).

God never refuses grace to those who honestly ask for it.
All He asks is that the vague thirst for the Infinite which has
urged the soul on to seek its good in a succession of pleasures
shall now be transformed into a thirst for God Himself. All
we need do is to voice these two petitions: Dear Lord, illumine my intellect to see the Truth, and give me the strength
to follow it. It is a prayer that is *always* answered. And it
makes no difference whether the desire for God we voice has
come from our disgusts, satieties, and despair or whether it
is born of our love of the beautiful, the perfect. God is willing to take either our old bones or our young dreams, for He
loves us, not because of the way we are, but because of what
we can be through His grace.

Curiously enough, it is a fear of how grace *will* change
and improve them that keeps many souls away from God.
They want God to take them as they are and to let them stay
that way. They want Him to take away their love of riches,
but not their riches — to purge them of the disgust of sin,
but not of the pleasure of sin. Some of them equate goodness with indifference to evil and think that God is good if
He is broad-minded or tolerant about evil. Like the onlook-
ers at the Cross, they want God on their terms, not His, and
they shout, "Come down, and we will believe." But the things
they ask are the marks of a *false* religion: It promises salvation without a cross, abandonment without sacrifice, Christ
without His nails. God is a consuming fire; our desire for God
must include a willingness to have the chaff burned from our

intellect and the weeds of our sinful will purged. The very fear souls have of surrendering themselves to the Lord with a cross is an evidence of their instinctive belief in His Holiness. Because God is Fire, we cannot escape Him, whether we draw near for conversion or flee from aversion: In either case, He affects us. If we accept His love, its fires will illumine and warm us; if we reject Him, they will still burn on in us in frustration and remorse.

As all human beings are touched by God's flaming love, so also are all touched by the desire for His intimacy. No one escapes this longing; we are all kings in exile, miserable without the Infinite. Those who reject the grace of God have a desire to *avoid* God, as those who accept it have a desire *for* God. The modern atheist does not disbelieve because of his intellect, but because of his will; it is not knowledge that makes him an atheist, but perversity. The denial of God springs from a person's desire not to have a God — from his wish that there were no Justice behind the universe, so that his injustices would fear no retribution; from his desire that there be no Law, so that he may not be judged by it; from his wish that there were no Absolute Goodness, that he might go on sinning with impunity. That is why the modern atheist is always angered when he hears anything said about God and religion — he would be incapable of such a resentment if God were only a myth. His feeling toward God is the same as that which a wicked person has for one whom he has wronged: He wishes the other were dead so that he could do nothing to avenge the wrong. The betrayer of friendship knows his friend exists, but he wishes he did not; the post-Christian atheist knows God exists, but he desires He should not.

We cannot escape God's justice by denying Him, but His friendship is easy to evade. He never forces our love. The surrender of the will to God is all-important in conversion because of this: God will not destroy our human freedom.

He will not even give proofs so absolutely overpowering as to destroy all choice, for He always leaves a margin for love. Therefore a necessary prelude to conversion is a spirit become docile, teachable, and humble. For if we think we know it all, not even God can teach us.

As soon as a person becomes humble, he recognizes his own long self-deception, the little tricks he has played on himself to conceal his unadmitted desire for God. Humility is truth, the recognition of ourselves as we are. That is why, when anyone accuses us of being a sheepstealer, we smile; but when we are accused of being a liar, we are apt to become angry, for it may be true. The penalty of pride is the inability to be really converted: "For the heart of this people is grown gross, and with their ears they have been dull of hearing, and their eyes they have shut; lest at any time they should see with their eyes, and hear with their ears, and understand with their heart, and be converted, and I should heal them" (Matt. 13:15).

Humility is so essential, indeed, that our Lord declared conversion to be dependent on our becoming childlike in affection and desire: "Amen, I say to you, unless you be converted, and become as little children, you shall not enter into the kingdom of Heaven. Whosoever therefore shall humble himself as this little child, he is the greater in the kingdom of Heaven" (Matt. 18:3, 4).

In conclusion, then: This tension between the flesh and the spirit, between the pull of time and the leash of eternity — this dialectic between the love of selfish pleasure and the desire for spiritual peace is in every single soul. The reason why more souls do not come to God is because they do not love God enough; they have placed a stronger longing on the side of the scales opposing Him. But they will never escape Him, even so; the tug of war continues while they live.

Every frustrated soul who is not insane is in this state because it has fought off the high summons of Divinity. " 'Tis vain to flee, for He is Everywhere. He that seems to be your Foe, is your only Fortress; He that seems to strike the blow, alone can stay it."

Will you continue this futile flight until it is too late? Will you die before your sins are dead? Or will you consent to desire God before all your passions are spent? What better time than now, with souls all unwashed, to come to His purifying hands? He alone is our way. Flee Him, and we are lost. He alone is our light. Depart from it, and we are blind. He alone is life. Leave Him, and we must die. Are we afraid that, if we shake the fires of our souls with desire, the ashes will choke our life? Do we say we have nothing to give — that our years have crackled and gone up in smoke? But if we cannot bring goodness to Him, we can bring Him our sins.

You say you are depressed and low in spirits? He brought you low only to make you want His heights!

Notes

1. *The Confession of St. Augustine,* p. 149, Peter Pauper Press, Mount Vernon, N.Y.

2. *Summa Theologiae,* I–2, q. 109, art. 3.

3. *Conversions,* edited by Maurice Leahy, pp. 68, 69, Benziger Bros., 1933.

Chapter 13

THE THEOLOGY OF CONVERSION

PSYCHIATRY IS ABLE to give a certain measure of peace of mind, for it adjusts the mind to the mood and temper of the world; but it never inquires whether we *ought* to adjust ourselves so completely to the present society. "I have taken you out of the world," said the Savior. It is now becoming evident, even to the cynic, that those who help the world most are the ones detached from the world. Peace of *soul* is a different and a finer thing; it results from justice, not from adjustment, from rebirth, not from integration to the values of the moment. *Pax opus justitiae.* Justice implies the subordination of the body to the soul and of the whole person to God and to neighbor. On the other hand, adjustment is to become acceptable to those around us, whether they are good or bad, wise or foolish, saints or such individuals as a saint would rather flee than emulate.

It is important to distinguish between the two kinds of peace. Peace of mind rests principally on what is called "sublimation," which psychology describes as a redirection of an instinct, passion, or energy from a crude, impulsive form to a creative activity that is social and, to some extent, ethical. There is nothing very new about sublimation except the name, for, throughout the ages, all wise teachers have recognized that it is important to divert man's interests from the base to the noble. Educators have always known that a child who is unduly curious can often have his curiosity sublimated into a healthy interest in science or history; the pugnacious instinct is sometimes sublimated through debating societies; the lawlessness of a boy can be sublimated by putting him in charge of a group, where he has to enforce the law. Such sublimations, useful as they are, can never give peace of soul, because this comes *only from God*. Psychological attempts to make man create this sort of peace — which he has no potentiality to create — are like trying to get a spinning top to begin spinning in the other direction.

No flat tire can fix itself, and no frustrated, unhappy person can get well without the introduction into his nature of something that is not already there. Something more is needed to cure a person than his own libido or instinct. Water can never rise above its own level, and no amount of drainage from the unconscious to the conscious can make the stream of thought clearer, cleaner, or stronger. When the patient attempts to accomplish sublimation on his own, he is very apt — rightly — to have the feeling that he is practicing autosuggestion, a rather dangerous experiment. If the energy for betterment is believed to come from an outside human source, such as the psychiatrist, he feels — sometimes rightly — that he is being manipulated by someone incapable of judging all the factors of his case; if the psychiatrist is one of those who deny the soul, this is nearly always true.

If a person is physically sick, he does not try to cure himself by expecting medicines to develop within his own body. Neither can a soul that is spiritually sick completely heal itself by its own efforts, without an energy and a power brought in from the outside. The sick person's own will is not sufficient; it is because the will and the instincts are at odds that he is suffering. Nor can human ideals alone cure him — these make no provision for the conflicts of those who cannot attain to them. Even the noblest of abstract ideals are of little use to a person who feels himself a failure, shut off from the possibility of success, and too weak to achieve virtue.

It is precisely because many individuals are painfully conscious of their weakness and frustration that they yearn for a compulsive system of life that will dispense them from all responsibility, without fully evaluating the reason for their flight.

There is something both good and bad in this, as the prodigal son was right in being hungry and wrong in feeding on husks.

The modern soul, too, is right in hungering for a law higher than its own will, wrong in taking that law from a dictator. With the denial of God, eternal destinies, and moral righteousness, it has become disgusted with its own inadequacy, its own unworthiness to serve as a proper object of narcissistic devotion. Like the child in the progressive school, it asks, "Must I always do whatever I want?" Having denied Eternal Love as the object of its choice, it now turns to something apparently greater than self. It is right in wanting something to adore and love with an intense passion; it is wrong in adoring a false god.

When one meditates upon the number of individuals who, in the midst of their frustrations, try to find healing without the aid of a Divine Physician, without an energy more powerful than themselves, one is reminded of the words of Carlyle, "The tragedy of life is not so much what men suffer, but rather how much they miss." The greatest opportunity they miss is that of becoming something more than their humanity. For it is possible for a human being to live on one of three levels. The first level is the subhuman, or the animal, in which a person is content to live only for his body, for his flesh and its pleasures; when a whole society lives thus, we have what Sorokin has called a "Sensate Culture." If reason is used at all on this lowest level, it is only to discover new techniques for providing thrills and amusements for the animal nature. A human can also live on a second, or higher, level, the rational; here he will pursue a good pagan life and will defend the natural virtues, but without great enthusiasm. Under the inspiration of reason alone, he is tolerant, philanthropic; he favors the underdog and contributes to community enterprises, but he refuses to believe that there is a knowledge beyond the reach of his own intellect or a strength exceeding his own will. High above these two levels there is a third, which is the Divine level; in this, a human being, thanks to the grace of God, is elevated to the supernatural order and is made a child of God.

These three levels might be compared to a three-story house: The first floor is hardly furnished at all; the second has some comforts; but the third is orderly, luxurious, and full of peace. An individual who lives for purely animal pleasures will take as sheer nonsense the suggestion that there is a level of reason above the first floor, where he lives according to his lusts. And to suggest to those who live on the second floor of reason that there is still a floor above, where peace of mind becomes peace of soul, is to invite them to ridicule the supernatural order. Those who dwell on the second floor have no understanding whatever of the supernatural; they regard it as a pious extra, as unessential as frost on a windowpane or frosting on a cake. They are willing to admit that there is assimilation in the universe and that the progress has been upward and vertical from the chemical to man, but when it comes to the development of man himself, they refuse to admit a continuation of the same vertical process. They see the past in terms of an upward process until man was produced; from that time on, they insist that it moves only on a horizontal plane and that man's progress is to be measured by his growing skill in the manipulation of nature and wealth and the acquiring of better material conditions — all of which are external to man. Those who refuse to mount to the third floor from the second are much like the two tadpoles who were one day discussing the possibility of a realm higher than that of the tadpoles. One little tadpole said to the other. "I think I will stick my head above the water to see what the rest of the world looks like." The other tadpole said, "Don't be foolish. You don't mean to tell me that there is anything in this world besides water!"

A reasonable being should ask himself why — if chemicals can enter into plants, and plants be taken up into animals, and animals be taken into man — why man himself, who is the peak of visible creation, should be denied the privilege of being assimilated into higher power? The rose has no right to say that there is no life above it — and neither has man, who has a vast capacity and unconquerable yearning for eternal life and truth and love.

The supernatural, the third level on which we may live, is not an outgrowth of the natural, as the oak develops from an acorn. It marks a complete break, a beginning anew. The development is not a gradual progress, in which a person becomes more tolerant, more broad-minded, more articulate about social justice, less hateful and less avaricious, until finally he reaches a point where he finds himself a Christian and a citizen of the supernatural order. That is not the way it happens.

It is a law of physics that a body continues in a state of rest or uniform motion in a straight line until it is compelled by outside forces to change that state; man, too, is subject to inertia, and he will remain in a merely natural state unless he is changed from the outside. Stones do not become elephants, nor elephants people. Man, by nature, is only a creature of God, almost as a stone or a bird is a creature of God — although man reflects some of the attributes of the Creator more faithfully than the stars and the plants do. In truth, the supernatural order is something to which man is not entitled; nevertheless it once belonged to our race. But the supernatural privilege of being a child of God, entitled to call Him Father, was always as unattainable to the nature of man as life is to a crystal. If a piece of marble suddenly burst into bloom, that would be a "supernatural" act, for it does not belong to the powers, the nature, or the capacities of marble to bloom. If a flower suddenly began to move from place to place, and to touch, and to taste, and to feel, that would be a "supernatural" act, for it does not belong to the flower's nature, its powers, or its capacities to possess the five senses. If a dog suddenly began to quote Shakespeare and Sophocles, that would be a "supernatural" act for a dog; it does not belong to the nature, the powers, or the capacities of a dog to reason. Man is by nature a creature of God, as humbly as a table is a creature of the carpenter; if he suddenly begins to throb with the very life of God, so that he can call God not his Creator but his Father, that is a supernatural act for a man. Man then *becomes* something which he *was* not; that elevation of his nature can come only as a gift from God.

A plant is more than the sum of the chemicals that enter into it, because a plant possesses an X quality that is not in the chemical order; an animal is something more than the sum of plant qualities, because it possesses an X that is not found in the antecedent order; and, in the same way, man possesses an X quality that makes him different from the animal, something that makes him able to laugh and think and freely love. But when a human enters the supernatural order, a new and greater X quality is introduced — something that is different in its nature from the sum of merely natural virtues he may have possessed before. That is why, throughout the Sacred Scriptures, man is constantly invited to become something that he is *not*. There is assumed, throughout the Scriptures, a difference between making and begetting: We make what is unlike us — for example, someone makes a table; but we beget what is like us — for example, a father begets a child. Inasmuch as we are made by God, we are unlike Him in His Divine Nature; inasmuch as we are begotten by God, we can become like Him, be partakers of His Nature, assume our place as His Children and the Heirs of the Kingdom of God. This is possible only because of a miraculous elevation, which is not ours by right or nature; for if the supernatural order were natural to man, then man himself would be God.

This raises the important question of *how* man may become more than he was — of what happens when a person is converted. The answer is this: A human is lifted to the supernatural order and is converted from a creature to a partaker of the Divine Nature. This can come about only through the grace of God, with which the person freely cooperates.

There is throughout nature a law that says that no lower order is ever lifted into a higher order without two things: There must be a descent of the higher order to the lower order, and, second, the lower order must surrender itself to the higher. Before the phosphates, the carbon, the sunlight, and the moisture can be absorbed into plant life, the plant must come down to the chemical order and take it up into itself; and the phosphates, the carbon, the sunlight, and the moisture must give up their lower existence when they are elevated. The plant cannot begin to live in the animal unless first the animal comes down to the plant life and lifts it up into itself; but the plant, too, immolates itself for the animal — it must be torn up from the roots and ground beneath the very jaws of death; then, and then only, does it begin to live in the animal kingdom and to share the joys of sentiency that it did not possess before. The animal begins to live in man only when man goes down to the animal and takes it unto himself; but the animal, in its turn, must submit itself to the knife and to the fire, for only by surrendering its lowly existence can it begin to live in the higher kingdom of man; then the animal participates in the life of a thinking, willing, and loving human being. If the plants and the animals could speak, they would say to the things that are below them, "Unless you die to yourself, you cannot live in my kingdom." Man, who *can* speak, says to the chemicals, the plants and the animals, "Unless you die to your lower nature, you cannot begin to live in my kingdom." The reward for the immolation of all these lower orders is that they now live in man a far more magnificent kind of existence than they could attain in themselves. They fall under a new government, their existence is ennobled, their life is enriched, their nature is elevated; this is the reward of their surrender.

How does man begin to live the higher life in God? First of all, God must come down to him, the Eternal must invade human history: This is the meaning of the Incarnation. Second, man must himself surrender his lower nature. But here there appears a difference between man and all other creatures — man is a *person,* which sunshine, grass, and cows are not. *Their* lower natures are destroyed by surrendering themselves to man, but since man is a person, his personality is indestructible. What man surrenders, then, is not his whole nature, but only that portion of it which is sinful, which is ungodlike. In conversion a man suffers a mortification, a kind of spiritual death, but his personality survives.

The specific act by which a human dies to his lower nature is the Sacrament of Baptism. This commencement of his supernatural life does not mark a mere change of direction, but an elevation or, better still, a re-generation. We can therefore understand why the old man in the Gospel story who asked what he must do to be saved was told by Our Blessed Lord that he must be born again. The aged Nicodemus thought that these words meant that he must enter again into his mother's womb; but Our Lord informed him that "...unless a person be born again of water and the Holy Spirit, he cannot enter into the kingdom of God. That which is born of the flesh is flesh; and that which is born of the Spirit, is spirit" (John 3:5, 6). The very heart of Christianity is the inspiration for man to strive to become something that he is not: "But as many as received him, he gave them power to be made the children of God, to them that believe in his name: Who are born, not of blood, nor of the will of the flesh, nor of the will of man, but of God" (John 1:12, 13).

As the soul gives life to the body, so does grace, or participation in the Divine Nature, give life to the soul. A body can be alive when its soul is dead. To the eyes of the spirit, every city and town is filled with such spiritual cadavers. The people seem to be alive; they eat, they go to movies, marry, talk politics, and they have one chance in 12,000 of being interviewed for a Kinsey Report — but their souls are dead. Yet this death need not be permanent, for while there is physical life, there is spiritual hope for everyone. So long as there is breath, there is still a possibility that the human nature will be divinized by grace.

Those who are spiritually alive do not see Jesus Christ as just a moral teacher or a great humanitarian; they know that He might be more appropriately called the Great Divinitarian, God in human flesh, true God and true man, whose purpose in coming to this earth was to give back to us that supernatural life which was lost through the original sin: "I am come that they may have life, and may have it more abundantly" (John 10:10). In the universe, seen from the Divine point of view, there are no races or nations; there are, however, two humanities. There are those who are born of the flesh, and they belong to the humanity of Adam; but those who are born of the spirit belong to the new and redeemed humanity of the new Adam, Christ, Who was mothered through Mary. What physical birth is to the child of nature, Baptism is to the spiritual child of God. Children resemble their parents because they share the same nature; so, thanks to Baptism, spiritual children begin to resemble God, for now they are born of His Nature.

There are other parallels between the physical and the supernatural: For the human race to carry on its natural life, seven conditions are required — they must be born; they must be nourished; some of them must grow to maturity and assume its responsibilities; if their bodies are wounded, the wounds must be healed; if there is disease, the traces of that disease must be driven out; there must be propagation, to perpetuate the race; and humanity, to survive, must live under some rule of order and government. In order that we may lead the supernatural life, Our Blessed Lord has instituted seven Sacraments, analogous to these seven conditions of physical life. Material signs are used in the Sacraments, as channels for the communication of His grace. If we were angels, we should need no such visible signs; but since we have bodies, as well as souls, and since nature rebelled through man's offense, it is fitting that nature, too, should be restored to God. Hence the use of oil, bread, water, hands, and wine in the administration of the seven Sacraments.

As a person must be born before he can begin to lead his physical life, so he must be born to lead a Divine Life. That birth occurs in the Sacrament of Baptism. To survive, the person must be nourished by Divine Life; that is done in the Sacrament of the Holy Eucharist. He must grow spiritually and assume his spiritual responsibilities; that is accomplished in the Sacrament of Confirmation. He must heal the wounds of sin; for this there is the Sacrament of Penance. He must wipe out the traces of sin at the end, to prepare for his journey to eternal life; for this there is the Sacrament of Extreme Unction. Man must also prolong and edify the Kingdom of

God, for which he is given the Sacrament of Matrimony. He must live under a spiritual government; this *is* provided through the Sacrament of Holy Orders in the Priesthood.

Nature *makes* human nature, but grace *remakes* human nature. Every person who has been born can also be regenerated, renewed, and revived if he establishes contact with new and divine sources of energy. Christianity puts a high value on human nature, but it does not trust its unaided powers too far. It says that man in his human nature is neither a saint nor a devil; he is neither intrinsically corrupt nor immaculately conceived. He needs divine assistance to perfect this nature. And it is available to him, no matter how wicked he has been in the past; even a man who stoned a martyr like Stephen, as Paul did, can still be saved, not of himself but by the grace of God — as Paul was. And since the new energy and new power to rescue him come from God, it is beside the point for anyone to plead, "I am not good enough." Of course not — no person is good enough. But hidden reserves of power are available to anyone who so desires. That was why Our Savior said, "Ask, and it shall be given you: seek, and you shall find: knock and it shall be opened to you" (Matt. 7:7).

Those who lack grace — that gift of God which is given so freely — have physical life but do not have spiritual life. This raises the question, "Why does not everyone accept grace?" The answer is to be found in the fact that man, alone in all nature, is free. The grass does not need to consult the moisture before it absorbs it to itself; the cow need not plead with the grass to come with it into the animal kingdom; but man is free, and God will break down no doors to force a higher destiny upon our wills. The Divine may only entreat and plead; He will show how much He loves us by dying to redeem us. But He will not use force, even to save us from our own shortsighted preference for a meaner share of life.

Some people in backward countries refuse vaccination;

they fear to be saved by a mystery they do not comprehend. Some sick people do not want to see a doctor; they are afraid the doctor may advise an operation as a condition of recovering their health. In the spiritual realm, too, we can refuse to be healed. We cannot initiate our own salvation — for the first movement of regeneration comes from God — but we can prevent it by our refusal to cooperate. Grace and human freedom are related like the two wings of a bird; both are needed for flight. Grace is a gift, and any gift can be rejected. Love is never imposed — to impose it would be to destroy love.

Because the acceptance of grace is a free act, implying a choice, it follows that some people will always be unwilling to accept it, especially since it invariably demands a sacrifice. The rich young man in the Gospel went away sad because he had great possessions; Saint Augustine, at one time in his life, said, "Dear Lord, I want to be good, but later on, not now." The great problem, facing every human, concerns not sublimation, but elevation. Are we willing to surrender the lower to find the ecstasies of the higher? Do we want God enough to overcome the obstacles that keep Him away? Do we love the sunlight enough to open the blinds our own agnosticism has drawn down?

The acceptance of grace is not a passive thing; it demands a surrender of something, even if it is only our pride. This fact alone should give pause to those naturalists who tell us that the supernatural is only a myth, for since when do myths and fantasies call for such sacrifices or make demands that are so hard to meet? Myths ask only for credulity — never for the plucking out of an eye or the cutting off of an arm, as does the Gospel. Yet these sacrifices must be made, this price paid, if we are to live full lives. No sculptor can chisel, no artist can paint, unless he detaches himself from noisy chatter in order to commune with the beautiful; so we can gain intimacy with the Divine only if we respond to God's invitation of grace with a willingness to give up some tawdry treasure, to surrender the field in order to buy the pearl of great price.

Then life can really begin, for, without the supernatural gift, every human is undeveloped still. Feed a person until he is "fed-up"; surround him with the materials to satisfy his every passion; give him license to do whatever he pleases; castle him; cage him; satiate him; cuddle him; amuse him! And invariably, time and time again, he will still be seeking for that which he has not, grasping for something already beyond his reach, hungering for the unworldly in the heart of the world. Without this great reality of God, man knows himself to be only half real and adequately describes himself as "I am not." Thus does he dimly perceive the great need of Him Who defines Himself as "Amen, amen I say to you, before Abraham was made, I am" (John 8:58).

The refusal of God's supernatural gift is the most tragic mistake a human being can make. Its acceptance is called conversion. Contrary to the common belief, a conversion is not caused by the emotions; emotions reflect only a mental state, and this change concerns the soul. Conversion, again, has nothing to do with sublimation; that process, too, is restricted to the order of nature. Conversion looks upward, not inward; it is an experience in no way related to the upsurge of unconsciousness into the consciousness. Conversion, first and foremost, and above all else, is due to Divine Grace, a gift of God that illumines our intellect to perceive truths that we never perceived before and strengthens our will to follow those truths, even though they demand sacrifices in the natural order. Conversion is due to the invasion of a new power, to the inner penetration of spirit and spirit, to the influence of the changeless upon the fluid character of man.

In his new awareness of the presence of a Divine Power, the individual turns over his *whole* personality, not to his "higher self," but to the higher new self, which is God. Those who have responded to that gift of grace begin to feel the presence of God in a new way. Their religion ceases to be "moralistic" in the sense that a person merely submits himself to a code, a law, and feels the necessity of obeying them as a duty. Religion also rises above the pietistic level on which there is a loving remembrance of Our Lord, a kind of sentimental fellow-traveling, through hymns and sermons, with One who lived 1900 years ago. For although some people have found a considerable emotional fulfillment on this pietistic plane, it is not Christianity and does not become so until one enters the third stage, the Mystical. Here at last — where Christ actually dwells in our hearts, and where there is an awareness rooted in love, and where the soul feels the tremendous impact of God working on itself — here is found the joy that surpasses all understanding.

Chapter 14

THE EFFECTS OF CONVERSION

THE TORMENTED MINDS of today are not the products of our tormented world. Rather, it is our upset minds that have upset the world. There is no such thing as the problem of the atomic bomb; there is, rather, the problem of those who make and use it. Only men and nations whose personalities were already atomized could join forces with external nature to use an atomic bomb in an attack on human existence. Man, by attempting to exist either apart from God or defiant of God, has made the world as delirious as his own mind is neurotic. The crisis today is so deep in its causes that all social and political attempts to deal with it are bound to be as ineffective as talcum powder in curing jaundice. It is man who has to be remade *first;* then society will be remade by the restored new man. The dictators that have been cast upon the shores of the twentieth century are not the creators of the disorder, but rather its creatures. They are symptoms, not causes, of the universal breakdown of a moral order in the heart of humanity. The constant refusal of man to allow a suprahistoric Divine Power to break into his closed mind is the pride that prepares catastrophe. Most people are intuitively aware that no change other than a spiritual change will be enough: The extreme sensitiveness and ready anger of those who urge revolutions against society and morality as their remedy are proof of the insecurity of their very position. The violence of their opposition to all criticism is a sure sign of the defenselessness of their own position; even they suspect that mankind stands less in need of revolution than redemption.

Humanity cannot redeem itself by its own human reason or power; but human beings can use both reason and power in cooperation with Divine Grace. This is what a person does when he becomes converted. It is time now to talk of the effect such a conversion has on the soul. The soul is now open to the working of Sanctifying Grace, which elevates our nature so that we *become* something we were not naturally — partakers of the Divine Nature Who descended to the level of our mortality to make us share His Life. This new grace, which adds Divine to human filiation so that we become Children of God as well as children of our parents, is not extrinsic to the soul or a mere imputation of the merit of Christ. There is a *reality* in the soul that was not there before — a created reality that comes directly from God Himself, a reality we ourselves cannot merit in the strict sense of the term. That is why it is called a grace; it is *gratis*, or free.

One effect of grace is that Our Divine Lord is no longer extrinsic to us, as He is for those who think of Him as only a historical figure Who lived over 1900 years ago. If Our Divine Savior had remained on earth, they would be right: He would be only an example to be copied, a voice to be heard. But once He ascended into Heaven and sent His Spirit to us, then He ceased to be only a model to be copied and became a Life to be lived.

Though we are more interested here in pointing out the psychological effects of grace on the soul than its many theological effects, two of these are too important to be omitted. These are the Divine Presence in the soul after Baptism and the incorporation of the individual into the Mystical Body of Christ. "Presence of God" is a phrase very loosely used today to cover anything from the Pantheism of the Lake poets to the vague sentimentalism of the Romanticist, who likes the woods because he "feels" God there. God is, indeed, present in the universe in many various ways, as any artist can be present in various ways, *e.g.*, in his painting, as its creator; in a museum, as a representative of culture; and in his children, as a father. God is present in the whole universe as Cause, and in this sense He is in the flowers and the trees. But a far more intimate presence was evidenced in the Incarnation, where God appeared as man in the heart of a new humanity that was to become His new Body.

The Incarnation (in the Hypostatic Union) made God man. The union of grace and nature makes us deified. As the actions of Jesus Christ were both Divine and human, so those of a person in the state of grace are God-like, being performed by both God and man; these acts are meritorious of heaven. The presence of God in such a soul is not a mere sentimental manner of speech, but a *real possession*. Because we have become adopted children of God by being born of Him, we now live by the Spirit of Christ. "For you have not received the spirit of bondage again in fear; but you have received the spirit of adoption of sons, whereby we cry: Abba, Father" (Rom. 8:15). The body has now become the Temple of God. "Or know you not, that your members are the temple of the Holy Spirit, who is in you, whom you have from God; and you are not your own" (1 Cor. 6:19).

Christ is the Head of such sanctified souls, and they stand in relation to Him as members of His Body. "And he has subjected all things under his feet, and has made him head over all the church, which is his body, and the fulness of him who is filled all in all" (Eph. 1:22, 23). The relation between Christ and His Body, the Church, was said by Christ Himself to be like that of the vine and its branches: "Yet a little while: and the world sees me no more. But you see me: because I live, and you shall live. In that day you shall know, that I am in my Father, and you in me, and I in you" (John 14:19, 20). "Now you are clean by reason of the word, which I have spoken to you. Abide in me, and I in you. As the branch cannot bear fruit of itself, unless it abide in the vine, so neither can you unless you abide in me. I am the vine; you the branches: he that abides in me, and I in him, the same bears much fruit: for without me you can do nothing" (John 15:3–5).

Jacques B. Bossuet has expressed this intimate relation of Christ with His Body, the Church, by describing the latter as the "prolongation of the Incarnation." Christ can have only one Body; therefore there cannot be many churches. Any church founded this morning or yesterday afternoon or even a hundred years ago is too remote from Pentecost to be Christ's Body. The Body and the Soul, the Church and the Holy Spirit — these must have been allied from the beginning.

The unity among the members of that Body cannot be a vague and undetermined association that any member is free to change, any more than a human body can be changeable, sometimes having one eye and one ear or no heart and seven lungs. The unity of the faithful in Christ's Body is not organizational, although an organization is necessary, and although those who admire the Church for its unity of belief and faith and liturgy attribute this to its organization. The Church is, rather, an organism. As a human body is one because it has one soul, one visible head, and one invisible mind, so the Church, the Mystical Body of Christ, is one because it has one soul — the Holy Spirit of God — one visible Head — Peter and his successors — and one invisible Head — Christ. As Christ took upon Himself a human nature from the womb of His Mother (overshadowed by the Holy Spirit), so He took from the womb of humanity (overshadowed by the Pentecostal Spirit) His Mystical Body, the Church. Christ teaches through His Body — therefore, His teaching is infallible. He governs through His Body — therefore, the authority is Divine. He sanctifies through His Body — therefore, the sanctification accomplished in the Sacraments does not depend on the personality or character of those who administer the Sacraments.

The Church is the *Totus Christus,* the Whole Christ, and it complements the individual Christ. In its physical aspect Christ's Body is perfect, but in its mystical aspect it is merely growing to perfection, for now it includes not only Him but us, with our imperfections. The prayers, sacrifices, and liturgy of the Church are offered not by the members alone — not by Christ, the Head alone — but by the *Head and members together* to the glory of God, the Everlasting Father. A new cell is added to the Mystical Body of Christ at every Baptism.

So much for the two most conspicuous effects of conversion in theological terms. But the *psychological* effects of conversion and incorporation into the Whole Christ are those of which the convert and his circle are sometimes more sensibly aware.

There is, first, *a recentering of life and a revolution of all its values.* This fresh, intellectual readjustment of thought to make room for God is one proof that conversion is not an emotional matter, for the emotions do not normally control the judgments. Before conversion, life is a confused and unintelligible blur, like the figures on a flattened Japanese lantern; afterward, it resembles that same lantern opened to its full height, with a candle inside to reveal the unity of pattern and design. Faith not only puts the candle into the lantern of life — it also lights it. A highly educated person before conversion may have had a vast knowledge of history, literature, science, anthropology, and philosophy, but these branches of his knowledge were divided into watertight compartments with no live correlation of one to the others; they were only isolated tidbits of information, a vast hors d'oeuvre of detail. After conversion the same facts are gathered into a unity, ordered in a hierarchy of knowledge that reveals an overwhelming evidence of Providence in history and also confers a new unity on one's personal life. What was before information has now become wisdom.

The unconverted soul was often exhausted, fatigued from having used up all its energies trying to find a purpose in life. It was tired in its mind and then tired in its body. A mind that cannot decide where it is going next soon exhausts itself by indecisiveness. Anxieties and fears possess the mind and fritter away the strength of the body. But once the goal of life is discovered, one does not need to waste his energy trying to discover it; the energy can now be spent in making the journey. The travel circulars are thrown away as one plunges into the joy of a voyage of discovery.

Many a young student in college is confused because he is without a philosophy of life or a pattern of existence. His education is but a substitution of this theory for that, a jettisoning of one relative point of view for another. The statistics he studied in his senior year are obsolete the year after graduation. His professors, who used the philosophy of Spencer as their inspiration twenty years ago, are now using Marx or Freud — within another ten years they will have found another substitute. Education has become little more than the mechanical replacing of one point of view by another, as the automobile displaced the horse and buggy. The mind is constantly solicited by contrary and contradictory points of view; it becomes more harassed than a body in constant oscillation between chill and fever. With conversion, education becomes an orderly progression from one truth that need never be discarded to the next. The student is given reasons and motives of credibility for an ordered philosophy of life; his education is now a growing penetration into a central mystery, a sounding of new depths of truth. His knowledge and understanding accrue, as life expands from cell to cell in the development of every living body.

Associated with the convert's sense of intellectual growth is a consciousness of being newly possessed of the intellectual heritage of the past, of having joined a living tradition of sound thinking. A past one respects is as essential for intellectual life as parenthood is essential for physical life. As an individual cannot think without a memory, neither can a society think without tradition. No longer uprooted from the past, but made the heir of its wealth, the convert ceases to visit the past as a mere antiquarian; he brings the past and the present into happy conjunction as the stepping-stone toward progress and enrichment in the future.

The convert's judgment of values in his personal life is no less radically transformed. Things that before seemed precious are now considered trivial, and things that before seemed inconsequential have now become the essence of real life. Without the Divine sense of values that conversion brings, the soul is like a department store where the wrong price tags are on everything; hairpins sell for a thousand dollars, and diamond rings for a nickel. Conversion hangs the right price tags on the right things and restores a true sense of values. That is why the outlook of a convert is entirely changed on such subjects as marriage, death, education, wealth, pain, and suffering. As a stained-glass window looks different from the inside of the church than it does from the outside, so all the great problems of life take on a new meaning and significance when one stands inside the Faith. Such a person now sees why religious education is essential — for unless the soul is saved, nothing is saved. Marriage is sacred to him because it is a symbol of the union of Christ and the Church. Suffering becomes bearable as a gift of God, to be offered in reparation for sin and for filling up the sufferings that are wanting to the Body of Christ; sickness is accepted in the knowledge that God is more concerned with what I *am* for Him than with what I *get done*. The old eagerness for economic security gives way to a serenity that does not worry about tomorrow before it comes and that trusts in *God* at all times. Peace is no longer understood to mean an escape from the crosses of life, but as the victory won over them by faith.

A second perceptible result of conversion is *a definite change in behavior and conduct of life*. Not only does conversion change one's values; it also reverses the tendencies and energies of life, directing them to another end. If the convert before conversion was already leading a good moral life, there is now less emphasis on keeping a law and more emphasis on maintaining a relationship of love. If the convert has been a sinner, his spiritual life frees him from habits and excesses that before weighed down the soul. He no longer need resort to alcohol or sleeping tablets. He often finds that these practices were not so much appetites as attempts to flee responsibility or to ensure, by plunging into unconsciousness, that he could avoid the necessity of choice. Before conversion, it was behavior that to a large extent determined belief; after conversion, it is belief that determines behavior. There is no longer a tendency to find scapegoats to blame for the faults of self, but rather a consciousness that the reformation of the world must begin with the reformation of self. There is still a fear of God, but it is not the servile fear a subject has for a dictator, but a filial fear, such as children have for a good parent whom they would never wish to hurt. From such a Love one does not ever need to run away, and the previous acts of dissipation, which were disguised forms of flight, are now renounced.

Once the soul has turned to God, there is no longer a struggle to give up these habits; they are not so much defeated, as crowded out by new interests. There is no longer a need of escape — for one is no longer in flight from oneself. The person who once did his own will now seeks to do God's will; the one who once served sin now hates it; the person who once found thoughts of God dry or even unpleasant now hopes above all else one day to behold the God Whom he loves. The transition the soul has undergone is as unmistakable as the passage from death to life; there has been, not a mere giving up of sin, but such a surrender to Divine Love as makes him shrink from sin because he would not wound the Divine Beloved.

Conscience, thus transformed in a convert, undergoes a paradoxical change: It is not nearly so harsh a master as before, in spite of the reform in conduct. It is true that behavior is changed — but that is only a surface proof of the fact that conscience is changed. Before conversion, conscience seemed to be a restraining, coercive power; God was a hostile and exacting judge; the commandments were prohibitions; and the Church was an inhibition. Responsibilities were identified with obligation; duty was seen as opposed to desire; the morally right was identified with the physically unpleasant; and love was opposed to morality. But after conversion the conscience no longer accuses; it never seems to command, or order, or inhibit, because there are no longer two wills in opposition. The will of the convert is the will of God. There is no need for a conscience to tell him what "ought to be done." Conscience is swallowed up in love, and there is no duty or "must" between lovers.

Duty, to the sinful mind, was the unwilling fulfillment of a command. Now, desiring only what God desires, the convert needs no restraint on his wishes; he is beyond good and evil, in that realm where there is no duty "*to* behave," but only the joy of living. What was previously a compulsory task is now a spontaneous pleasure. Converts who have had the habit of sleeping late are fearful at first that they will not be able to rise early enough for Sunday Mass —

and certainly not, they tell you, early enough for daily Mass. But once possessed of Divine Love, they find that early rising is a joy, for nothing is hard to one who loves. Before, life was based on self-determination, and the will always worked to safeguard self-interest and selfishness. Afterwards, life is Christ-determined; the convert wants no other mind than that of Christ, no other will than Christ's will. Behavior has changed at its source; now it issues from a relationship of love. Generosity is easy; sharing apples will not make people brothers and sisters, but if they are conscious of their relationship, they will gladly share an apple.

The new moral life is not austere or arduous, because there is no longer a feeling that one has to live up to a hated contract; instead, the convert is motivated by a feeling that he can never do enough for Him Whom he loves. The nagging reminder that one ought to avoid sin has been replaced by the desire that nothing must hinder us from drawing nearer to God. From this new orientation come the passion and zeal of a Saint Paul: "For I am sure that neither death, nor life, nor angels, nor principalities, nor powers, nor things present, nor things to come, nor might, nor height, nor depth, nor any other creature shall be able to separate us from the love of God, which is in Christ Jesus our Lord" (Rom. 8:38, 39).

But even this does not end the list of the convert's new benefits. He also receives *certitude*. Philosophy gives a proof for the existence of God; the science of apologetics gives the motives for believing in Christ, the Son of God; but all the incontrovertible proofs they offer fall short of the certitude that actually comes to a convert through the gift of Faith. Imagine a young man whose father has been lost for years. A friend, returned from a trip, assures him that he has certain evidence that his father really exists on another continent. But the young man is not fully satisfied with the evidence, however convincing it is; until he is restored to his father's actual presence, he will not have peace. So it is with conversion: Before, one knows *about* God; afterward, one *knows* God. The first knowledge the mind has is notional and abstract; the second is real, concrete, and it becomes bound up with all one's sentiments, emotions, passions, and habits. Before conversion, the truths seemed true but far off; they did not touch one personally. After conversion, they become so personalized that the mind knows that it is through with the search for a place to live; it can now settle down to the making of a home. The convert's certitude is so great that his mind does not feel that *an* answer has been given, but *the* answer — the absolute, final solution, which one would die for rather than surrender.

As a result, all the doubts and despair of the intellectual vanish — and here the Church differs from all other world religions. In other religions, doubts increase with the development of reason, but in the Church faith intensifies as reason develops. This is because our reason and our faith in Christ and His Mystical Body both derive from the same God of Light, whereas reason and belief in a pagan teacher often have different sources. Reason is from God, but a belief in pagan teaching comes merely from the external environment or through propaganda. It is historically true that an age of great faith in Christ is always an age of profound reason; the *Summa* of the thirteenth-century Thomas Aquinas is an example. This relation is a logical one: Just as reason is the perfection of the senses, so faith is the perfection of reason. A person neither sees nor walks as well when he is drunk as when he is sober; his senses lack the perfecting power of reason. In the same way, a mind reasoning without faith does not function as well as reasoning with faith.

Those who have never gone through the experience of a complete conversion imagine that reason must be completely abdicated for such a step. We hear them make such remarks as, "I cannot understand it; he seemed like an intelligent man." But those who have gone through the experience of conversion see that just as the eye winks, closing itself to the light for an instant that it may reopen and see better, so, too, one winks his reason for that brief instant in which he admits that it may not know *all* the answers. Then, when faith comes, the reason is found to be intact and clearer-sighted than before. Both reason and faith are now seen as deriving from God Himself; they can never, therefore, be in opposition. Knowing this, the convert loses all his doubts. His certitude in his faith becomes unshakable — indeed, is his old notions are now apt to be shaken by the earthquake of his faith.

Now the certitude in the Divinity and infallibility of Christ, in all that that implies, surpasses even the evidence and the arguments for it, for the certitude is derived from God Himself. "Flesh and blood has not revealed it to you, but my Father who is in heaven" (Matt. 16:17). Now the convert understands that there are three lights to guide humanity to happiness: there is the light of the sun for our senses, the light of reason for our sciences, theology and the light of faith for our religion and salvation. Those who lack the gift of faith and those who have it are like two persons looking at a rainbow: One of them is blind, and the other is blessed with eyesight. There are little children in our parochial schools who could never answer the objections of learned professors who might attack their faith; yet such objections would no more shake their faith than if they attempted to prove that their eyes could not see color nor their ears hear sounds.

This absence of confusion, this absolute conviction of Divine and Absolute Truth, is one of the greatest consolations of the faithful. The converted soul sees itself as the man born blind — now restored to vision and to light. As a result the soul becomes bolder in his judgments; the blinkers are now removed, and he has a Divine standard by which to judge not only his own actions but world events about him. Only a person of faith can understand the present world situation; such a person alone appreciates that it is not the clash of conflicting political systems, but a moral judgment on the way people think and live. Even in the midst of such tribulations as today's, his faith begets patience and productivity; thanks to the magnet of faith, all his scattered fragments of ideas are like iron filings, made of one piece and suffused with one energy.

But some will surely ask, "Don't conversion and the acceptance of the authority of the Church as the authority of Christ destroy human freedom? Doesn't the acceptance of the absolute of the Church imply authoritarianism?" The answer is negative. To myopic eyes, there may, indeed, seem to be a superficial resemblance between accepting the authority of the Church and accepting the authoritarianism of a Stalin. But there are three profound differences between the two.

First, the authoritarianism of modern politics is *external;* the authority of the Church is *internal.* The dictator's rule is imposed from without, is pressed on one as insistently as a dog barking at the heels of the sheep, and it is accepted coweringly and under pressure. Submission to arbitrary rules that do not coincide with our own best judgment leads to the complete destruction of personality. But the authority of the Church is never arbitrary, never communicated entirely from without; it coincides with the Truth of Christ, which is already in the soul and which has been accepted on evidence our reason approves. Here the authority accords with our conscience, and it completes the personality that submits to it. The relationship of the Christian and the Church is very much like that of a student and a professor: The more the student accepts the authority of the professor, the more the student learns, and the smaller the gap dividing them becomes; one day the student may himself become an associate of that teacher. It was such submission to this spiritual authority of which Our Lord spoke to His Apostles: "I will not now call you servants: for the servant knows not what his lord does. But I have called you friends: because all things whatsoever I have heard of my Father, I have made known to you" (John 15:15).

There is a second difference: The totalitarian state, to make its whimsical rulings accepted, must always aim at suppressing freedom of choice. For example, it will tell a citizen that he is not free to work at what he likes, to live where he pleases. But the authority of the Church tries, through training her children in the proper use of freedom of choice, to develop the freedom of perfection. Far from discouraging individuals from following their own preferences, the Church devotes much of her energy to teaching them *how* to choose, and to choose wisely.

An instructor in aviation teaches a candidate the laws of flight, the principles of gravitation and navigation. Then the student is given full freedom of choice; he can either obey the laws of flight or disobey them. If he uses his freedom to disobey, he will crash; if he uses his freedom to obey the laws he has learned, he will enjoy flying. The Church, likewise, teaches us the laws that govern reality and the consequences of breaking them. This is what Our Lord meant when He said, "And you shall know the truth, and the truth shall make you free" (John 8:32). For moral freedom — like every other freedom — is limited by the order of the universe. You are free to draw a triangle (provided that you give it three sides instead of thirty); you are free to draw a giraffe (provided that you respect its nature, giving it a long neck and not a short one); you are free to teach chemistry (provided that you tell the students that water is H_2O and not H_2SO_4). So with the Church: We are free to reject the teachings of Christ in His Church, just as we are free to ignore or disobey the laws of engineering; but we will find that the rejection of her laws never leads us to the perfection of our personality, as we foolishly hoped. It results, instead, in a morbid affirmation of the ego, which can even lead to self-destruction.

Life may be likened to children playing. The totalitarian would build them a playground where all their movements are supervised, where they are ordered to play only those games that the state dictates — games that the children nearly all detest. The result is that freedom of choice is, of course, taken away. Moreover, all hope and spontaneity are lost to the children. But the playground established by the Church might be a rock in the sea, surrounded by great walls; inside of those walls the children may dance and sing and play as they please. Liberals would ask the Church to tear down the walls on the grounds that they are a restraining influence; but if this were done, you would find all the children huddled in the center of the island, afraid to play, afraid to sing, afraid to dance, afraid of falling into the sea. Spiritual authority is like those beneficent walls. Or, again, it is like a levee that prevents the river of thought from becoming riotous and destroying the countryside of sanity.

The third difference between the discipline of the authoritarian state and the Church concerns the effect their authority has on the subject. Totalitarianism begets fear in the hearts of its subjects, because it habitually enforces its will by the whip, the chain, the concentration camp, and the false charge, which slanders a man; it thus develops hostility within the hearts of its subjects. Church authority, since it is internal, uses absolutely no threat or fear or compulsion; it relies, rather, on the echo each of its rulings raises in the heart and mind of the individual. Any one of its subjects is as free to reject the Church as Judas was; like Judas, at his moment of departure he is asked to return with the kindly word "Friend." One submits to the authority of the Church as a child submits to the authority of his parents — because he loves them — and from this love flows an ardent admiration and gratitude. In the light of these differences, it is evident that the real choice offered today is not between freedom from authority and submission to authority; it is rather a matter of choosing which *kind* of authority we will accept.

The modern person is so confused that, for all his talk about freedom, he is often eager to renounce this gift in favor of security. Even when no greater security is offered him in exchange, he is eager to give up his freedom of choice; he cannot bear the burden of its responsibility. Weary of being alone and afraid and isolated in a hostile world, he wants to surrender himself to something or to somebody — to commit a kind of mayhem of the will. Will he surrender to the anonymous authority of a collective state, or will he accept a spiritual authority that restores his freedom with the acceptance of truth?

The Church makes none of us less free than we were before. But we chiefly value freedom in order to give it away; everyone who loves surrenders his freedom, whether his passion be the love of another person, the love of a cause, or the love of God. When a man loves a woman, he says, "*I* am yours," and the surrender of freedom gives him into a sweet slavery. Every person in love with God says, as Paul did, "What will you have me to do?" (Acts 9:6) and adds, as we do in the Our Father, "Thy Will be done on earth as it is in Heaven." In both instances, freedom is surrendered for the sake of a greater joy. Freedom hoarded is of little value — spent, for something we love, it brings peace and perfects one's personality in the law and love of God.

The new certitude of the convert, then, is a precious thing and very different from the abandonment of will and intellect some imagine it to be. But the full tale of the benefits from conversion is not ended. We must speak of another christening gift — *peace of soul*. There is a world of difference between peace of mind and peace of soul. Peace of mind is the result of bringing *some* ordering principle to bear on discordant human experiences; this may be achieved by tolerance, or by a gritting of one's teeth in the face of pain; by killing conscience, or denying guilt, or by finding new loves to assuage old griefs. Each of these is an integration, but on a very low level. This kind of peace Our Lord calls false, and He likens it to living under the dominion of Satan: "When a strong man fully armed guards his palace, his possessions are safe" (Luke 11:21). It is the peace of those who have convinced themselves they are animals; the peace of the stone-deaf whom no word of truth can pierce; the peace of the blind who guard themselves against every ray of heavenly light. It is the false peace of the slothful servant who had the same talent at the end as at the beginning because he ignored the judgment that would demand an account of his stewardship. It is the false peace of the man who built his house on the shifting road, so that it vanished with the floods and the storms. With such false peace of mind, Satan tempts his victims; he makes it seem refined to the refined, sensual to the sensual, and coarse to the coarse.

Conversion brings the soul out of either chaos or this false peace of mind to true peace of soul. "Peace I leave with you, my peace I give unto you: not as the world gives, do I give unto you. Let not your heart be troubled, nor let it be afraid" (John 14:27). This true peace is born of the tranquillity of order, wherein the senses are subject to the reason, the reason to faith, and the whole personality to the Will of God. The true peace that follows conversion is deepened, not disturbed, by the crosses, checks, and disquietudes of the world, for they are all welcomed as coming from the hands of the Loving Father. This true peace can never come from adjustment to the world, for if the world is wicked, adjustments to wickedness make us worse. It comes only from identification of one's own will with the Will of God.

The peaceful soul does not seek, now, to live morally, but to live for God; morality is only a by-product of the union with Him. This peace unites the soul with his neighbor, prompting him to visit the sick, to feed the hungry and clothe the naked; for by loving another soul one gives to God.

The only real pain the convert now has is his inability to do more for the love of God. It is easy to fulfill the claims of lesser ideals, such as Humanism, and their disciples very quickly become complacent; they are already as virtuous as their code asks them to be. It is very easy to be a good Humanist, but it is very hard to be a true follower of Christ. Yet it is not the memory of *past* sins that creates this pain amid the peace, but present shortcomings: Because the convert loves so much, he feels as if he had done nothing. What gift can ever be an expression of this new love? If he could give God the universe, even that would not be enough.

All the energy that was previously wasted in conflict — either in trying to find the purpose of life or in trying alone and futilely to conquer his vices — can now be released to serve a single purpose. Regret, remorse, fears, and the anxieties that flowed from sin now completely vanish in repentance. The convert no longer regrets what he might have been; the Holy Spirit fills his soul with a constant presentiment of what he can become through grace. This spiritual recuperation is accompanied by hope, at no matter what age the change occurs — although the convert always regrets that he waited so long. As Saint Augustine said, "Too late, O ancient beauty, have I loved thee." But since grace rejuvenates, it quickens even the old to consecrated service.

And there are many other ways in which peace of soul will manifest itself after conversion: It makes somebodies out of nobodies by giving them a service of Divine Sonship; it roots out anger, resentments, and hate by overcoming sin; it gives the convert faith in other people, whom he now sees as potential children of God; it improves his health by curing the ills that sprang from a disordered, unhappy, and restless mind; for trials and difficulties, it gives him the aid of Divine power; it brings him at all times a sense of harmony with the universe; it sublimates his passions; it makes him fret less about the spiritual shortcomings of the world because he is engrossed in seeking his own spiritualization; it enables the soul to live in a constant consciousness of God's presence, as the earth, in its flight about the sun, carries its own atmosphere with it. In business, in the home, in household duties, in the factory, all actions are done in the sight of God, all thoughts revolve about His Truths. The unreasoning blame, the false accusations, the jealousies and bitterness of others are borne patiently, as our Lord bore them, so that love might reign and that God might be glorified in the bitter as in the sweet. Dependence on Him becomes strength; one no longer fears to undertake good works, knowing He will supply the means. But above all else, with this deep sense of peace, there is the gift of perseverance, which inspires us never to let down our guard, or to shrink from difficulties, or to be depressed as the soul presses on to its supernal vocation in Christ Jesus, Our Lord.

A final effect of complete conversion is less pleasant: One becomes the target of opposition and hate. A person can join any other movement, group, or cult without provoking hostile comment from his neighbors and friends; he can even found some esoteric sun cult of his own and be tolerated as a citizen exercising his legitimate freedom and satisfying his own religious needs. But as soon as anyone joins the Church, hatred and opposition appear. This is because his friends intuitively know that he no longer shares the spirit of the world, that he is now governed by Spirit, is lifted into a truly supernatural order, is united with Divinity in a special way, which is a challenge and reproach to those who would make the best of two worlds.

This reaction is not difficult to understand. Forget, for a moment, that the Church exists; and suppose there should suddenly appear on earth an institution equally Divine, which claimed to teach Truth as unerringly as God teaches it; which summoned children every morning to schools where they would begin and end their lessons with prayer; which forbade its married members to dishonor their marriage ties; which taught purity in a carnal environment; which, in all its decisions on society, on human rights, on politics and economics, started with the principle that nothing *really* matters except the salvation of a soul. How would the world receive it? With defiance, hatred, vilification, persecution, and unremitting attacks. Whenever the Voice is heard, the Presence felt, there is such violent opposition as has been promised: "But because you are not of the world, but I have chosen you out of the world, therefore the world hates you" (John 15:19).

As a consequence of this opposition to Christ, those who know a convert invoke a thousand far-fetched explanations to avoid the true reason — namely, the appeal of Divinity. The conversion of the young is explained as a phenomenon of adolescence; in the slightly older, it is blamed on a disappointment in love; the mature are called guilty of a mental aberration due to change of life; the old are accused of senility; in the unlearned, it is due to ignorance; in the learned, it causes raised eyebrows and the reflection, "Surprising! I thought he was too intelligent for that sort of thing."

It is this fear of provoking the enmity of the world that discourages many from becoming converts. Of this Our Lord Himself warned: How else could Heaven be known but by the enmity it would provoke among the worldly? "For I came to set a man at variance against his father, and the daughter against the mother, and the daughter-in-law against her mother-in-law" (Matt. 10:35). In this sense, Our Lord, indeed, brought a sword, causing division among human beings; but the peace He also brought recompenses those who, apparently giving up everything, find all that is.

Who are the prospects for conversion? How are the men and women set apart who will, in a year or two, seek out the Church? What kind of people need conversion? There is no special temperament, no unique mood that marks the next year's convert. Everyone in the world is looking for certitude, peace of soul, and freedom of spirit. In the quest of every pleasure, even in the pursuit of the unlawful, all people pursue their ceaseless quest of the Infinite. *Where* they look for God is the only question on which they differ. In this they are divided, as music lovers are: The music we love is the music we already have in our souls. The disordered soul likes discordant music; the unregulated will enjoys unregulated dissonances and rejects the finer, better-orchestrated symphonies. It might take considerable education and self-discipline to make jive-loving minds appreciate the "Leonore," No. 3, overture, or any work of Handel, Mozart, or Beethoven. Yet the love of some kind of music is in everyone; it is in the *kind* of music one loves that the difference lies, and no one enjoys good music without training and discipline.

Everyone wants the things that only a love of God will bring, but most people today seek them in the wrong places. That is why no one comes to God without a revolution of the spirit; a person must stop seeking his good in Godlessness. "And this is the judgment: because the light is come into the world, and men loved darkness rather than the light: for their works were evil. For everyone that does evil hates the light, and comes not to the light, that his works may not be reproved" (John 3:19, 20). Anyone who turns his face toward the light will be converted; but the turning must be done of his own free will. One can bribe tyrants, coax Quislings, flatter dictators, but there is no way to win God's love except by love. To each soul, He is forever saying, "Behold, I stand at the gate, and knock" (Apoc. 3:20). Shall we refuse to open it? To each mind, he reiterates, "I am the way and the truth and the life" (John 14:6).

Are we ashamed to receive the truth, lest it expose our ignorance and perversity — even though that exposure bring us to glory and peace? To every heart, Our Lord says, "I am the Good Shepherd" (John 10:11). Shall the frightened lambs lost in the brambles and thickets of modern life refuse His saving Hand? There is one simple way of beginning a conversion: Cease asking what God will give you if you come to Him, and begin to ask what you will give God. It is not the sacrifice it sounds, for, in having God, you will have everything besides.